Huntsville

MADISON COUNTY

TO THE EDGE *of*

Huntsville
MADISON COUNTY
TO THE EDGE OF THE UNIVERSE

Introduction by Jan Davis

Art Direction by Enrique Espinosa

Sponsored by the Chamber
of Commerce
of Huntsville/Madison County

Towery Publishing, Inc.

URBAN
TAPESTRY
SERIES
TOWERY
PUBLISHING, INC.

Contents

LIBRARY OF CONGRESS CATALOGING-IN-PUBLICATION DATA IS AVAILABLE ON PAGE 272

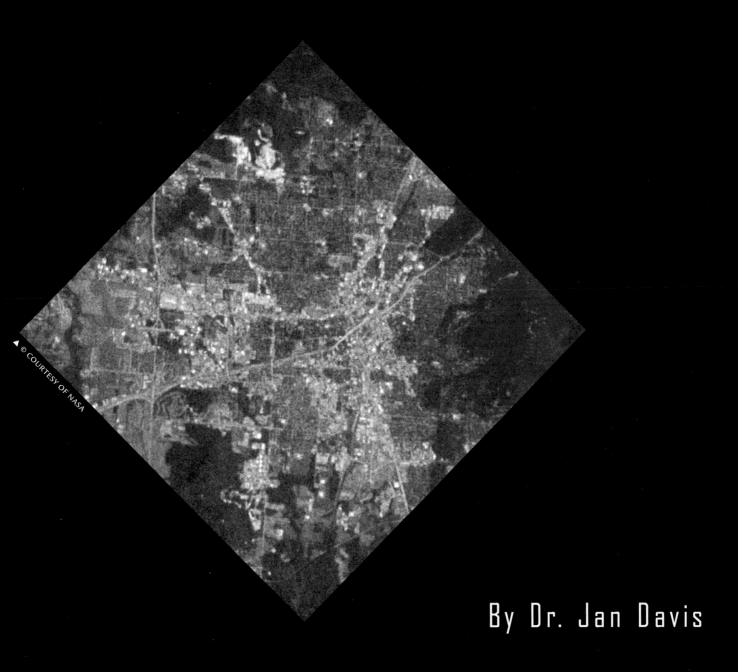

By Dr. Jan Davis

I t goes without saying that being in Earth orbit—more than 200 miles high, as the space shuttle flies—does some profound things to you. I have had the honor of being in space aboard the space shuttle three times now, yet I still am amazed at the majesty, the strangeness, and the profound sense of connectedness that such a perspective has given me.

I tell people that the most lasting revelation, among the many gleaned during my spaceflights, was looking down at Earth, and seeing just how small and connected our planet really is. We are of one world, and as the space shuttle orbits—circling Earth once very 90 minutes or so—you see this clearly.

When you're passing over an area in daylight, you see the blue oceans and the swirl of clouds and the nearness of the continents to each other. The immensity of deep space puts all of this into perspective, and reminds you in an indelible way that we are, indeed, just one group of people who share one small planet circling one small star.

When you fly over those parts of the earth where night reigns, though, you get an altogether different view. The clouds and oceans and green rippling hills disappear. Cities light up, like so many stars. These lights gather into man-made constellations. You see the outlines of the West Coast, the eastern seaboard, and the Great Lakes as blaring strings of brightness from the big cities. You see the huge individual metropolises like Houston, Dallas/Fort Worth, Atlanta, Miami, and New York. And you see the hundreds of smaller towns and cities—each one a point of starlike brightness—scattered without pattern in between.

Not far to the west of Atlanta, I was able to see a small city located in the ripple of foothills that rise into the Appalachians—Huntsville. Down there was the place where the country's rocket program was born and developed. Without Huntsville, the space program would have taken a completely different and more difficult path, or perhaps would have been impossible altogether. ✏➤

I had another name for the tiny speck nestled in the northern Alabama hills—home. Down there were also the streets of my past, the places where my dreams of going into space had taken shape and had been nurtured in countless ways. Without Huntsville, my own personal path to the heavens would have been a lot more difficult.

As a nation, we owe much to this small, unpretentious community. It is here that people have dreamed large, and where confidence, community, and steadfast determination have made those dreams unfurl in magnificent triumphs for us all. Looking down from Earth orbit, Huntsville may have looked small, but it's always been a major part of me.

Growing up in Huntsville—this mountainous city worthy of Norman Rockwell's insights—I was shadowed by the giants of the rocket and space programs. NASA's George C. Marshall Space Flight Center is here, as are a huge number of related military and government institutions, as well as private businesses, all of which make up one of the world's most formidable complexes of aerospace organizations. It is almost impossible to grow up in Huntsville and *not* develop a fascination with space travel and exploration.

That's not everyone's dream, of course, but it was mine ever since women were first selected as astronauts. As mentioned, Huntsville enabled and nurtured this dream all the way from my years in grade school through Huntsville High School, then, later, through my doctoral degree at the University of Alabama in Huntsville. Throughout, the city's excellent schools, colleges, and universities have worked with the various space-related businesses and government agencies to create an environment in which it was possible for me to earn my way aboard three space shuttle missions—*Endeavour* in 1992, *Discovery* in 1994, and *Discovery* again in 1997.

In all, I have logged nearly 700 hours in space, during which I retrieved and deployed satellites with a gigantic robotic arm; performed many scientific experiments; and worked hard to keep up with my socks in the strange environs of microgravity, where socks tend to disappear almost as quickly as they do in the family laundry room down home on Earth.

In many ways, though, Huntsville's emphasis on space takes a bit of explaining. The city is full of contradictions. It's a small, idyllic community that hosts all of the Mayberry-like virtues of a small southern town. The past is avidly protected here, and the city's history is learned early by all of its schoolchildren. There's a down-home quality to Huntsville that is fitting for a town of just 175,000. But don't be deceived by the laid-back veneer. Huntsville is also Rocket City, thanks to the twin industries of military and space, which set the pace for the future in a city that has so fervently and passionately cherished and preserved its history. You have the

Marshall Space Flight Center, Redstone Arsenal, and any number of high-tech industries thriving alongside pristine historic communities such as the Twickenham Historic District, which features Alabama's largest group of pre-Civil War era homes. You have the city's political players—the people who help determine Huntsville's future—powwowing and power-breakfasting at a place like Eunice's Country Kitchen, a no-frills, unassuming diner that's been keeping Huntsvillians well fed for decades.

As I said, a city of wonderful contradictions, always unpredictable and capable of delight.

Huntsville was founded by a pioneer named John Hunt, who built a cabin near the big spring that still flows through the city near the old Regions Bank. The state of Alabama was actually begun in Huntsville, when, in 1819, the leaders of the Alabama Territory met here and agreed to petition the United States

for statehood. The city's trailblazing accomplishments include the state's first school, library, newspaper, bank, and Protestant church. It was also the state's first capital, before that distinction went to Montgomery in 1847.

In the early years of World War II, in July 1941, Huntsville was selected by the U.S. War Department as the location for a chemical munitions manufacturing and storage plant. Its inland location would ensure sufficient protection from enemy attack, and its proximity to water, road, and rail transportation—Huntsville occupies the heart of the Southeast—also made it an attractive site. The Huntsville Arsenal, as the facility was named, produced more than 27 million chemical-munitions items during the war, with its staff winning several production awards. With the 1942 addition of the Redstone Ordnance Plant (renamed the next year as simply Redstone Arsenal), Huntsville became an invaluable munitions supplier to the U.S. military, producing such items as chemical artillery ammunition, bombs, and rifle grenades. ⋙

DR. WERNHER VON BRAUN

After the war, the city's trajectory turned skyward. Alabama state Senator John Sparkman—a native of Huntsville who lived in Twickenham—enticed a team of German scientists, led by rocket pioneer Dr. Wernher von Braun, to settle at Redstone to help put together the U.S. military's Ordnance Guided Missile Center. This is where von Braun's team developed the rocket that orbited the first U.S. satellite. From its serene location near the farmland of central Huntsville—about as unlikely a spot as you could find for such futuristic research—the center expanded to accommodate the U.S. Army Ballistic Missile Agency, which contained the U.S. Army Missile Command, the U.S. Army Space and Strategic Defense Command, and the Marshall Space Flight Center.

Suddenly, what was then a small town of about 16,000 took off, shortly to become the U.S. capital for space and military research, development, and production. In a very short time, Huntsville went from being known as the Watercress Capital of the World to Rocket City. Its population took off quicker than one of the missiles von Braun and his team were testing, and ever since, Huntsville has maintained its position at the forefront of space exploration.

KONRAD DANNENBERG, MEMBER OF DR. WERNHER VON BRAUN'S ROCKET TEAM.

Huntsville's education community flourished following the arrival of von Braun's Paperclip Group (so named after the government code words Operation: PAPERCLIP). As a result, the city today boasts many respected institutions—such as the University of Alabama in Huntsville and the Alabama Agricultural and Mechanical University—that have helped pave the way for numerous discoveries and innovations in the fields of biotechnology, nutrition, medicine, science, and engineering.

The Huntsville City School System, meanwhile, has picked up *Expansion Management* magazine's Best in Alabama rankings for three straight years, and its teachers have amassed an impressive list of awards and commendations. And fittingly, the names of many of these schools salute the city's aerospace heritage, from Challenger Middle School to Roger B. Chaffee Elementary School, so christened in honor of the astronaut who lost his life in the 1967 Apollo I fire at Cape Kennedy. One of the things I remember most proudly about my shuttle missions was the opportunity to talk from outer space with students from Randolph School, my old elementary school. ✺

In business as in education, Huntsville has excelled, garnering a reputation for having one of the strongest economies in the country—strong enough to be consistently designated by *Employment Review* magazine as one of the best places in the United States to live and work. It's not surprising, then, that Huntsville has attracted scores of national and international companies—from Boeing and Engelhard Corporation to DaimlerChrysler, SCI Systems, and NekTek Inc.; from Dunlop and Intergraph to ADTRAN, a homegrown manufacturer of telecommunications equipment. In all, more than 50 Fortune 500 companies have operations here, and the Chamber of Commerce of Huntsville/Madison County *Industrial Directory* includes 1,300 industrial firms and organizations. A study by the Massachusetts-based Cognetics, Inc. economic consulting firm recently ranked Huntsville as the best small metropolitan area in which to start a business.

Still, Huntsville is best known around the world as the United States' main hub for space research, from the early postwar days of Redstone to the work going on today at NASA's Marshall Space Flight Center, where engineers are building the country's first permanent space station. NASA's flagship organization in the ✍

development of space propulsion systems and space transportation, the Marshall Space Flight Center team has excelled in the fields of microgravity, biotechnology, and space optics research and manufacturing. From developing new disease-curing drugs to constructing ever more powerful computer microchips, the Marshall Space Flight Center is an invaluable citizen of both Huntsville and the world.

Nearby Madison, which I'm told is the fastest-growing town or city in Alabama, offers its residents easy access to all the pleasures of Huntsville as well as all the advantages of living in a smaller, incorporated city. Located just five miles to the east of Huntsville, Madison has a new library, recreational facilities, and its own school system. Ever since the growth created in the late 1940s and early 1950s by Redstone Arsenal, the development of Huntsville International Airport, and the establishment of Cummings Research Park, family-oriented Madison has been booming. Today, its 26,000 residents enjoy one of the highest per capita incomes in the Southeast, a culturally diversified population, a low crime rate, and activities for residents of all ages.

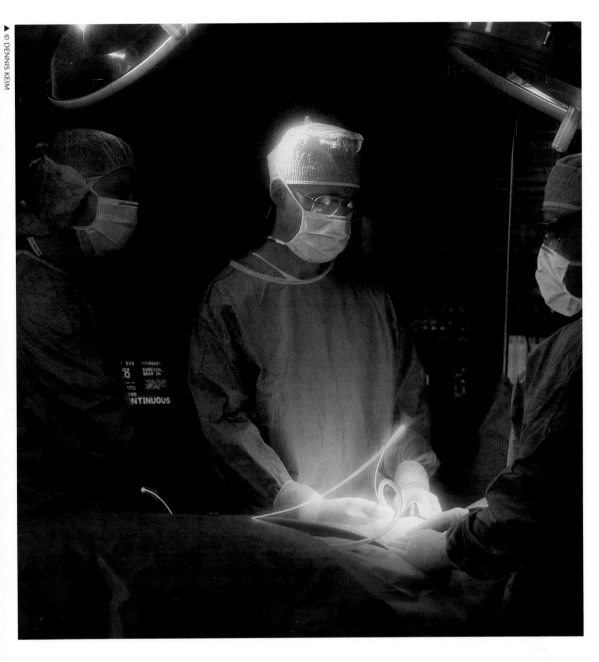

Despite all of its high-tech presence, Huntsville is still very much—and quite proudly—a town built on the foundation of agriculture, with its rich soil perfect for the growth of cotton and soybeans, among other crops. In addition to the farmland's being productive and profitable around here, it's also simply beautiful to the eye, with the expansive livestock pastures and surrounding mountains and sloping hills boasting the feel of a countryside getaway just a few miles from Huntsville's downtown center. The very location of the city—situated between the Tennessee River and the gorgeous Appalachian Mountains—offers an awe-inspiring view from just about any direction you face.

Equally beautiful is the view of the city from atop Monte Sano Mountain, 1,600 feet above sea level. The state park there covers nearly 2,200 acres, and features everything from a lush Japanese garden (perfect for afternoon strolls) to the Burritt Museum and Park. Housed in the uniquely designed Burritt mansion (imagine a building in the shape of a Maltese Cross and you get the picture), the museum contains a storehouse of ✦

historic treasures from Huntsville's rich past, from Native American artifacts to a wide array of antique medical and pharmaceutical equipment. The grounds of Burritt Park also feature seven reconstructed log cabins complete with vintage furniture from the 1800s. And it's a hot spot among couples in search of an idyllic setting to stage a wedding.

More than 1,750 acres of parkland help to enhance Huntsville's natural beauty and provide a location for bringing the community together for a variety of events, not to mention golfing, boating, and myriad sporting activities. When the crowds of European scientists and engineers arrived just after World War II, one of the things they wanted most was a full plate of cultural and recreational offerings. Being the resourceful lot that they were, they set out building parks and establishing orchestras with almost the same zeal as they had applied to developing rocket engines and guidance systems.

The most popular of the city's parks, Big Spring International Park, is located on the site where settler John Hunt first built a cabin in 1805. Big Spring is the home to numerous arts and music festivals, including the Concerts in the Park summer series and PANOPLY, a four-day celebration of the performing and visual arts that draws more than 100,000 folks each April. Founded in 1843, Big Spring is a favorite among locals and visitors alike for its Swiss rose garden, its glowing Yoshino cherry trees, and its Norwegian light beacon and fog bell.

There is a wide array of other diversions throughout the city, something for cave explorers and history buffs, green-thumbed gardeners and lovers of art, opera, and trains. If you need a respite from the rigors of the workweek, a stroll through the Alabama Constitution Village should do the job nicely. A vivid and painstaking re-creation of life as it was in the 19th century, Constitution Village commemorates Alabama's 1819

The Early Works Museum is Alabama's largest hands-on history center.

entrance into the Union, and you can still walk down the same block where city delegates wrote the constitution that made Alabama a state. Villagers here dress in period clothing, and the heavily gardened area is cloaked in the tantalizing aroma of fresh-baked bread, cookies, and a variety of tempting confections.

If you walk just a bit east from Constitution Village, you'll be amid the architecturally dazzling Twickenham Historic District, home of more than 65 antebellum structures. Twickenham (which was Huntsville's original name) is an outdoor museum of architecture, with overwhelmingly beautiful homes built in the early to mid-1800s, many of which have been included in the Historic American Buildings Survey since the mid-1930s. And if you're still yearning for a journey back in time—or just a hammer, a rocking chair, or something to spruce up your garden—drop by Harrison Brothers Hardware, a delightful emporium near Courthouse Square that has kept Huntsvillians supplied with the tools they need since 1879. ✥

The finer things in art are in abundant display here. The Huntsville Museum of Art contains five galleries loaded with works from celebrated local and regional artists such as Helen Vaughn, Yvonne Wells, and Janice Kluge, and an impressive gallery geared to children. The Huntsville Opera Theater regularly plays host to such revered productions as *Madama Butterfly*, *Cosi Fan Tutte*, and *La Traviata*, while the city's theater scene flourishes at a number of playhouses. We also have a respected symphony orchestra and the dazzling Huntsville Civic Ballet, which has thrived for nearly 30 years.

Sports plays a large role in the lives of locals, whether they're working up a sweat themselves or kicking back at the ballpark or football field. Runners from across the globe converge here every December for the Rocket City Marathon, which winds throughout our streets. On a less strenuous level, there are enough golf courses here to provide both weekend warriors and full-time professionals a spot on the links, and public parks and community centers boast everything from swimming pools to basketball and tennis courts.

There are few better ways to make a humid Huntsville summer night bearable than cracking peanuts and taking in the national pastime at Joe W. Davis Stadium, home of the Huntsville Stars. The longtime Class AA farm team for the Oakland A's, and one of the teams in the Southern League, the Stars hooked up in 1998 with the Milwaukee Brewers. Locals over the years have had the privilege of watching several respected major leaguers hone their skills on the Davis diamond, including Jose Canseco and Mark McGwire. Additionally, the Stars were the Southern League's Western Division champions in 1997.

And oddly enough for this warm, southern city, ice hockey—long a favorite sport of mine—has also become a local obsession. Mostly it's because of the University of Alabama in Huntsville's wildly successful Chargers, who consistently sell out their games at the Von Braun Center Arena. And no wonder: They're the 1996 and 1998 NCAA Division II national champions (not to mention national runners-up in 1997). ✺

And for anyone who just likes tying on the blades and cutting figure eights, there's the Benton H. Wilcoxon Municipal Ice Complex, a double-rink facility that hosts everything from the Huntsville Amateur Hockey Association to pickup hockey games for adults and children. The complex also offers lessons and fine party facilities. It's a great place, and something of a throwback to my childhood days spent on the ice at the old Ice Palace.

There is much more to Huntsville, of course, than I can hope to mention here. In particular, there are those dozens of little things that usually get left off of lists of this sort, things that bring pleasure and give character in small but impressive ways. Memories of cold, crisp nights watching football games. The beautiful dogwoods and azaleas that always popped up come Easter. Camping and boating with my family

around all of the city's nearby state parks and waterskiing on Lake Guntersville. The citywide rumbling during the rocket-engine testing for the Saturn V rockets that took Apollo missions to the moon.

But most of all, I like to stop now and then and look skyward on one of those country-clear nights we get, when the enormity of space seems so close you could reach out and grab it. It is then that I remember those giants whose shoulders I stand on, and I remember that many of those giants lived and worked and dreamed right here in Huntsville. I remember what it felt like to be 200 miles up in space, looking down from Earth orbit at Huntsville, and I remember—at times like these—what an extraordinary place it is that I call home.

A T THE U.S. SPACE & ROCKET Center, a space shuttle replica aims its sights at a bit of space history—a Saturn 1B rocket draped in Christmas lights.

HISTORIC NASA
REDSTONE TEST SITE

BUILT FROM $25,000 WORTH OF scrap metal, the Redstone Test Site (OPPOSITE) stands as a testimonial to the ingenuity of the rocket pioneers. The ideas gathered from the test site were instrumental in launching the first American—Alan Shepard—into space. Reminiscent of this historic event, icons of man's fantastic voyage are strewn throughout the city of Huntsville.

I N A 1952 *COLLIER'S* MAGAZINE article, Dr. Wernher von Braun wrote: "Development of the space station is as inevitable as the rising of the sun; man has already poked his nose into space and he is not likely to pull it back." Thanks to the early efforts of von Braun and his fellow scientists, the space station is becoming a reality, just like the Mercury and Apollo missions of years past.

THE U.S. SPACE AND ROCKET CENTER houses hundreds of space-age artifacts including historic rockets such as the Saturn 1B (OPPOSITE) and the mammoth Saturn V (ABOVE). Listed on the National Register of Historic Places, the three-stage Saturn V test vehicle was instrumental in landing man on the moon.

Nasa's Marshall Space Flight Center, located on Redstone Arsenal, is at the forefront of advanced technology. The lead organization for developing propulsion systems (OPPOSITE RIGHT) and conducting microgravity research (OPPOSITE LEFT), the center also oversees the X-33 and X-34 programs—vehicles that will enhance the reliability and safety of space travel (ABOVE).

O NE OF THE NATION'S PREMIER engineering schools, the University of Alabama in Huntsville offers degrees in a wide variety of engineering options, including chemical, civil, mechanical, and aerospace. The technologically rich environment of Huntsville provides future engineers with opportunities to experience firsthand the research occurring within various fields.

IN ORDER TO INSPIRE THE NEXT generation of space travelers, von Braun suggested that the U.S. Space & Rocket Center create an intensive program focused on math and science. The result was U.S. Space Camp, a weeklong program that draws hundreds of thousands of young people—including first daughter Chelsea Clinton—to experience space flight training and mock shuttle missions.

SAVING THE LIVES OF THOUSANDS and protecting the lives of millions: Huntsville Hospital's MedFlight (OPPOSITE) embarks on a mission while helicopters of Redstone Arsenal's Aviation and Missile Command (AMCOM) prepare for a military operation (THIS PAGE).

S PACE TRAVEL IS REFLECTED IN ALL aspects of Huntsville life. Posing alongside the city's towering church steeples, the pointed profiles of the early manned space vehicles reflect a secular way to reach the heavens.

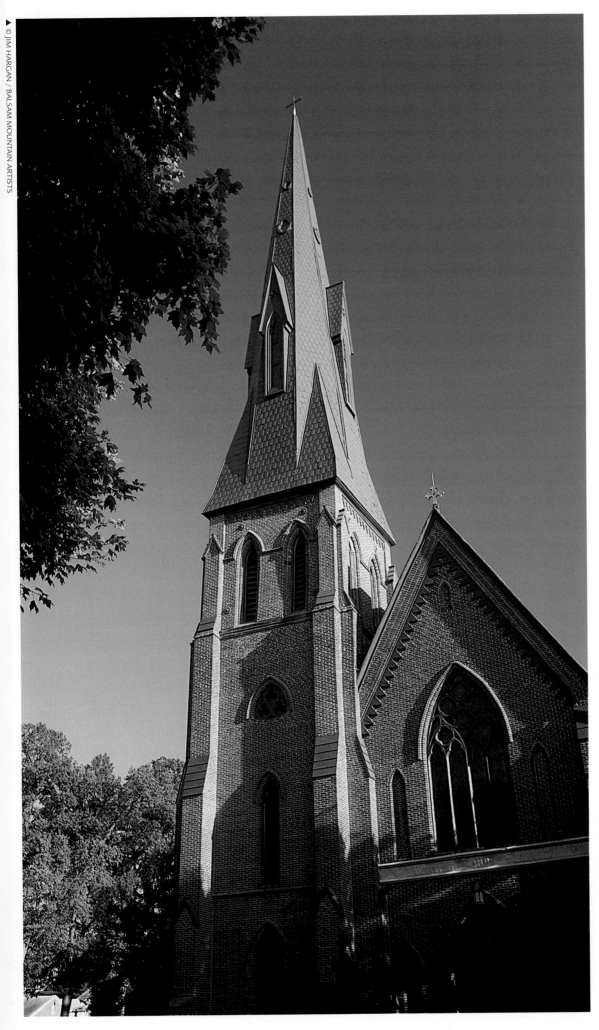

LOCATED IN THE TWICKENHAM Historic District, the Church of the Nativity is an elegant Gothic Revival building dating from 1859. Along with St. Mary of the Visitation (OPPOSITE), it is listed on the National Register of Historic Places.

I N SUNDAY MORNING GATHERINGS across the city, congregations such as those at the First Missionary Baptist Church (OPPOSITE) and St. Mary of the Visitation (ABOVE) make a joyful noise. Located in the heart of the Bible Belt, Huntsville has approximately 328 houses of worship.

P LACES OF NATURAL BEAUTY AREN'T
restricted to Huntsville's many
gardens. At historic Maple Hill
Cemetery, a reverent angel holds
her silent-yet-constant vigil over
those who have come to rest there.

UNTIL THE DAY BREAK AND THE SHADOWS FLEE AWAY

MAPLES

THE REMAINS OF FIVE ALABAMA
governors, 200 Confederate sol-
diers, and many others fill Maple
Hill Cemetery, established in 1818.

LONG AFTER THE LAST VICTIM HAS fallen, the pain and strife of civil war are manifested in local reenactments and memorial tombstones.

FROM CONCERTS IN THE PARK featuring brass bands dressed in Civil War garb to the brassy tunes of the Virgil I. Grissom High School's award-winning Tiger Marching Band, Huntsville enjoys a steady stream of musical salutes.

H ARRISON BROTHERS HARDWARE, established in 1879, not only carries hardware, cast-iron cookware, and rocking chairs, but also has the best selection of glass marbles around. A throwback to another era, the store is heated by a potbellied stove; tall, rolling ladders lead to treasures stored high along the walls.

BECAUSE HUNTSVILLE BUSINESSMEN remained allied to the Union cause at the start of the Civil War, their beautiful mansions were spared destruction. The result today is the scenic Twickenham Historic District, an area rich in *Gone With the Wind* ambience and filled with the largest number of pre-Civil War homes in the state of Alabama.

ORIGINALLY THE RETIREMENT HOME of Dr. William Henry Burritt, the Burritt Museum and Park is a repository of regional history. Constructed in the shape of a Maltese cross, the mansion offers a panoramic view of the Tennessee Valley.

Each year the Huntsville Polo Club meets for the Museum Cup, a benefit for the Huntsville Museum of Art. The polo grounds are located on the sprawling fields of Harris Hills Farms, a 60-acre horse ranch found within the city limits.

THE CLASS AA HUNTSVILLE STARS have been a fixture in the community since 1985, when officials built Joe W. Davis Stadium (ABOVE) on the site of the old airport. Named after the late mayor, the facility has been witness to the developing talents of today's home run hero Mark McGwire, as well as Jose Canseco, affectionately known to Huntsvillians as Jose Parkway for his ability to send home runs careening toward the nearby highway. Kids with dreams of baseball in their futures "batter up" at McGucken Park (OPPOSITE BOTTOM).

WITH A NOD TO THE BOYS OF SUM-
mer, the boys of winter take
to the ice. The self-proclaimed
Ice Hockey Capital of the South,
Huntsville boasts both a professional team, the Central Hockey
League's Channel Cats, and the
NCAA Division II 1998 Champion,
the University of Alabama in Huntsville Chargers. After the successful
completion of their 1998 season,
the Chargers began the transition
to Division I, where they will compete with such prominent oppo-
nents as Michigan, Boston College,
and Ohio State.

CHARGING AROUND THE VON BRAUN Center arena, cowboys and cowgirls from across North America compete in the annual Longhorn World Championship Rodeo. The competition consists of six major events, including bareback bronco riding and steer wrestling, each sanctioned for world championship points by the International Pro Rodeo Association.

THE TRUMPET OF MARCHING BANDS is resoundingly echoed in the energetic cheers of spectators in Huntsville's Milton Frank Stadium. During high school football season, laureled youth meet head-to-head in a frenzy found only in a state renowned for its love of the gridiron.

PART OF HUNTSVILLE'S ANNUAL Memorial Day Celebration, the Cotton Row Run starts in Big Spring International Park and travels through the city's downtown. The turnout is always considerable, not only of athletes testing their prowess, but also of those supporting their heroes.

A TRUE GOLFER'S PARADISE, THE UP-scale Hampton Cove community is home to an acclaimed course that is part of the Robert Trent Jones Golf Trail. The 324-hole trail is noted for its impressive design.

THE BEAUTY OF HUNTSVILLE IS
readily apparent in the colorful
foliage that brightens a day of outdoor activities.

T HE SIMPLE PLEASURES OF FAMILY life are an important part of the Huntsville community. Week-end traditions include relaxing during a picnic at one of the area's numerous playgrounds or feeding the ducks in Big Spring International Park.

P ART OF THE UNIVERSITY OF ALA- bama System, the University of Alabama in Huntsville (UAH) offers a broad range of under- graduate degree programs, while remaining focused to meet the specific needs of the city's technology-driven industries.

B ACKDROPS OF THE DEEPEST
southern blue sustain a variety
of floating fantasies. Climbing
through the sky or drifting lazily
in a pool, Huntsville-area living is
the stuff dreams are made of.

SOME LIKE IT

HOT!

T HE WOODS ARE LOVELY, DARK AND deep," remarked Robert Frost as he stopped to survey the scenery on a snowy evening. While Hunts- ville is beautiful under an icy blanket, sometimes not even a wishful thermometer can counteract the chill in the air.

G EARING UP FOR THEIR NEXT CAMP-oree, local Boy Scouts gather the necessities of survival. Huntsville youngsters take to camping with a relish and enthusiastically practice the illustrious Scout motto: Be Prepared.

S PRING IGNITES THE CITY IN A flurry of color. The 112-acre Huntsville-Madison County Botanical Garden invites enthusiasts to explore woodland paths; broad, grassy meadows; and a NASA-influenced Center for Biospheric Education and Research.

Built in 1860, the two-story, brick Huntsville Depot is one of America's oldest railroad terminals. Visitors to the depot—now a museum—can literally read history's writing on the wall in the form of graffiti left by Civil War prisoners and troops.

FIRE ST

ALTHOUGH HUNTSVILLE'S FIRE-fighters find time to relax between fires, they are all business when it comes to protecting and saving lives and property.

G. W. JONES & SONS

Huntsvillians know the joys of a quiet afternoon of relaxation, whether from the convenient perch of a sunny windowsill or a less orthodox spot atop the hood of a curbside car

BEGUN IN 1994, THE ANNUAL TRAIL of Tears Memorial Ride commemorates the historic significance of a route along Highway 72 used during the forced removal of Native Americans from the eastern United States.

P ATRONS OF RODEOS FAMILY DANCE club get their thrills atop the club's mechanical bull. Crash test dummies Vince and Larry, on the other hand, tell the woes of one wild ride too many during a visit to Huntsville's Safety City.

Kᴇᴇᴘɪɴɢ ᴛʜᴇ ᴄɪᴛʏ sᴀꜰᴇ: Hᴜɴᴛs-
ville's finest patrol the streets
while Judge Loyd H. Little Jr. (ᴏᴘ-
ᴘᴏsɪᴛᴇ) does his part to ensure
justice is upheld. And at Safety
City, children rely on hands-on
activities to learn the dos and
don'ts of living safely.

CAROLE RECORD, OWNER OF THE Kaffeeklatsch, entertains her customers with bistro dining to the tunes of local jazz and blues talent (OPPOSITE). And at Eunice's Country Kitchen, Aunt Eunice serves up her hot ham and biscuits with a hug and a smile. Legendary in Huntsville, Aunt Eunice counts the city's major political players among her devoted clientele. It is said that if you don't go to Eunice's, you can't win the election.

LOCAL NEWCOMER THE JAZZ FAC-
tory tempts restaurant-goers
with a variety of San Francisco-style
fare by Chef Gevara Teebi (OPPO-
SITE). The restaurant, housed along
the cobblestone sidewalks of
downtown, showcases local jazz
musicians, as well as art deco
surroundings. But if fast food is
more your style, nothing could be
more tempting than a familiar
McDonald's burger, advertised
on an original, single-arched,
Speedee road sign.

FUJI RA

36 ▷9A

9

9

10

RA-654

10   36 ▷ 10A

O N AN AVERAGE NIGHT DOWNTOWN, regulars at Bubba's kick back, relax, and shoot the breeze, enjoying the down-home atmosphere of a classic southern bar with a classic southern name.

15 16

FUJI-RDP ▷ FUJICHROME-R.

FUJI-RDP▷

S OME 50 YEARS AGO WHEN DR. Wernher von Braun and his team of rocket scientists came to Huntsville, the area was an unassuming farm town of around 20,000 citizens. Today, agriculture is still a part of the local economy (PAGES 120-125).

T HE BRIDGES OF MADISON COUNTY
stand steadfast in their role
as the connecting link between
Huntsville and its surrounding
communities.

THE RURAL SILHOUETTES THAT DOT the local landscape reflect a time when life was simpler. Built in the 1930s, the community center and museum in Monte Sano State Park succumbed to a fire that left only the walls and chimney standing. Now referred to as the Old Tavern, the ruins are the picturesque setting for picnics and snowdrifts.

T O ESCAPE FROM THE STRESS OF day-to-day living, Hunstvillians retreat to the numerous parks in the area, from nearby Monte Sano State Park—Latin for "mountain of health"—to William B. Bankhead National Forest, a 180,000-acre paradise in northwestern Alabama.

THE JAPANESE GARDEN ON MONTE Sano Mountain celebrates the diversity of cultures found in the Tennessee Valley. There, amid the lush foliage and carefully sculpted greenery, visitors can travel halfway around the world in a matter of a few short steps.

U NDER THE DIRECTION OF CONDUC- tor Taavo Virkhaus (SEATED, ABOVE) and Concertmaster Mark Reneau, the Huntsville Symphony Orchestra approaches the new millennium with a crescendo.

With three different series per season—classical, chamber, and pops—the symphony inspires the love of classical music in everyone. On a different note,

local jazz great and Wynton Marsalis protégé Ken Watters (OPPOSITE) entertains music lovers with his own form of high-energy modern jazz.

THE 1993 BRAINCHILD OF HUNTS-
ville's civic leaders, September's
Big Spring Jam has quickly become
one of the top events held in the
South. With headliners such as Al
Green, Foo Fighters, Travis Tritt,
and the Four Tops, the Jam brings
a diverse group of people to Big
Spring International Park for a week-
end of relaxation and good music.

THIS MECCA OF TECHNOLOGY AND engineering proves, at times, that it is also capable of relaxing and enjoying a beautiful day.

Pausing mid-arabesque, Nikki Drake and Community Ballet Association Artistic Director David E. Herriott rehearse for a local production. As sponsor of the only nonprofit dance school in North Alabama, the ballet organization has taught hundreds of the area's young people the art of concentration, skill, and grace.

P ASSIONATE AND TALENTED, YOUNG
artists Dwight Pope (OPPOSITE)
and Everett Young enliven Huntsville's arts scene with life-size
cultural imagery.

WITH VIBRANT STROKES OF PASTELS, artist Pamela Daugherty-Watters captures the energy and life of her subjects. A native of northeast Alabama, she builds upon the techniques of the Impressionists to describe the landscapes of her beloved South.

Huntsville native Tallulah Bankhead once said, "If you really want to help the American theater, don't be an actress, dahling. Be an audience." For- tunately, Huntsville has its share of both. From the dramatic talents displayed in a Theatre Huntsville production of Tennessee Williams' *Night of the Iguana* (OPPOSITE) to the mythical quality of a Fantasy Playhouse rehearsal, Huntsville's amateur theater groups have been dazzling audiences for decades.

B IG SPRING JAM'S OLDER SISTER, Panoply, enjoys a distinguished place as Huntsville's leading festival of the arts. Highlights of the event include musical acts such as Dave Gallaher of Microwave Dave & the Nukes (OPPOSITE).

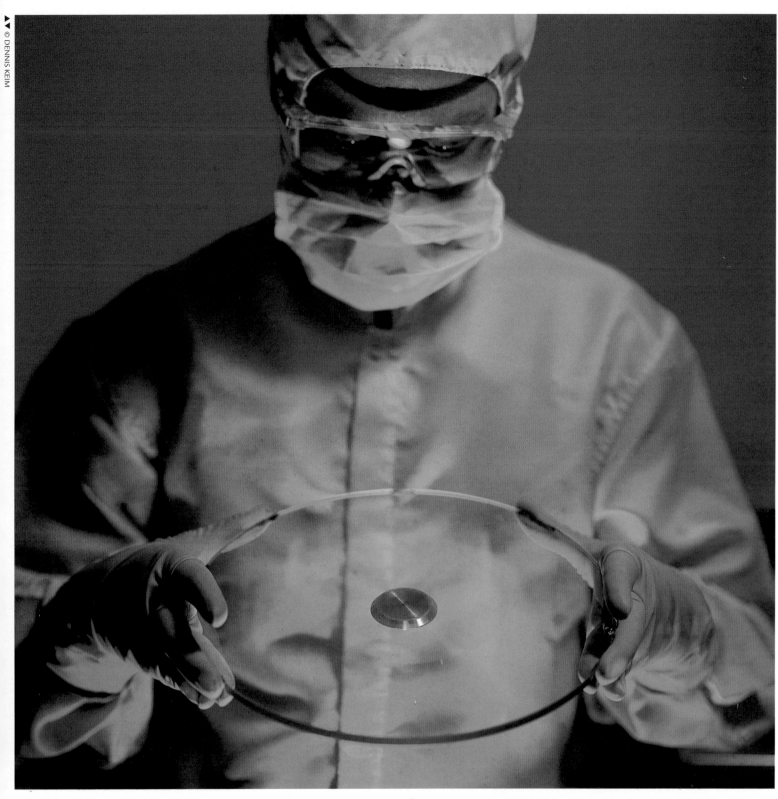

A FRIEND OF LEGENDARY BLUES-
men Howlin' Wolf and Muddy
Waters, James Wherry keeps the
music alive through a memorabilia
collection that includes numerous
vinyl recordings (OPPOSITE). On a
more high-tech audiovisual front,
local companies, such as Cinram,
capture sights and sounds on
formats including compact discs
and DVDs.

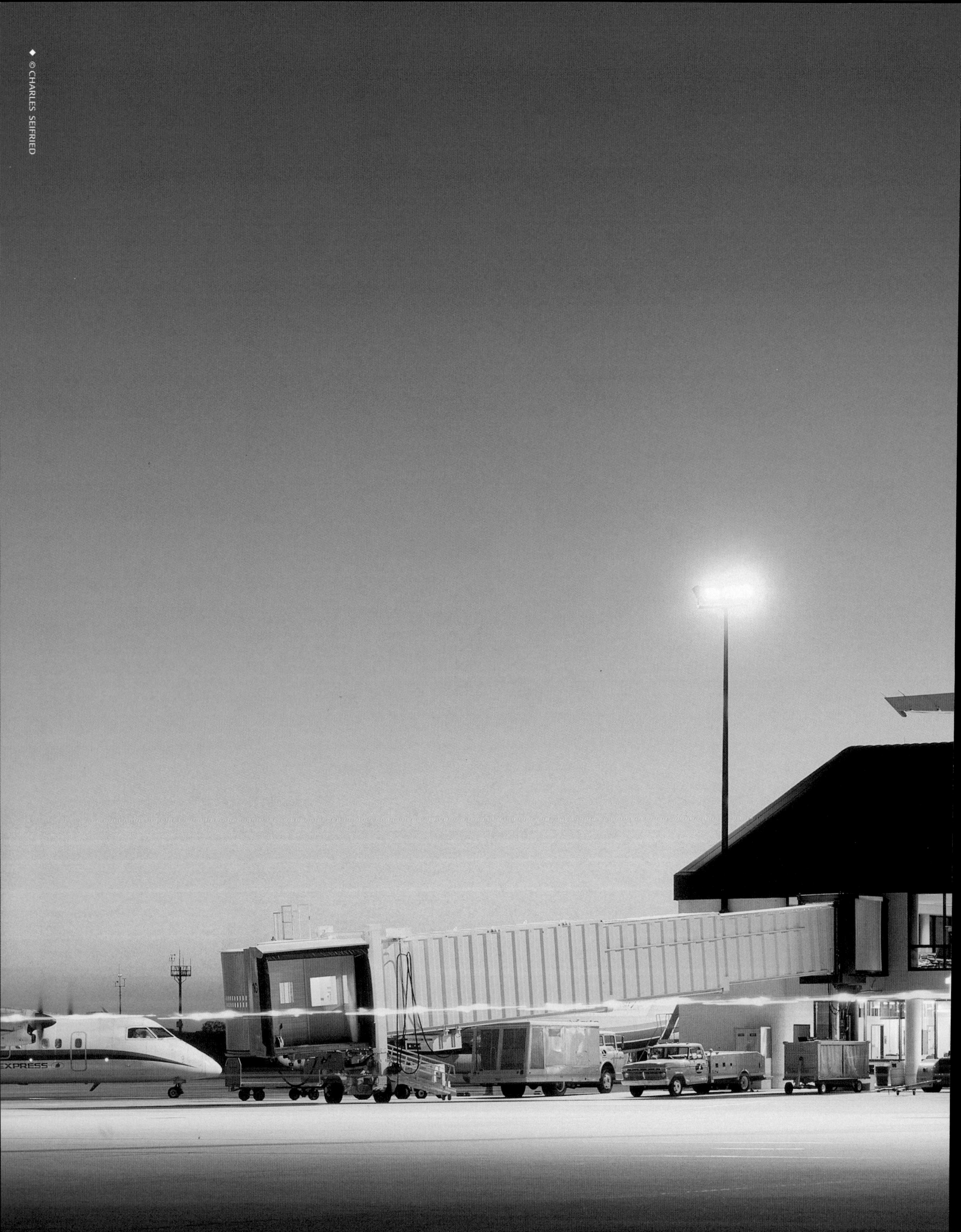
EXPRESS

ERVING APPROXIMATELY 900,000 passengers per year, Huntsville International Airport is on the road to becoming a transportation hub for the Southeast. Travelers can choose from more than 70 flights a day (PAGES 152-155).

DURING THE WING DING LIGHT Parade, motorcycle owners replace headlights with neon and fiber-optic beams, creating patterns of permanent glowing streaks in the night.

The parallel lines of a nearby highway and the converging symmetry of intersecting train tracks speak to the bewildering harmony of the area's transportation system (PAGES 158-159).

A S THE SUN SETS AMID A BRILLIANT
   wash of color, Huntsville aims
its sights toward the edge of the
universe. For this community, the

PROFILES IN EXCELLENCE

A LOOK AT THE CORPORATIONS, BUSINESSES, PROFESSIONAL GROUPS, AND COMMUNITY SERVICE ORGANIZATIONS THAT HAVE MADE THIS BOOK POSSIBLE. THEIR STORIES—OFFERING AN INFORMAL CHRONICLE OF THE LOCAL BUSINESS COMMUNITY—ARE ARRANGED ACCORDING TO THE DATE THEY WERE ESTABLISHED IN HUNTSVILLE/MADISON COUNTY.

ADTRAN, INC. ✳ ALABAMA A&M UNIVERSITY ✳ AMSOUTH BANK ✳ APAC-ALABAMA, INC. ASHBURN & GRAY DIVISION ✳ AVEX ELECTRONICS INC. ✳ BELLSOUTH ✳ THE BOEING COMPANY ✳ CALHOUN COMMUNITY COLLEGE ✳ CAMPBELL & SONS OIL CO., INC. ✳ CAS, INC. ✳ CHAMBER OF COMMERCE OF HUNTSVILLE/MADISON COUNTY ✳ CITY OF HUNTSVILLE ✳ COLONIAL BANK ✳ COLONIAL PROPERTIES TRUST ✳ COLSA CORPORATION ✳ COMCAST CABLEVISION OF HUNTSVILLE ✳ COMPASS BANK ✳ COMPUTER SYSTEMS TECHNOLOGY, INC. ✳ CRESTWOOD MEDICAL CENTER ✳ CYBEX COMPUTER PRODUCTS CORPORATION ✳ DUNLOP TIRE CORPORATION ✳ EER SYSTEMS INC. ✳ ENGELHARD CORPORATION ✳ EXECUTIVE LODGE SUITE HOTEL ✳ HERITAGE BANK OF HUNTSVILLE ✳ HILTON HUNTSVILLE ✳ HUNTSVILLE HOSPITAL SYSTEM ✳ THE HUNTSVILLE TIMES ✳ J.F. DRAKE STATE TECHNICAL COLLEGE ✳ LANGE, SIMPSON, ROBINSON & SOMERVILLE LLP ✳ LG ELECTRONICS ALABAMA, INC. ✳ MADISON COUNTY COMMISSION ✳ MADISON RESEARCH CORPORATION ✳ MAGNETEK, INC. ✳ MEADOW GOLD DAIRIES ✳ MEVATEC CORPORATION ✳ OAKWOOD COLLEGE ✳ PARKER HANNIFIN CORPORATION ✳ THE PORT OF HUNTSVILLE ✳ POWERTEL, INC. ✳ QUALITY RESEARCH, INC. ✳ QUANTUM RESEARCH INTERNATIONAL, INC. ✳ QUANTUM TECHNOLOGIES, INC. ✳ REDSTONE FEDERAL CREDIT UNION ✳ REGIONS BANK ✳ RISE REAL ESTATE, INC. ✳ RUSS RUSSELL COMMERCIAL REAL ESTATE ✳ SAINT-GOBAIN INDUSTRIAL CERAMICS ✳ SIGMATECH, INC. ✳ SOUTHERN BANK OF COMMERCE ✳ SOUTHTRUST BANK, N.A.-HUNTSVILLE ✳ SUMMA TECHNOLOGY, INC. ✳ TEC-MASTERS, INC. ✳ TELEDYNE METALWORKING PRODUCTS ✳ TIME DOMAIN ✳ TOCCO, INC. ✳ TRIAD PROPERTIES CORPORATION ✳ TRW, INC. ✳ THE UNIVERSITY OF ALABAMA IN HUNTSVILLE ✳ U.S ARMY CORPS OF ENGINEERS, ENGINEERING AND SUPPORT CENTER, HUNTSVILLE ✳ U.S. SPACE & ROCKET CENTER ✳ UWOHALI INCORPORATED ✳ VMIC ✳ VON BRAUN CENTER ✳ WOLVERINE TUBE, INC. ✳

1805-1950

1805	City of Huntsville
1808	Madison County Commission
1835	Regions Bank
1875	Alabama A&M University
1883	BellSouth
1895	Huntsville Hospital System
1896	Oakwood College
1907	AmSouth Bank
1910	The Huntsville Times
1915	Chamber of Commerce of Huntsville/Madison County
1923	Lange, Simpson, Robinson & Somerville LLP
1935	Compass Bank
1935	TOCCO, Inc.
1944	Meadow Gold Dairies
1946	APAC-Alabama, Inc. Ashburn & Gray Division
1947	Calhoun Community College

Huntsville is a tale of two cities. It is the home of Alabama's first constitutional convention, while also being one of the nation's foremost locations for the development of space travel and technology. Well known for its hospitable residents, the city is also recognized nationwide for its entrepreneurs and its emerging and fast-growing companies. It is a place where the traditional values of family, church, and home thrive among the foothills of the economically productive Tennessee Valley.

Mayor Loretta Spencer has the best of both worlds: She lives in and works for a thriving high-technology city that is steeped in Alabama history. For Spencer, Huntsville is an easy product to sell to prospective companies, new families, and visitors. Working with a staff of 2,000 dedicated employees who share her pride in the community's achievements, it is not difficult for Spencer to promise the best of city services to Huntsville residents.

"Huntsville has so much to offer the people who make this city their home. There are many employment opportunities, quality education for both schoolchildren and college students, and a standard of living that provides wonderful cultural and recreational activities," says Spencer. "My job is to make the world aware of the opportunities in Huntsville. I am proud of the advantages our city has to extend to its residents and companies."

A Place of Prosperity

Today, more than 175,000 people call Huntsville home. In addition, about 15,000 small businesses and large corporations have located and prospered here because of the city's affordable cost of living; easy access to the nation's interstate system; availability of national and international air transportation; supportive business, government, and educational relationships; and mild winter climate. The city provides new and existing businesses with the potential for growth.

"Cummings Research Park, the second-largest research and development park in the nation, offers high-technology companies an environment where they can thrive in the synergy and knowledge base that is available to them," Spencer says. "The downtown area is attractive to companies interested in furnishing employees with a working environment that combines historic buildings with today's technology. The Jetplex Industrial Park at Huntsville International Airport provides an excellent location for companies needing to transport their goods both nationally and internationally."

The Next Century

By promoting Huntsville's quality community services and affordable cost of living, Spencer is ensuring the future growth and diversification of the city. Providing such services as utilities, park maintenance, police and fire protection, sanitation, and recreational activities, city employees are focused on delivering a quality of life that will rocket Huntsville into the 21st century as one of the South's leading business, government, and research centers.

"I think the most important thing that city leaders can do for their constituents is to build strong, collaborative ties with companies that will provide good employment opportunities, while also contributing to the community's quality of life," says Spencer. "For Huntsville, that means continuing to provide an excellent business environment for space, technology, and industrial companies and government agencies, while also encouraging the establishment and growth of new businesses."

◄ JENNIFER & COMPANY

"Huntsville has so much to offer the people who make the city their home. There are many employment opportunities, quality education for both schoolchildren and college students, and a standard of living that provides wonderful cultural and recreational activities," says Mayor Loretta Spencer.

THE MADISON COUNTY COMMISSION HAS A UNIQUE PARTNERSHIP IN THE RESIDENTIAL AND INDUSTRIAL GROWTH OF MADISON COUNTY. WHILE CITY GOVERNMENTS FOCUS ON GROWTH WITHIN THEIR BORDERS AND LOCAL FEDERAL GOVERNMENT AGENCIES CONCENTRATE ON THEIR PUBLICLY FUNDED PROJECTS, THE RESPONSIBILITIES, OPPORTUNITIES, AND CHALLENGES FACING THE MADISON COUNTY COMMISSION ENCOMPASS ALL OF THE AREA'S GOVERNING ENTITIES AND MUCH MORE. IN FACT, NO OTHER LOCAL

government organization has as broad a role.

The traditional responsibility of the Madison County Commission starts with roads—maintaining, repairing, and adding to the road system. These efforts are essential to the well-being of the county's 280,000 residents, as well as those from the Tennessee Valley who travel into Madison County to work, shop, dine, or enjoy community events. Yet, the roles of the county's elected commissioners go far beyond its basic infrastructure.

"We are a partner in all public projects that affect the residents of Madison County," says Mike Gillespie, Madison County Commission chairman. "We have many responsibilities when it comes to maintaining our industrial and research parks. Within the county, we are accountable for managing and promoting international trade development. And we are responsible for allocating the budgets for a whole range of services, from the Madison County Sheriff's Department and Madison County Public Works to the Madison County Tax Assessor's Office and the Madison County Rural Recreation Department."

Since 1988, the commission has been composed of the chairman (elected at large) and six district commissioners (elected by district every four years). In his role as chairman, Gillespie works to manage the county's more than $50 million annual budget along with the district commissioners—Harold Harbin, District 1; Faye Dyer, District 2; Jerry Craig, District 3; Dale W. Strong, District 4; Morris J. "Mo" Brooks, District 5; and Prince Preyer, District 6. They are joined by the 1,000 employees who provide county services.

Focusing on Quality Growth

When Madison County's governing body was established by

law and charged with responsibility for roads and revenue in 1821, the county became a leader in Alabama's development. Today, covering 806 square miles from the southernmost ridges of the Appalachians to the Tennessee River, Madison County is Alabama's third most populated county, with a per capita income that ranks second in the state.

Elected to his first term in 1980, Gillespie says the commission's top priority during his years as chairman has been to maintain a high level of county service amid rapid population growth. In 1950, there were about 20,000 residents countywide, compared to 280,000 today.

"With the tremendous growth, the county continues to become more and more urbanized," Gillespie says. "Known primarily as a high-technology community, there are also a significant number of manufacturing jobs here. The commission is proud of Madison County's diverse industrial base."

Although the commission is not directly responsible for city services, it does work with area communities to maintain and expand road systems, support countywide services, and recruit new industry. "We want our community to flourish," Gillespie says. "The commission is employed to serve both city and county residents in Madison County. The services we provide the public are designed to work for the safety, health, educational opportunities, and economic prosperity of our residents."

THE MADISON COUNTY COMMISSION HAS A UNIQUE PARTNERSHIP IN THE RESIDENTIAL AND INDUSTRIAL GROWTH OF MADISON COUNTY. THE COMMISSION IS EMPLOYED TO SERVE THE PUBLIC TO PROVIDE A SAFE AND HEALTHY ENVIRONMENT WITH EDUCATIONAL OPPORTUNITIES AND ECONOMIC PROSPERITY (TOP).

MADISON COUNTY IS KNOWN AS A HIGH-TECHNOLOGY COMMUNITY, BUT THERE ARE ALSO A SIGNIFICANT NUMBER OF MANUFACTURING JOBS IN THE AREA. THE COMMISSION IS PROUD OF MADISON COUNTY'S DIVERSE INDUSTRIAL BASE (BOTTOM).

BOB GATHANY

BOEING DEFENSE & SPACE GROUP

WISDOM HAS IT THAT THE MOST SUCCESSFUL CORPORATIONS ARE BUILT ON A SOLID FOUNDATION OF EXPERIENCE, COMMITMENT, AND INTEGRITY. THERE IS NO BETTER SYMBOL OF SUCH WISDOM IN HUNTSVILLE THAN THE GREEK REVIVAL BUILDING ON THE WEST SIDE OF THE CITY'S DOWNTOWN SQUARE. AS ONE OF THE OLDEST BUILDINGS IN THE STATE, THIS ANTEBELLUM STRUCTURE REPRESENTS MORE THAN 150 YEARS OF BANKING HISTORY IN HUNTSVILLE. TODAY, ITS PRESENCE REMAINS

as impressive as the interstate banking institution it houses: Regions Bank.

"Regions Bank is the oldest financial institution in Madison County," says Steve Monger, Huntsville CEO for Regions Bank. "We have a long-standing commitment to sound business practices throughout Regions Bank. We've had a lot of stability in management over the past 20 years and our banks maintain a lot of local autonomy. As a result, we have been recognized nationally as a leading banking institution."

LOCATED IN THE GREEK REVIVAL BUILDING ON THE WEST SIDE OF HUNTSVILLE'S DOWNTOWN SQUARE, REGIONS BANK IS THE OLDEST FINANCIAL INSTITUTION IN MADISON COUNTY. WITH A CONSUMER AND COMMERCIAL CUSTOMER BASE, REGIONS HAS A LONG-STANDING COMMITMENT TO SOUND BUSINESS PRACTICES, PROVIDING MORTGAGE BANKING, INSURANCE, SECURITIES BROKERAGE, AND MUTUAL FUNDS.

Legacy of Financial Strength

Beginning in 1835 as the State Bank of Alabama, Regions' predecessors include the Northern Bank of Alabama, which became the National Bank of Huntsville. It became the First National Bank of Huntsville in 1899, the First Alabama Bank of Huntsville in 1975, and, in 1997, Regions Bank.

"We are still the same bank we've always been," Monger says. "As First Alabama Bancshares grew and took its banking services to other states in the Southeast, we realized we needed to change the

name to encompass our position as a multistate banking institution which also provides mortgage banking, insurance, securities brokerage, and mutual funds."

Continuing Its Local Commitment

Our customer base is both consumer and commercial," Monger says. "We work to ensure that we provide quality services to both the individual and the large and small businesses that make up the majority of our business in Madison County." To maintain and improve Regions Bank's services, the local offices have joined in a bankwide program known as Excellence Through Quality Service, which emphasizes quality improvements in the bank's relationships with employees, customers, and stockholders.

To better serve growing areas of the country locally, Regions Bank operates branches throughout Madison County, including Huntsville, Madison, Meridianville, Redstone Arsenal, and Marshall Space Flight Center. "We offer a lot of convenience with our branches," Monger says. "And our virtual banking allows customers to bank with us without ever going to the bank."

The economic growth of Huntsville and Madison County has provided Regions Bank several opportunities for growth in its customer base, employment, and services. The bank's financial strength allows it to give back to the Huntsville community through programs that support education, economic growth, and the community's quality of life.

"Where better in Alabama to do business than Huntsville and Madison County?" Monger asks. "The growth here has given us the opportunity to grow in many areas. It has also given us the opportunity to be involved in a dynamic, exciting community."

REGIONS BANK

THERE IS A SPECIAL BOND THAT EXISTS BETWEEN HUNTSVILLE HOSPITAL AND THE PEOPLE IT SERVES. IT'S A BOND THAT IS OFTEN FORMED IN CRISIS—WHEN A CRITICALLY ILL NEWBORN IS RUSHED TO THE NEONATAL UNIT, WHEN MEDFLIGHT TRANSPORTS AN ACCIDENT VICTIM TO THE REGION'S ONLY TRAUMA CENTER, OR WHEN A MAN'S CHEST PAINS LEAD TO EMERGENCY OPEN-HEART SURGERY. THIS BOND BETWEEN HUNTSVILLE HOSPITAL AND ITS PATIENTS IS BUILT ON CARING AND TRUST. ✳ HUNTSVILLE HOSPITAL'S

commitment to its patients began in 1895, when a group of volunteer women opened Huntsville Infirmary. A century later, the hospital continues to serve as a lifeline for those in medical need and a health care safety net for the less fortunate in the community. Today, thanks to the efforts of its medical staff, hospital employees, volunteers, and supporters, Huntsville Hospital is fulfilling its mission of "improving the health of those we serve."

"We are the community hospital, and we recognize our responsibility to provide our community with the very best medical care possible," says Joe Austin, CEO of Huntsville Hospital System since 1978. "We are also a regional referral center for North Alabama. What this means is that families in our area do not have to travel to Birmingham or Nashville to receive the quality care that they need and deserve. It's here in Huntsville. In fact, one-third of our patients come from outside of Madison County."

As one of the nation's largest community, not-for-profit hospital systems, the 901-bed Huntsville Hospital System serves nearly 300,000 patients a year in two acute care facilities, an outpatient Medical Mall, and a 50-bed rehabilitation hospital that is leased to HealthSouth. Comprehensive services provided by the hospital include the region's leading obstetric program; the area's only neonatal unit; MedFlight; and an advanced emergency/trauma program, which includes a chest pain center and a pediatric ER.

Huntsville Hospital pioneered cardiac care in North Alabama and is also home to the Comprehensive Cancer Institute. Thirty-four operating rooms are available in the system, offering the full range of specialties, including cardiac,

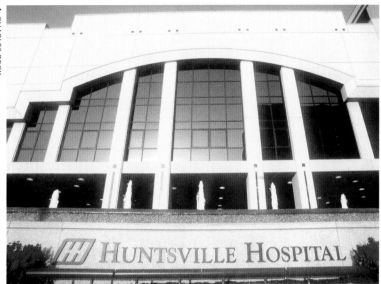

CHARLES BECK

neurosurgery, and orthopedic. Specialty programs available include the region's first sleep center, the Wellness Center, The Women's Center, Joint Camp, Congestive Heart Failure Clinic, Business Health Services, and Madison FirstCare urgent care facility.

With 4,800 employees and an annual payroll of $125 million, Huntsville Hospital's annual economic impact in the community exceeds $325 million. The hospital's medical staff includes more than 500 highly trained physicians representing more than 55 clinical specialties.

Huntsville Hospital is governed by the Health Care Authority of the City of Huntsville. The authority is an all-volunteer board and is responsible for representing the community in the governance of the hospital. The authority is not a department of the City of Huntsville. Huntsville Hospital does not receive any tax support from city, county, state, or federal governments.

"Our community is very unique," says Austin, "and so is our community hospital. We are very proud of the quality care that we provide and the medical technology which we offer at Huntsville Hospital. You will not find this true in many cities of a similar size."

THANKS TO THE EFFORTS OF THE MEDICAL STAFF, HOSPITAL EMPLOYEES, VOLUNTEERS, AND SUPPORTERS, HUNTSVILLE HOSPITAL IS FULFILLING ITS MISSION OF "IMPROVING THE HEALTH OF THOSE WE SERVE."

HUNTSVILLE HOSPITAL SYSTEM IS THERE WHEN A CRITICALLY ILL NEWBORN IS RUSHED TO THE NEONATAL UNIT, WHEN MEDFLIGHT TRANSPORTS AN ACCIDENT VICTIM TO THE REGION'S ONLY TRAUMA CENTER, OR WHEN A MAN'S CHEST PAINS LEAD TO EMERGENCY OPEN-HEART SURGERY.

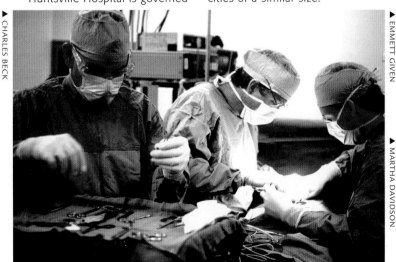

CHARLES BECK

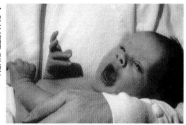

EMMETT GIVEN

MARTHA DAVIDSON

F OR STUDENTS, FACULTY, AND ALUMNI OF ALABAMA A&M (AGRICULTURAL AND MECHANICAL) UNIVERSITY, THE PHRASE "CLIMBING THE HILL" CARRIES MANY MEANINGS. IT CAN REFER TO ACHIEVING ACADEMIC SUCCESS, PARTICIPATING IN ATHLETIC AND EXTRACURRICULAR ACTIVITIES, OVERCOMING OBSTACLES TO ACHIEVE PERSONAL AND PROFESSIONAL GOALS, OR, QUITE SIMPLY, CLIMBING TO THE TOP OF THE HILL ON WHICH THE SCHOOL IS SITUATED TO CAPTURE A BREATHTAKING VIEW OF THE CAMPUS AND THE CITY OF HUNTSVILLE.

While the view at Alabama A&M is indeed unmatched, so too are the opportunities to learn and expand personal horizons. Nearly 5,500 students attend the university, which is one of the largest and oldest historically African-American universities in the nation.

"Before students graduate from Alabama A&M University, they are well prepared and well educated, and reflect well on the university," says President Dr. John T. Gibson. "We are interested in the development of the whole student, both academically and personally. We want each student to have the capabilities and confidence to be successful in his or her chosen career."

A Proud Academic Heritage

E stablished in 1875 as a land-grant university charged with teaching, research, and public service functions, Alabama A&M was founded by Dr. William Hooper Councill, a former slave who became an educator, lawyer, publisher, and statesman.

Although the university's charter called for a focus on agriculture and mechanical—or engineering—programs, Alabama A&M has diver-

sified to offer educational excellence in many areas. Today, it offers numerous educational programs through five academic schools: Agricultural and Environmental Sciences, Arts and Sciences, Business, Education, and Engineering and Technology.

In addition, the graduate school offers master's degrees in science, social work, business, urban and regional planning, and education, as well as doctoral degrees in ap-

plied physics, plant and soil sciences, and food science. The university also maintains nearly a dozen research and service centers, where activities include plant genetics and breeding, rural transportation, location of clean water sources, teacher training, and small-business development.

"We are a comprehensive, four-year university that offers many things not available anywhere in the region," Gibson says. "We are home to the first baccalaureate degree program in computer science offered in the state of Alabama. We are the only institution in Huntsville that gives certificates in teaching, which has caused our School of Education to have the largest enrollment of any school on campus. And we are the only university in the area that offers a master's degree in business and social work."

Gibson credits the school's 250 full-time faculty members, nearly 70 percent of whom hold doctoral degrees, for Alabama A&M's academic success. "The caliber of our academic programs has been possible because of the highly trained and dedicated faculty members

ALABAMA A&M UNIVERSITY IS INTERESTED IN THE DEVELOPMENT OF THE WHOLE STUDENT, BOTH ACADEMICALLY AND PERSONALLY. THE UNIVERSITY WANTS EACH STUDENT TO HAVE THE CAPABILITIES AND CONFIDENCE TO BE SUCCESSFUL IN HIS OR HER CHOSEN CAREER (TOP).

ALABAMA A&M STRIVES TO CREATE THE ULTIMATE ENVIRONMENT FOR EXCELLENCE IN EDUCATION AND PERSONAL GROWTH WITH HANDS-ON TRAINING, A HIGHLY DEDICATED FACULTY, AND NEW FACILITIES (BOTTOM LEFT AND RIGHT).

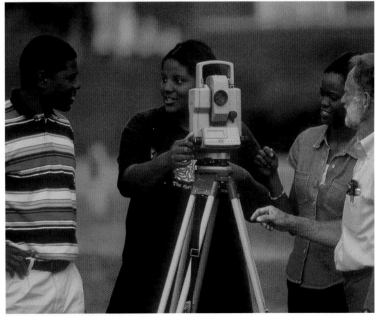

who work with students to help them to be successful in their studies," Gibson says.

Excellent Educational Opportunities

The School of Agricultural and Environmental Sciences offers nationally recognized centers of excellence in nonlinear optics, forestry and ecology, hydrology, soil climatology, and remote sensing. More traditional areas of study utilize 1,300 acres of university land for research and demonstrations of fruits and vegetables; forestry; and crop, soil, environmental, and animal sciences.

The university's state-of-the-art Telecommunications Center has expanded the traditional classroom by offering multidisciplinary distance-learning classes involving videoconferences, computer chat sessions, and E-mail communications. In addition, Alabama A&M offers many cooperative and internship programs to provide premed students, 85 percent of whom go on to medical school, with on-the-job training.

Students in the School of Business augment their formal education with hands-on training through the Alabama Small Business Development Consortium, the Northeast Alabama Region Small Business Development Center, and the campus-based Center for Entrepreneurship and Economic Development.

The School of Engineering and Technology has forged teaching relationships with Huntsville's high-technology government agencies and industries to ensure that students receive the best and most up-to-date technical education possible. Of the more than 330 engineering programs nationwide, Alabama A&M's curriculum is among only 83 such programs targeted by the Boeing Company as a resource for recruiting engineers and engineering technologies.

A Well-Rounded Education

More than 80 percent of Alabama A&M students participate in extracurricular activities, and the university's commitment to intercollegiate and intramural athletics is evidenced by its new, $10 million, 21,000-seat Louis Crews Stadium, the sixth-largest sporting facility in the state of Alabama. For those who want to exercise their minds, the university is building a $12 million, 80,000-square-foot library, which will be equipped with a computer network that allows students to access files and resource materials from their dorm rooms.

Alabama A&M University is indeed an international university, in both its curriculum and its student makeup. Students from 60 foreign countries come to Huntsville for the school's strong programs in physics, agriculture, and business.

Regardless of their field of study, students benefit from the relationship between Alabama A&M and Huntsville's business and technical communities. Says Gibson, "We get a lot of assistance from the community with the development of our academic programs, especially those in the technology field. Then, our students also benefit from obtaining jobs upon graduation with companies in Huntsville."

On the Hill, Alabama A&M strives to create the ultimate environment for excellence in education and personal growth. And, upon graduation, all Alabama A&M students are encouraged to live by the university's motto—Service is Sovereignty—through lifelong contributions both in their professions and in the communities where they live and work.

BEING THE SERVICE PROVIDER OF CHOICE IS THE GOAL OF BELLSOUTH AS IT LEADS THE TELECOMMUNICATIONS INDUSTRY INTO THE 21ST CENTURY. IN THIS ERA OF AGGRESSIVE COMPETITION AND RAPIDLY EVOLVING TECHNOLOGY, BELLSOUTH STANDS AS THE LEADING PROVIDER OF TELECOMMUNICATIONS, WIRELESS COMMUNICATIONS, DIRECTORY ADVERTISING AND PUBLISHING, VIDEO, INTERNET, AND INFORMATION SERVICES NOT ONLY IN HUNTSVILLE AND MADISON COUNTY, BUT ALSO WITHIN ITS NINE-STATE

region and among the 30 million customers it serves in 20 countries.

BellSouth has broken growth records across the South, adding more than 1 million U.S. access lines annually since 1995. The company also has won multiple highest customer satisfaction rankings in the J.D. Power and Associates Residential Local Telephone Customer Satisfaction Study.

BellSouth's operating cash flow in the domestic cellular business has increased annually, while its international cellular business more than doubles every year. BellSouth's data services continue to explode, with revenues from its digital services for business and carrier customers increasing more than 25 percent annually. Bellsouth.net is one of the fastest-growing Internet access services in the United States and provides 24-hour customer assistance on-line and by telephone.

In Huntsville and North Alabama, BellSouth offers the service and technology that have brought it repeated success in a high-tech market that demands advanced telecommunications services. For BellSouth, the Huntsville market is—and always has been—on the leading edge of the company's telecommunications technology.

BELLSOUTH'S SOPHISTICATED NETWORK EMPLOYS ASYNCHRONOUS TRANSFER MODE (ATM), A HIGH-BANDWIDTH, HIGH-SPEED DIGITAL TRANSPORT TECHNOLOGY.

Committed to State-of-the-Art Services

BellSouth has a profound commitment to Huntsville and Madison County to provide state-of-the-art telecommunications services," says Gary Pledger, BellSouth's regional director in North Alabama. "We know technology. We have a unique customer base in this area of high-technology consumers who not only use advanced telecommunications, but who are creating advanced telecommunications. In many cases, our employees have set standards for the rest of the company, as Huntsville is often

the market where new technological advances are deployed."

Second only to Birmingham in size in Alabama, the Huntsville District has historically been at the top or near the top in performance within BellSouth's nine-state region. That reputation continues a history of telecommunications service that began in 1883 when Southern Bell, as it was then called, established the Huntsville telephone exchange with 34 customers. The number of customers increased to 251 in 1900, 1,652 by 1925, and 4,129 in 1945. Five former Southern Bell states became a part of the newly created South Central Bell in July 1968,

and records show it had 133,524 customers in Huntsville by 1975.

Today, BellSouth provides local telephone service, data transmission service, enhanced services, long-distance access, and BellSouth Long Distance service in the Huntsville/Madison County area. Since 1988, BellSouth has invested more than $15 million annually in technology to serve the local area.

Leader in Wireless Technology

Today's BellSouth offers far more than wired telephone services. BellSouth Mobility—which entered the Huntsville market in 1986—is the world's leader in wireless phone

service, and this leadership is evident in the Huntsville market as well. "We have done extremely well in Huntsville because we have good support here within the community," says Barry Gillespie, general manager for BellSouth Mobility in the Huntsville District. "We have grown in this market as the industry has evolved since the time when all wireless communications companies could only offer analog services with one or two price plans. Today, we have an array of analog and digital services and numerous pricing plans to support all kinds of customer needs."

Unlike other personal communications services, BellSouth Mobility digital phones work on any analog or 800 MHz cellular system in the country. This allows consumers to use their phones throughout Alabama or any other state. Consumers can also make calls worldwide, using the most sophisticated equipment over the largest communications network in history.

BellSouth Mobility is the leader in digital technology for its advanced calling features, such as voice mail, caller ID, message waiting alert, privacy, flexibility, and call-carrying capacity. This division has also won the J.D. Power and Associates highest customer-service award for setting the benchmark in customer service for the industry.

"We offer the highest-quality technical support and 24-hour,

seven-day-a-week customer service," Gillespie says. "In addition, we offer some of the most competitive rates available. Although more competitors are entering the market, BellSouth Mobility will remain competitive with our customer offerings, various pricing plans, and customer service. We will do what it takes to maintain our competitive edge."

Supporting all that BellSouth does is BellSouth Advertising & Publishing Corporation, which is one of the largest and most progressive publishers of telephone and classified advertising directories in the world. This division is responsible for compiling, printing, and distributing eight different community directories in North Alabama. More than 800,000 copies of these directories—all printed on recyclable paper—are distributed in North Alabama, with more than 380,000 directories going to customers in Huntsville/Madison County. BellSouth also offers a myriad of voice information services, such as Consumer Tips and Real Talking Ads, designed to help Yellow Pages advertisers reach specific, relevant target audiences.

BellSouth Technologies Maintain Competitive Edge

Since the Telecommunications Act of 1996, BellSouth has been allowed to offer more integrated services to its customers," Pledger says. "Our aim is to be a one-stop

shop for all telecommunications and entertainment services so that all customer services are handled with one call to one company, and that is very important to future competitiveness for BellSouth. Our customers can now get Internet access, home service, and wireless service from one company. Future expansions in our technology and services will allow us to offer digital cable television and broader bandwidth digital services."

BellSouth's legacy of more than a century as telecommunications supplier to Huntsville and North Alabama makes it uniquely qualified to respond to customer needs. Having been an integral part of Huntsville and its growth for so long, local BellSouth employees easily exemplify their company's slogan: Nobody Knows a Neighbor Like a Neighbor.

BELLSOUTH'S REAL YELLOW PAGES GIVES USERS QUICK ACCESS TO THE MOST CURRENT AND ACCURATE DIRECTORY LISTINGS, BOTH IN PRINT AND ON-LINE (LEFT).

THE BELLSOUTH MOBILITY AIR BALLOON MAKES APPEARANCES AT MANY COMMUNITY EVENTS (RIGHT).

E NGRAVED ON THE BRICK ENTRANCE LEADING TO HUNTSVILLE'S OAKWOOD COLLEGE ARE THE WORDS "ENTER TO LEARN. DEPART TO SERVE." THIS FOUR-YEAR LIBERAL ARTS INSTITUTION IS DISTINGUISHED BY ITS COMMITMENT TO BOTH ACADEMIC EXCELLENCE AND CHRISTIAN INSTRUCTION. AT OAKWOOD, THE ADMINISTRATION AND FACULTY ARE DEDICATED TO FURTHERING STUDENTS' EDUCATION THROUGH SOUND CHRISTIAN PRINCIPLES THAT WILL SUMMON GRADUATES INTO ROLES OF SERVICE IN THEIR COMMUNITIES.

"A sense of service—that's the primary value we want our students to leave here with," says Dr. Delbert W. Baker, president of Oakwood College. "We want them to have a sense of service toward their local and national communities, as well as to the global community. To prepare them for that service, our focus here is on three molding principles: education, excellence, and eternity."

▼ FRED PULLINS

Offering Academics and Christian Education

A s a private, historically black, Seventh-day Adventist college of more than 1,800 students and 300 faculty and staff members, Oakwood offers excellent educational opportunities in 38 degree concentrations within 15 departments. The college's top-notch instruction is carried out in an environment that is concerned with the academic and spiritual development of each student.

"We believe that what we bring to the table is a value-added perspective," says Baker, who himself is a 1975 graduate of Oakwood.

"We have a unique educational system that is grounded in values that are consistent with Christian tradition. As a private institution, we can bring Christian values into our education and can make it part of the classroom. And the students that we attract are sensitive to their own spiritual, as well as academic development."

Huntsville became the site for a Seventh-day Adventist college in 1896, following a decision by the church leadership to establish a college to educate blacks in the

South. Ellen G. White, a church leader, cofounded Oakwood on a 360-acre tract that had once been home to a slave plantation. "Back then, Huntsville was viewed as being a receptive city for the college training of blacks. And that has proven to be true," Baker says.

One of the Nation's Strongest Black Colleges

T oday, Oakwood boasts a 1,200-acre campus that attracts students from nearly 40 states and more than 30 countries. The college

has developed educational strengths in the fields of biology and life science, business, education, religion, and music. Oakwood's choir—known as the Aeolians—and many of its talented musicians are nationally recognized. In addition, the college has added the Institute for Research and has made technology integral to the educational program. The Oakwood College board of trustees, along with its faculty, staff, and students, have recently voted to pursue university status by the year 2002 with a curriculum with graduate programs.

Oakwood is the third largest of the nation's 15 Seventh-day Adventist colleges and universities. As the only one of those that is historically black, it is also the only one that qualifies for membership in the United Negro College Fund (UNCF).

"We are one of the strongest colleges in the United Negro College Fund," Baker says. "We have had increasing enrollment over the last nine years, we are financially strong. We, also have one of the largest campuses with real estate that has great potential for development and expansion. But more than anything else, Oakwood is one of the best in terms of educational standards. We rank among the top colleges in the United States in terms of producing the most black graduates accepted to medical schools."

As a UNCF member, Oakwood participates in and benefits from fund-raising campaigns for the nation's historically black colleges. The membership also allows Oakwood access to international educational opportunities, such as participation in a $28 million project to offer assistance to black institutions of higher education in Africa.

The college is very much a part of the Huntsville community, with students carrying out their mission of service by participating in local tutoring, community improvement, and child development programs.

Opening Doors for All Students

Building on a commitment to diversity, Oakwood is open to all races. The college also offers an evening adult education program that is broad in its enrollment. Says Baker, "We are interested in

nurturing and importing diversity to our campus. Oakwood is receptive to all cultures."

In addition to its own degree offerings, Oakwood is involved in cooperative programs with the University of Alabama in Huntsville, Alabama A&M University, and the University of Wisconsin in Madison. These affiliations allow Oakwood students to obtain degrees in civil, computer, electrical, mechanical, and industrial engineering. Premedical students can also participate in the early selection program, which includes instruction at Loma Linda University Schools of Medicine and Dentistry in California. In addition, the college helps individuals with degrees in other areas to pursue medical school admission by first obtaining the additional instruction needed from Oakwood.

"At Oakwood College we look for ways to open doors for our students in whatever career they choose," Baker says. "Black people in U.S. society have faced numerous challenges in access and opportunity. As a historically black institution, Oakwood College has a unique opportunity to produce the kind of students who are needed in society and can really make a difference. With a strong education and a deep Christian faith, our students have what it takes to obtain success in their careers and to be of service to their community."

"A SENSE OF SERVICE—THAT'S THE PRIMARY VALUE WE WANT OUR STUDENTS TO LEAVE HERE WITH," SAYS DR. DELBERT W. BAKER, PRESIDENT OF OAKWOOD COLLEGE. "WE WANT THEM TO HAVE A SENSE OF SERVICE TOWARD THEIR LOCAL AND NATIONAL COMMUNITIES, AS WELL AS TO THE GLOBAL COMMUNITY. TO PREPARE THEM FOR THAT SERVICE, OUR FOCUS HERE IS ON THREE MOLDING PRINCIPLES: EDUCATION, EXCELLENCE, AND ETERNITY."

TODAY, OAKWOOD BOASTS A 1,200-ACRE CAMPUS THAT ATTRACTS STUDENTS FROM NEARLY 40 STATES AND MORE THAN 30 COUNTRIES. THE COLLEGE HAS DEVELOPED EDUCATIONAL STRENGTHS IN THE FIELDS OF BIOLOGY AND LIFE SCIENCE, BUSINESS, EDUCATION, RELIGION, AND MUSIC.

KNOWN THROUGHOUT THE BANKING INDUSTRY AS THE RELATIONSHIP PEOPLE, AMSOUTH BANK BELIEVES THAT CUSTOMER RELATIONSHIPS GO FAR BEYOND FINANCIAL STATEMENTS AND LOAN APPLICATIONS. AMSOUTH ADHERES TO A BUSINESS PHILOSOPHY THAT IS SUMMED UP IN SIX BASIC VALUES: DO MORE THAN IS EXPECTED; IMPROVE SOMEONE'S LIFE; MAKE A DIFFERENCE; MAKE TIME FOR PEOPLE; IF SOMETHING'S WRONG, MAKE IT RIGHT; AND DO THE RIGHT THING. THESE BASIC VALUES HAVE MADE AMSOUTH ONE OF THE REGION'S leading financial institutions.

"AmSouth has set a standard for itself with six basic values that make it unique from other banking institutions," says Craig Holley, president of AmSouth in Huntsville. "We feel very strongly about being relationship oriented and about paying attention to our basic values as they relate to doing business. AmSouth is also committed to offering the latest innovations in financial products and services."

Huntsville Banking Tradition

With total assets of $20 billion, AmSouth is one of the best-capitalized, large bank-holding companies in the United States. Much of its success in Alabama, Tennessee, Florida, and Georgia stems from its commitment to consumer and business banking, trust and private banking, and commercial banking. With 12 offices in Huntsville—including the 168,000-square-foot AmSouth Center, which has dominated the downtown skyline since opening in 1990—the employees of AmSouth continue a legacy of service that can be traced back nearly a century.

During a business venture to Huntsville in 1907, south Alabama businessman Fox Henderson decided that the city needed a local financial institution that would provide farmers and small businesses with a reliable and continuous source of financing to ensure economic growth. With the support of several prominent business leaders, Henderson organized Henderson National Bank. Nearly a half century later, that same entrepreneurial spirit inspired another group of civic and business leaders to establish the American National Bank of Huntsville. Eventually, both institutions merged as part of the AmSouth banking family.

Commitment to Customers and Community

Within Alabama, Huntsville and the North Alabama region make up the second-largest banking area for AmSouth. Says Holley, "The Huntsville market is clearly one of the fastest-growing markets for our bank. To remain on top of the growth potential, it is important to stay on the cutting edge with new and innovative banking services. That's why AmSouth has invested more than $70 million in technical upgrades. But even though we believe in innovation, we are also committed to traditional values and to building long-term relationships with our customers."

For that reason, AmSouth is represented by its employees in nearly every community organization in Huntsville. It is through these volunteer positions that employees build the bank's relationship with the Huntsville community.

"Our main interests in the community are education, the arts, health and human services, and community revitalization," Holley says. "The work our employees do in the community is an extension of our commitment to building a personal relationship with Huntsville's residents. Giving back in terms of both time and resources brings us back to our basic values. And being involved in making our community a better place is the right thing to do."

Recognized across the South as the Relationship People, AmSouth Bank is working to better the lives of its customers and its communities.

◀ GIL BRADY

AMSOUTH BANK'S MANAGEMENT GROUP (FROM LEFT): DAVID NAST, CONSUMER AND BUSINESS BANKING; CRAIG HOLLEY, PRESIDENT; LEE HOEKENSCHNIEDER, TRUST AND PRIVATE BANKING; AND MIKE ALLEN, COMMERCIAL BANKING (LEFT)

THE FIRM OF LANGE, SIMPSON, ROBINSON & SOMERVILLE LLP HAS A PROUD HERITAGE IN HUNTSVILLE, RICH IN THE QUALITY LEGAL SERVICES PROVIDED TO CLIENTS, THE HIGH ETHICAL STANDARDS PRACTICED BY ITS PARTNERS AND ASSOCIATES, AND ITS DEDICATED INVOLVEMENT IN THE CITY'S GROWTH AND PROSPERITY. THIS LONG LEGACY OF HIGH-QUALITY CLIENT REPRESENTATION AND COMMUNITY SERVICE WAS FIRST ESTABLISHED BY CLARENCE L. WATTS WHEN HE FOUNDED THE FIRM IN 1923. ✱ WATTS WAS JOINED IN 1950

by M. Louis Salmon, creating the firm of Watts and Salmon. Salmon was a recipient of the Distinguished Service Award presented annually by the Chamber of Commerce of Huntsville/Madison County, an award recognizing his efforts with such organizations as the community's Industrial Development Board and the University of Alabama in Huntsville Foundation.

Six years later, Roscoe O. Roberts Jr. joined the firm, and it was renamed Watts, Salmon and Roberts. Frank K. Noojin Jr. became a partner in 1967, and Glenn F. Manning joined in 1973, whereupon the firm became Watts, Salmon, Roberts, Manning and Noojin.

In 1989, the firm took on an even higher level of expertise when it merged with Lange, Simpson, Robinson & Somerville of Birmingham. As part of the merger, the Huntsville firm took on a new name, and gained a depth of experience and professional strength that comes with its affiliation with a large law firm.

The Strength of a Large Firm

Established in Birmingham in 1919, Lange, Simpson, Robinson & Somerville is a general civil practice law firm, representing businesses, individuals, financial institutions, governmental entities, and utilities. Its Birmingham office provides clients with a full range of services, including banking, corporate and business practice, labor and employment law, real estate, bankruptcy, securities, municipal bonds, and health care.

The Huntsville office has a considerable practice in the areas of civil litigation and appeals, employment law, banking, corporate law, real estate, tax law, estate planning, and administration of estates. The firm is general counsel for Regions Bank in Huntsville, Smith Engineering, and the Spencer

DENNIS KEIM

Companies Incorporated, and local counsel for such companies as ADTRAN, AVEX Electronics, BellSouth Telecommunications, Crestwood Hospital, Dunlop Tire Corporation, and Strategic Mortgage Services.

Noojin, who continues as the firm's senior partner in Huntsville, practices in the areas of civil litigation, commercial transactions, and banking law, while partner John R. Barran practices in the areas of corporate and public and private financing law, and partner David R. Pace practices in the area of civil litigation, employment law, creditors' rights law, and commercial law. Resident partner Harald E. Bailey practices in the areas of real property, corporate, and commercial law; and resident associate Jana Jawan Smith practices in the areas of real estate, creditors' rights law, commercial law, probate, and general litigation.

Working with clients and within the community, partners and associates at the Huntsville office of Lange, Simpson, Robinson & Somerville strive to provide the

highest-quality legal counsel possible with the highest ethical standards, continuing a legacy started more than 75 years ago.

Alabama State Law Disclaimer
"No representation is made that the quality of the legal services to be performed is greater than the quality of the legal services performed by other lawyers."

THE STRENGTH OF LANGE, SIMPSON, ROBINSON & SOMERVILLE LLP LIES WITHIN ITS HIGH-QUALITY CLIENT REPRESENTATION AND COMMUNITY SERVICE PERFORMED BY (TOP ROW/LEFT TO RIGHT) RESIDENT PARTNER HARALD E. BAILEY; ASSOCIATE JANA JAWAN SMITH; PARTNER DAVID R. PACE; (BOTTOM ROW/LEFT TO RIGHT) PARTNER JOHN R. BARRAN; AND THE FIRM'S SENIOR PARTNER, FRANK NOOJIN.

THE FIRM OF LANGE, SIMPSON, ROBINSON & SOMERVILLE HAS A PROUD HERITAGE IN HUNTSVILLE, RICH IN THE QUALITY LEGAL SERVICES PROVIDED TO CLIENTS, THE HIGH ETHICAL STANDARDS PRACTICED BY ITS PARTNERS AND ASSOCIATES, AND ITS DEDICATED INVOLVEMENT IN THE CITY'S GROWTH AND PROSPERITY (BOTTOM).

DENNIS KEIM

The Huntsville Times

COMMUNICATIONS IS A TWO-WAY STREET FOR THE EDITORIAL STAFF OF *THE HUNTSVILLE TIMES*. FOR MORE THAN 85 YEARS, THE NEWSPAPER HAS BEEN COMMITTED TO BEING ONE OF THE STATE'S BEST IN PROVIDING COVERAGE OF COMMUNITY EVENTS, ACTIVITIES, PEOPLE, AND BREAKING NEWS. BUT THIS NEWSPAPER GOES BEYOND ITS TRADITIONAL ROLE AS A NEWS SOURCE FOR THE TENNESSEE VALLEY BY ALSO OFFERING ITS READERSHIP THE OPPORTUNITY TO COMMUNICATE THEIR VIEWS WITHIN THE PAGES OF THE PAPER.

The Times has introduced several forums that encourage readers to share their opinions on community issues. The "Talk to *The Times*" column, where readers can call in and record their opinions for use in the newspaper; the more traditional Letters to the Editor section; and the easy reader access offered by *The Times*' Internet site at www.al.com turn into a viable communications tool for the entire North Alabama area the paper serves.

"This newspaper is the community's newspaper," says Bob Ludwig, publisher of *The Huntsville Times*. "It is not the publisher's or the editor's or anyone else's. In every way possible, we allow people to communicate with each other. We want the community to be proactive in their newspaper. In our news coverage, we routinely report on the actions of 75 to 100 people in the community. But there are so many others out there whom we want to hear from, and we want to share their opinions with all *Times* readers."

Changing with the Times

Viable newspapers are also evolving newspapers that change with the needs of the communities they serve. At *The Times*, that evolution has meant the addition of several special sections to focus on subjects pertinent to Tennessee Valley residents. Those sections include the Life & Science section on Tuesday and the Federal and Military news page on Wednesday; the Extra Credit education section and *react*, an interactive magazine for teens, on Tuesday; the Food page on Wednesday; the Out and About entertainment section and the Prep Sports section on Thursday;

the TV Times on Friday; and the Life & Family section on Saturday. The Sunday edition features expanded Business, Sports, and Life sections, as well as Real Estate Sunday, Travel, Entertainment, and Forum editorial sections, along with *Parade* magazine.

"THIS NEWSPAPER IS THE COMMUNITY'S NEWSPAPER," SAYS BOB LUDWIG, PUBLISHER OF *THE HUNTSVILLE TIMES* (TOP).

WITH MORE THAN 300 FULL- AND PART-TIME EMPLOYEES, *THE TIMES* IS THE THIRD-LARGEST NEWSPAPER IN THE STATE, WITH A CIRCULATION OF 85,000 ON SUNDAY AND A DAILY CIRCULATION OF 65,000 (BOTTOM).

In addition, *The Times* runs a series of focused business sections, covering such topics as personal finance in Money Matters on Monday; technology news in Access features on Tuesday; features on locally owned businesses and entrepreneurs in the Made in the Tennessee Valley section on Thursday; and general business pages on Wednesday and Saturday. Other news features—such as Sports, Life, the editorial page, local and syndicated columns, and weather forecasts—are also a daily feature of *The Times*. The Associated Press and the Alabama Press Association consistently recognize *The Times*' award-winning sections.

"In many ways, what we have done is taken news and features that have been spread throughout the paper and repackaged them in special sections," Ludwig says. "This gives a higher profile to the news that we think is important to our readers. And it also gives them easier access to the parts of the paper they are interested in."

Giving Readers the News

Coverage and placement of local news also have a high priority within the pages of *The Times*. Thorough and accurate coverage of local news is essential to giving readers the information they need to make decisions that affect the way they live.

"We really are trying to focus on what's happening in the community," Ludwig says. "The front page is dedicated to local news. But we are always conscious about the need to have a good mix of local, national, and international news so that our readers are well informed on current events and issues around the world."

The Times, owned by the newspaper and magazine conglomerate Advance Publications, is the third-largest newspaper in the state, with a circulation of 85,000 on Sunday and a daily circulation of 65,000. With more than 300 full- and part-time employees, *The Times* has the largest staff of any news organization in the region. To provide thorough coverage of

news outside of Huntsville, *The Times* has full-time reporters at satellite offices in Washington, D.C.; the state capitol in Montgomery; and a number of regional bureaus in several nearby counties.

Giving Back to the Community

The Times also supports the North Alabama community by participating in a number of local activities and organizations, including Big Spring Jam, PANOPLY, United Way of Madison County, Huntsville/Madison County Botanical Garden, Huntsville Museum of Art, Huntsville Symphony Orchestra, and Chamber of Commerce of Huntsville/Madison County.

But nowhere is the newspaper's community spirit more evident than in its *Times* in Education program, which recruits sponsors to purchase newspapers for classroom instruction. Participating classrooms in city and county schools use the newspapers as a living history book, following lesson plans developed to encourage newspaper reading among students.

Since 1910, *The Huntsville Times* has been a daily force in the lives of Huntsville and North Alabama residents. Today, more than ever, the employees at *The Times* are working to provide its readers with the best in local, national, and international news coverage. In all aspects of the newspaper business, *The Times* strives to fulfill its slogan: We've Got You Covered.

FOR MORE THAN 85 YEARS, *THE TIMES* HAS BEEN COMMITTED TO BEING ONE OF THE STATE'S BEST NEWSPAPERS, PROVIDING COVERAGE OF COMMUNITY EVENTS, ACTIVITIES, PEOPLE, AND BREAKING NEWS.

ECONOMIC DEVELOPMENT IS ABOUT QUALITY OF LIFE. IT'S ABOUT CREATING OPPORTUNITIES FOR FINANCIAL WELL-BEING AND PROSPERITY. AND IT'S ABOUT OPENING DOORS FOR EDUCATIONAL, CULTURAL, ARTISTIC, RECREATIONAL, AND COMMUNITY OFFERINGS THAT TRANSFORM A CITY OF BUILDINGS AND HIGHWAYS INTO A VIBRANT, EXCITING PLACE FOR PEOPLE FROM ALL WALKS OF LIFE. ✸ SINCE 1915, THE MISSION OF THE CHAMBER OF COMMERCE OF HUNTSVILLE/MADISON COUNTY HAS BEEN TO IMPROVE THE STRONG

THE CHAMBER OF COMMERCE OF HUNTSVILLE/MADISON COUNTY IS LOCATED IN A 28,000-SQUARE-FOOT, THREE-STORY BRICK BUILDING LOCATED ON A TWO-ACRE SITE IN DOWNTOWN HUNTSVILLE. THE FACILITY, BUILT IN 1986 AT 225 CHURCH STREET, WAS EXPANDED BY 7,000 SQUARE FEET FOR A NEW ECONOMIC DEVELOPMENT CENTER IN 1996 TO ADD STATE-OF-THE-ART ECONOMIC DEVELOPMENT SERVICES. THE CHAMBER OF COMMERCE HAS BEEN ACCREDITED BY THE UNITED STATES CHAMBER OF COMMERCE SINCE 1971.

business environment by helping recruit, retain, and expand businesses and by enhancing the quality of life in the community. As a result of the Chamber's efforts to increase economic growth, the organization has had a great impact on the livelihood of businesses and industries and on the lives of those in Huntsville/Madison County, North Alabama, and southern Tennessee.

"Generating economic development brings prosperity to the community. The number one reason for the existence of this Chamber of Commerce is to promote the community for business growth and increased employment so that we can offer an enhanced quality of life for all citizens," says Brian Hilson, president and CEO of the Chamber.

Building on a Vision for Growth

Since the early years as a cotton farming community, Huntsville/Madison County has emerged as a leading industrial and technological environment. The University of Alabama in Huntsville and the U.S. Space & Rocket Center evolved with the early and ongoing support of NASA's Marshall Space Flight Center and local high-technology industries. The Huntsville Museum of Art, the annual Panoply arts festival, and the Huntsville Stars baseball team are all augmented by the financial and political support of local businesses and industries. Without the vision of local business and government leaders, along with the needs of local industry, the Huntsville International Airport, Cummings Research Park, and Chase Industrial Park would not

exist. The Chamber of Commerce supports all of these key initiatives, which collectively make Huntsville/Madison County the unique community it is.

"Through the years, we have maintained a very strong commitment and focus on traditional economic development activities, including support of existing businesses, aggressive business recruitment, and by fostering growth of new companies," Hilson says. "To this long-standing commitment, we have added workforce development and community image enhancement."

These areas of focus are all part of a five-year economic development initiative organized by the Chamber called EDGE (excellence in marketing the region, development of the workforce to meet the needs of a quality-conscious regional economy, growth in local enterprises, and enhancement of the region's image both nationally and internationally). The program will raise $1.2 million annually to continue the Chamber's work in both traditional and new economic development efforts.

"Madison County has led the state of Alabama in the percentages of new jobs and expanding industries for several years," Hilson says. "The Chamber is positioning Huntsville/Madison County as a world-class business location that is increasingly attractive in the global marketplace. We are emphasizing diversified growth, the development of quality jobs, and the growth of technology-based career opportunities."

Excellence in Marketing

Working together with such organizations as the City of Huntsville, Madison County Commission, City of Madison, Industrial Development Board of the City

of Huntsville, Huntsville/Madison County Airport Authority, Madison Industrial Development Board, Cummings Research Park Board, University of Alabama in Huntsville Foundation, Huntsville Electric Utility Board, and Tennessee Valley Authority, as well as state and regional organizations, the Chamber is able to effectively market the local business climate.

"When the Chamber is working with industry prospects, they are speaking for all areas of the city and county involved in economic development," says Joe Hinds, a Chamber board member, and chairman of the Industrial Development Board of the City of Huntsville. "Presenting a unified front is essential to recruiting industries, especially when they want to work with one community representative to address all their industrial needs. The Chamber is a catalyst that draws all other entities together and represents these organizations with one voice."

While the Chamber focuses on assisting and recruiting companies for Huntsville's traditional industries of defense, space, and electronics, efforts are also concentrated on diversifying the local business base into other fields. With the support of EDGE, the Chamber is working toward recruiting companies in search of locations for manufacturing, diversified engineering, research and development support operations, and administrative and service office activities. These efforts can lead to recruiting companies in other industrial sectors, such as biomedical production, equipment and machinery manufacturing, and design and manufacturing of electronic devices for the medical industry and other fields.

Development of the Workforce

Despite a long list of collective efforts, Hilson and other leaders know the local workforce is the one key factor that could tremendously affect the Chamber's economic development objectives. With the establishment of new industries comes a growing need for more employees with engineering or technology backgrounds.

"Our community is experiencing tremendous job growth," Hilson says. "The employment requirements of our companies are unique because of the need for technically trained, capable workers."

Keeping pace with the workforce needs of corporate expansions can be achieved effectively through a close partnership between the local educational systems and the area's business and industrial sectors. All levels of education—including the city and county school systems and the local colleges and universities—have a tremendous impact on the type of employees available in Huntsville/Madison County. For that reason, the Chamber has formed a Workforce Development Council made up of private sector leaders who work to ensure that education and training efforts complement the employment needs of the advanced regional economy.

"Business, education, and the workforce must be closely attuned to one another, and the Chamber can help facilitate the understanding that must exist between these entities," Hilson says. "If our companies are to continue to provide some of the best long-term career opportunities available anywhere, then the workforce of tomorrow must understand what's required to fill those jobs."

The Chamber's efforts to enhance workforce development are crucial to the growth of the Huntsville/Madison County economy, as well as the economy of North Alabama. "Workforce development is tantamount to where our future lies," says Bob Ludwig, the Chamber's 1999 chairman of the board. "The quantity and quality of our workforce are critical to our growth. That's why it's so important for the Chamber and the business community to have a partnership

THE FIRST DOCUMENTED OFFICE OF THE CHAMBER OF COMMERCE WAS THE ELK BUILDING, LOCATED ON EUSTIS STREET NEAR THE EAST SIDE OF THE SQUARE. RECORDS SHOW THAT THE CHAMBER HELD OFFICE SPACE THERE FROM 1916 TO 1923. HISTORICAL DOCUMENTS HAVE INDICATED THERE WAS A CHAMBER OF COMMERCE OF HUNTSVILLE FROM 1896 TO 1906, WHICH BECAME KNOWN AS THE HUNTSVILLE BUSINESS MEN'S ASSOCIATION FROM 1911 TO 1912.

with education. Schools need to strengthen technical training programs because those skills are highly marketable."

The Chamber is also working to find ways to recruit new employees to Huntsville/Madison County. "The Chamber has traditionally been well known for recruiting companies, yet through EDGE, we are now also involved in the recruitment of employees," Hilson says.

Growth in Business

Representing more than 2,000 members, the Chamber addresses issues that affect local businesses, supports business owners with services that can improve their profit margin, and provides members with learning and networking opportunities that can change a company's future or an individual's career. EDGE complements these activities by addressing potential barriers to local growth, aggressively pursuing opportunities for expansion, and supporting entrepreneurial development.

In several ways, EDGE works to enhance business development programs already under way through Chamber programs, which include Workforce Development, Technology Development, Small Business Development, Governmental Affairs, Leadership Huntsville/Madison County Training, and Membership and Communications. These programs work to improve the business climate by coordinating such efforts as Welfare to Work, Small Business Awards Celebration, Northeast Alabama Regional Small Business Development Center, Government Update Luncheons, Special Issues Task Forces, Legislative Alerts, Youth Leadership, Chamber Pak, and several networking events.

"The Chamber's economic development programs are focused on helping existing businesses because we want to take care of them first," Hilson says. "Although attracting new businesses tends to gain more headlines, we also want to concentrate on enhancing growth opportunities and helping remove

any obstacles for expanding companies. While executing these efforts through our Existing Industry committee and professional staff, we actually find great opportunities for business attraction. Our existing companies are the best source for identifying leads to companies that might consider Huntsville/Madison County as a future location."

The Chamber's ability to effectively support existing industry includes the assistance it provides to the community's small businesses. "Supported by the Chamber, the Northeast Alabama Regional Small Business Development Center is our single most important resource," Ludwig says. "More than 85 percent of Chamber members are small businesses, and 90 percent of our expanding job base comes from existing industry, which is mostly made up of small businesses. It is important that the Chamber support this large source of business growth by assisting with development plans, enhancing op-

THE CHAMBER OF COMMERCE OF HUNTSVILLE/ MADISON COUNTY HAS BEEN A PART OF THE BUSINESS COMMUNITY SINCE 1915. THE CHAMBER OCCUPIED THE O.M. HUNDLY HOUSE ON 113 SOUTH JEFFERSON FROM 1924 TO 1925 (LEFT); THE FIRST FLOOR ANNEX OF THE RUSSELL ERSKINE HOTEL FROM 1943 TO 1952 (TOP RIGHT); AND THE "OLD" CHAMBER OF COMMERCE BUILDING AT 305 CHURCH STREET FROM 1965 TO 1986 (BOTTOM RIGHT).

portunities, and helping solve business issues."

Enhancing the Region's Image

Through efforts funded by EDGE, the Chamber is working to improve the image of Huntsville/Madison County in order to intensify the recruitment of new industries and employees. To effectively compete in the global marketplace, the region's economic development marketing efforts must project the type of positive image associated with other leading technology-based communities. In Huntsville/Madison County, that means organizing a promotional campaign that emphasizes quality of life, employment opportunities, business climate and economy, and technology-based companies.

"It is not well known that Huntsville/Madison County is one of America's most advanced technology-based communities, and it provides an ideal place to live, work, and do business. To get that message out, we need to create a positive perception of our community. At the state, national, and international levels, the Huntsville/Madison County region is perceived to be a community within itself," Hilson says.

The Chamber is focused on promoting Huntsville/Madison County to a higher level of recognition, ensuring that the community is known not only for its space program and missile industry, but also for its quality of life. The goal is to make people aware of all the attributes that make the area a unique location for companies and their employees. "We are taking Huntsville/Madison County to a level where we are considered among the country's finest business cities," Hilson says.

Promoting Business Success

Years ago, leading volunteers from all sectors of the business community saw the potential for economic growth in the cotton fields of North Alabama. Since then, Huntsville/Madison County's ongoing progress has been based on their vision and on the efforts of the Chamber.

"The Chamber has taken a very proactive stand to accomplish economic development, and to continue that approach, all facets of the Chamber touch on EDGE," says Linda Green, 1998 chair of the board. "By attracting new business and supporting existing business, the Chamber continues to be an effective organization for all business entities in Huntsville/Madison County."

Always remaining on the edge of economic development, the Chamber of Commerce of Huntsville/Madison County is continuing to prove that The Sky Is Not The Limit when it comes to local economic growth.

THE CHAMBER OF COMMERCE WAS LOCATED IN THE TENNESSEE VALLEY BANK AT 102 WEST CLINTON STREET TWICE OVER THE YEARS (LEFT). OCCUPATION THE FIRST TIME WAS FROM 1926 TO THE EARLY 1940S. THE SECOND MOVE TO THE BUILDING, WHICH ULTIMATELY BECAME KNOWN AS THE TERRY HUTCHINS BUILDING, WAS FROM 1962 TO 1964. THE RUSSELL ERSKINE HOTEL AT 115 WEST CLINTON STREET HOUSED BOTH THE CHAMBER OF COMMERCE AND THE HUNTSVILLE INDUSTRIAL EXPANSION COMMITTEE FOR THE FIRST TIME IN 1946 (TOP RIGHT). A SECOND FLOOR SUITE AT THE HOTEL TWICKENHAM LOCATED ON 121 EAST CLINTON WAS THE HOME OF THE CHAMBER FROM 1953 TO 1961 (BOTTOM RIGHT).

DOING BUSINESS THE COMPASS BANK WAY IS A UNIQUE EXPERIENCE FOR CUSTOMERS WHO WANT INNOVATIVE, COMPETITIVELY PRICED PRODUCTS AND SUPERIOR CUSTOMER SERVICE. COMMITTED TO CUSTOMERS' NEEDS, COMPASS IS DEDICATED TO BUILDING STRONG CUSTOMER RELATIONSHIPS AND IS FOCUSED ON OUTSTANDING FINANCIAL PERFORMANCE AND TREMENDOUS GROWTH. ✳ COMPASS BANK HAS LED OTHER FINANCIAL INSTITUTIONS IN HUNTSVILLE, AS WELL AS IN ALABAMA, IN OFFERING THE MOST INNOVATIVE BANKING

products. It was the first to expand its services to cover all the regions of the state and the first bank in Alabama to purchase an out-of-state bank. Compass was also the first bank in Alabama to offer Saturday banking and on-line banking services. It was one of the first to offer telephone banking and a bank debit card, and the first bank in the nation to offer on-line brokerage trading services through its affiliate CompassWeb Brokerage.

"We try to differentiate ourselves from the competition by offering the best in innovative products to our customers. We combined those products with a high level of customer service," says Clay Vandiver, Huntsville city president of Compass Bank. "We are committed to satisfying all the banking needs of our customers through the development of innovative products that help them in their personal and business banking."

Many Innovations

Another innovation is Compass Bank's Web site, ww.compassweb.com. Compass Bank is not only one of the first banks to offer a Web site, but it is also one of the first to offer interactive services where customers can apply for loans; obtain information on interest rates for CDs, loans, and mortgages; and, through CompassWeb Brokerage, utilize stock portfolio services.

Compass Bank is an SBA Preferred Lender and offers business customers services such as commercial checking and savings, commercial money market accounts, treasury management services, business banking software, investment and brokerage services, equipment financing and leasing, retirement programs and pension plans, trust services, and interest rate protection products. Compass Bank's professional financial plan-

ners provide businesses with innovative financial solutions to help them move forward on the local, regional, or national level.

In Huntsville, Compass Bank has seven convenient locations, including its four-story, 32,000-square-foot city headquarters on Governor's Drive. Compass Bank now has 247 banking locations that offer full services to customers in Alabama, Florida, and Texas, and more than $14 billion in assets.

"Compass has a great concentration of banks in North Alabama," Vandiver says. "And localized decision-making is our strength. The markets that we are in have a local management team that is given autonomy."

That commitment to local autonomy also allows the bank's employees to connect on a personal basis with the communities it serves. In Huntsville, Compass Bank donates more than $85,000 annually to local charities. Among its community projects, the bank has sponsored Fifth Grade Days during the Panoply arts festival, and the Run for Hope 5K race to raise funds for local nonprofit organizations.

High-Tech in a High-Tech City

In a city known for its own contributions to the country's technological age, Compass Bank's innovative use of leading-edge technology has served customers well. "Huntsville is one of the best markets that Compass Bank is affiliated with," Vandiver says.

The technology used by Compass Bank gives its employees the flexibility and experience to assist with a variety of customer needs, and has helped Compass Bank employees and customers fully realize its banking motto: Where There's Compass, There's a Way.

DENNIS KEIM

COMPASS BANK IS DEDICATED TO BUILDING STRONG CUSTOMER RELATIONSHIPS AND IS FOCUSED ON OUTSTANDING FINANCIAL PERFORMANCE AND TREMENDOUS GROWTH. "WE ARE COMMITTED TO SATISFYING ALL THE BANKING NEEDS OF OUR CUSTOMERS THROUGH THE DEVELOPMENT OF INNOVATIVE PRODUCTS THAT HELP THEM IN THEIR PERSONAL AND BUSINESS BANKING," SAYS CLAY VANDIVER, HUNTSVILLE CITY PRESIDENT OF COMPASS BANK.

TOCCO, Inc. is one of the world's few ISO 9001 tooling- and equipment-accredited International Standards of Operations 9001 manufacturers of quality induction heating systems and equipment. For more than 60 years, the company has helped manufacturers worldwide improve their business and save money with custom-designed induction heating equipment. ✶ From its home base in Boaz, Alabama, TOCCO provides industrial companies with engineering and metallurgical expertise to develop, design, manufacture, test, and support equipment that meets customers' production and process requirements. Induction heating systems offer a fast, efficient, and economical method of heating any electrically conductive material to a precise temperature. Through computerized technology, these systems allow manufacturers to heat selected areas of a workpiece or the entire material with precise control of temperature and heat depth.

"TOCCO's induction heating systems can be used to thermally enhance products," says Denis Liederbach, president and general manager. "Many manufacturing processes that use heat induction systems involve products that require surface hardening, primarily in the automotive industry. After heating metal to above 1,600 degrees Fahrenheit, and subjecting the material to a controlled cooling rate, the result is an exceptionally hard surface with better wear characteristics."

Leading Today's Heat Treating Industry

Although surface hardening is a major feature, TOCCO systems can also be used for annealing, stress relieving, tempering, brazing, bonding, shrink fitting, forging, forming, and many other processes that require fast, localized, efficient, and economical heat. These processes can be applied to virtually any shape of part, ranging in size from fractions of an inch to substantial lengths and diameters. Most heat processes involve metal parts, but TOCCO equipment can also accommodate plastic and rubber components that need to be removed, bonded, or shrink fitted. TOCCO leads the way in induction vacuuming and controlled atmosphere induction brazing, offering a more cost effective and controlled alternative to furnace brazing.

"In the past, the heat treating business was similar to the blacksmith industry—heat it and beat it," Liederbach says. "With today's technologies, the demands for using heat induction have changed. We are committed to providing customers with the right system for their products by analyzing needs and recommending a system of maximum value."

Once TOCCO engineers design a system, it is tested in a production environment to ensure that the processed parts meet customer requirements. The company also installs and interconnects its systems on production lines, examines and verifies processed parts, conducts operating and maintenance training, and provides field application assistance throughout the life of the system.

World's Most Reliable Heat

Owned by Park-Ohio Industries of Cleveland, Ohio, TOCCO has six manufacturing operations and 21 sales offices in 13 countries, with annual sales reaching more than $50 million. The company relocated from Cleveland to the 100,000-square-foot headquarters and manufacturing operation in Boaz, which today has 200 employees. In 1997, the Alabama headquarters was awarded ISO 9001 certification for meeting international quality standards.

While TOCCO has made a name for itself by providing heat induction systems for manufacturing processes, its technology has found other innovative applications as well. "The automotive industry is our biggest market," Liederbach says. "But the benefits of TOCCO's technology are moving into other fields, such as food packaging, water faucets and fixtures, tools, and environmental operations."

As engineers and developers become more familiar with the benefits of thermally enhanced products, TOCCO expects its market share will continue to grow domestically and internationally. And that bodes well for TOCCO's ongoing commitment to providing customers with the most reliable heat in the world.

From its headquarteres in Boaz, Alabama, TOCCO, Inc. provides industrial companies with engineering and metallurgical expertise to develop, design, manufacture, test, and support equipment that meets customers' production and process requirements (left).

TOCCO and its employees are proud of the company's designation as an ISO 9001 Tooling- and Equipment-accredited manufacturer of quality induction heating systems and equipment (right).

▼ TERRI HUBERT, CORPORATE VIDEO

Meadow Gold Dairies

IN 1997, WHEN MEADOW GOLD DAIRIES' BLACK-AND-WHITE MILK COW WAS TEMPORARILY REMOVED FROM HER PERCH HIGH ATOP A SILO TO RECEIVE A NEW COAT OF PAINT, THE COMPANY'S EMPLOYEES WERE OVERWHELMED WITH PUBLIC CONCERN. PHONES RANG CONSTANTLY, EMPLOYEES ON THEIR ROUTES HEARD COMMENTS, AND THE LOCAL MEDIA EVEN ASKED THE QUESTION: "WHERE IS THE MEADOW GOLD COW?" ✳ TODAY, THE BELOVED ICON IS AGAIN A PERMANENT PART OF HUNTSVILLE'S SKYLINE—A REMINDER OF

MEADOW GOLD DAIRIES' FAMOUS BLACK-AND-WHITE COW SITS ON HER PERCH ATOP THE HIGHEST MILK TANK AT THE FACILITY (LEFT).

FOR MORE THAN 50 YEARS, QUALITY AND SERVICE HAVE MADE MEADOW GOLD A HOUSEHOLD NAME IN NORTH ALABAMA. THE FACILITIES ARE LOCATED CLOSE TO THE DOWNTOWN AREA OF HUNTSVILLE (RIGHT).

a simpler day when farming was just as much a part of downtown commerce as the five-and-dime and the soda fountain. Several generations of Huntsville-area children have grown up searching for those ubiquitous black-and-white spots during trips around the city. For 20 years, the cow has not only been a popular landmark, but has also represented one of the healthiest products manufactured in Madison County—clean, cold, wholesome milk.

A Heritage of Quality

Although established during the 1940s, Meadow Gold Dairies can trace its heritage back to 1890, when a Swiss dairyman started Monte Sano Dairy. Production under the Monte Saymo label began in 1914, and the dairy moved to its present location in 1928 under the ownership of the Huntsville Ice Cream and Creamery Company. But it wasn't until 1944, when Beatrice Foods purchased the local business, that the Meadow Gold label debuted in North Alabama.

During the next 40 years, Meadow Gold established itself as the milk of choice in 13 North Alabama counties. Although the dairy changed ownership a number of times in the late 1980s and mid-1990s, the Meadow Gold label remained intact until Barber's Milk purchased the company in 1997. The ownership and label change were short lived, and in 1998, the dairy was sold to Southern Foods Group of Dallas, which reinstated the Meadow Gold label as the milk product of choice for North Alabama. While the Huntsville operation is now part of a national company with dairies in 26 locations throughout the United States, it is still very much a homegrown success story.

Dairy Products for Today's Families

From Gadsden to Cullman, from Florence to Nashville, Meadow Gold is the most popular choice of area milk lovers. In fact, Huntsville's Meadow Gold Dairies produces and distributes about 40 million gallons of milk and milk products annually for wholesale and retail customers throughout North Alabama, North Georgia, and south-central Tennessee. With the help of its 250 employees, the company offers whole, 2 percent, skim, and fat-free milk, as well as buttermilk, pure juices, flavored drinks, and cultured products, such as cottage cheese and sour cream. To help ensure the quality of its popular products, Meadow Gold has invested more than $5 million to upgrade the Huntsville facility.

For more than 50 years, quality and service have made Meadow Gold a household name in the North Alabama area. That type of brand recognition—combined with the company's long-term commitment to customer, employee, supplier, and community satisfaction—has helped position this Huntsville success story as "Meadow Gold—Your Hometown Dairy."

F OR MORE THAN 50 YEARS, THE ASHBURN & GRAY DIVISION OF APAC-ALABAMA, INC. HAS PAVED, RESURFACED, AND OVERLAID THE ROADWAYS AND HIGHWAYS OF HUNTSVILLE AND NORTH ALABAMA. FROM I-65 AND I-565 TO THE U.S. HIGHWAY 231 AND 431 OVERPASSES, FROM THE REDSTONE ARSENAL ROADWAY SYSTEM TO THE RESIDENTIAL ROADS CRISSCROSSING THE CITY OF HUNTSVILLE, AND FROM THE HUNTSVILLE INTERNATIONAL AIRPORT RUNWAY AND APRON EXPANSION TO THE STREETS, CURBS, AND GUTTERS OF NEW SUBDIVI-

sions, APAC's Ashburn & Gray Division continues to meet the area's road construction needs.

As a division of the nation's largest highway contractor, APAC's Ashburn & Gray is backed by the financial and operational stability of a major corporation, while also providing the service and attention of a locally managed company. Started in Huntsville in 1946 by the uncle-nephew team of Cecil Ashburn and Pat Gray, Ashburn & Gray Construction was purchased by APAC in 1988, making it a part of a subsidiary of Ashland Incorporated, a Kentucky-based, worldwide energy, chemical, and construction company.

Building North Alabama's Roads

The Ashburn & Gray Division is one of four APAC divisions in Alabama and among 42 APAC divisions in Alabama, Georgia, Florida, Mississippi, Tennessee, Kentucky, North Carolina, South Carolina, Virginia, Texas, Arkansas, Kansas, Missouri, and Oklahoma. Ashburn & Gray's territory stretches from the Mississippi state line to the Georgia state line, and from the southern part of Tennessee to Cullman, Alabama. While its highway and roadway construction projects give Ashburn & Gray its most significant local profile, the

company is also involved in private development and environmental projects.

Paving and base operations and resurfacing and asphalt overlay are areas of expertise for the 200 employees of Ashburn & Gray. They also have extensive experience in the construction of drainage, storm, sewer, and utility systems; the preparation, excavation, and stabilization of soil at construction sites; and the installation of landfill liners and leachate collection systems.

The company assists customers with determining a project's construction methods, preconstruction costs, quality control, and environmental impact. Ashburn & Gray takes an innovative approach in the use of new asphalt blends, designs, and construction alternatives, all determined by the company's goal to provide the best quality products and service to meet customer needs.

To better serve the western section of its territory, Ashburn & Gray maintains the Holland & Woodard Branch in Decatur. The division also operates asphalt plants in Huntsville, Decatur, and Fort Payne, and a sand and gravel operation in Guntersville to provide construction materials for its projects and to sell to other contractors.

Though providing quality roads and construction projects is the division's goal, its number one priority has always been the safety of its employees and the public it serves. The division's low accident and injury rates are unparalleled in the industry, and it also strives to protect the environment, provide clean air and water, and research new construction and recycling technologies.

Offering competitive costs and inventive solutions for its customers, providing quality roads and construction for its public and private users, and ensuring safety and job security for its employees, Ashburn & Gray continues APAC's tradition of being a company built on a century of innovation.

CLOCKWISE FROM TOP:
FOR MORE THAN 50 YEARS, THE ASHBURN & GRAY DIVISION OF APAC-ALABAMA, INC. HAS PAVED, RESURFACED, AND OVERLAID THE ROADWAYS AND HIGHWAYS OF HUNTSVILLE AND NORTH ALABAMA.

APAC ASSISTS CUSTOMERS WITH DETERMINING A PROJECT'S CONSTRUCTION METHODS, PRECONSTRUCTION COSTS, QUALITY CONTROL, AND ENVIRONMENTAL IMPACT.

WHILE ITS HIGHWAY AND ROADWAY CONSTRUCTION PROJECTS GIVE ASHBURN & GRAY ITS MOST SIGNIFICANT LOCAL PROFILE, THE COMPANY ALSO STRIVES TO PROTECT THE ENVIRONMENT, PROVIDE CLEAN AIR AND WATER, AND RESEARCH NEW CONSTRUCTION AND RECYCLING TECHNOLOGIES.

THERE IS A DISTINCT BOTTOM LINE AT CALHOUN COMMUNITY COLLEGE, BUT IT HAS LITTLE TO DO WITH NUMBERS IN AN ACCOUNTING LEDGER. THAT BOTTOM LINE—THE GOAL OF EVERY CALHOUN STAFF AND FACULTY MEMBER—IS THE NURTURING OF THE STUDENTS WHO GRADUATE FROM THIS TWO-YEAR COMMUNITY COLLEGE AND FILL THE EMPLOYMENT NEEDS OF AREA BUSINESSES AND INDUSTRY. ✳ CALHOUN'S COMMITMENT TO PROVIDING AN EDUCATED WORKFORCE FOR THE GROWING NUMBER OF TECHNICAL

AS CALHOUN COMMUNITY COLLEGE FURTHER DEVELOPS ITS TECHNOLOGICAL PROGRAMS, THE COLLEGE IS ALSO SOLIDIFYING ITS POSITION AS THE LARGEST TWO-YEAR COLLEGE IN ALABAMA. "OUR QUALITY OF EDUCATION IS RECOGNIZED AMONG THE BEST OF TWO-YEAR COLLEGES THROUGHOUT THE COUNTRY, AND WE ARE NUMBER ONE IN THE COUNTRY FOR THE NUMBER OF STUDENTS RECOGNIZED AS ACADEMIC ALL-AMERICANS," SAYS PRESIDENT RICHARD CARPENTER.

jobs in North Alabama has made the college a tremendous asset to local business and industry. In many ways, Calhoun is a partner in the economic development of North Alabama—providing educational opportunities to students from all backgrounds, working with industry to offer courses needed to fill technical jobs, developing entire customized training programs, and building state-of-the-art facilities for hands-on learning.

"Workforce development is our number one priority. Everything else we do is secondary," says Calhoun President Richard Carpenter. "Economic development is exploding in North Alabama, and we are part of that explosion. We support economic development by offering our facilities, our faculty, and our expertise to fill industry needs for

employees trained in technological fields."

In the past year alone, Calhoun has worked on a fee basis with more than 100 companies to develop specialized training that is quick, efficient, and cost effective. Those companies include ADTRAN, SCI Systems, Teledyne Brown Engineering, 3M, Saginaw/Delphi, and the Tennessee Valley Authority. Calhoun's most significant industry partnership involves providing Boeing with technological training for employees at its new rocket booster plant in Decatur, Alabama.

Technological Growth at Calhoun

The Boeing partnership has spurred unprecedented growth at Calhoun's Decatur campus, where construction has begun on a $28 million Boeing Aerospace

Training Center. The center is part of a $40 million construction project that also includes a $7.5 million Advanced Manufacturing Center and a $5 million Center for Visualization Technology (virtual reality).

"As an institution, 10 years ago Calhoun didn't think about specialized training being a major thrust of the college," Carpenter says. "Since 1992, workforce development that includes customized training programs has been a priority. It is being done in different parts of the country, and North Alabama has the most potential for these kinds of programs."

Alabama's Largest

As Calhoun further develops its technological programs, the college is also solidifying its position as the largest two-year college in the state. With nearly 8,000 students, Calhoun offers a vast range of degreed programs at its Decatur campus, including programs of study in business, fine arts, health and physical education, mathematics, language arts, social sciences, and natural sciences, in addition to technical programs. Calhoun also has a campus in Huntsville's Cummings Research Park, as well as teaching facilities at Redstone Arsenal and Limestone Correctional Facility.

"We are the state's most cost-efficient educational institution," Carpenter says. "Our administration costs per student are the lowest in the state. Our quality of education is recognized among the best of two-year colleges throughout the country, and we are number one in the country for the number of students recognized as Academic All-Americans." Six of Calhoun's graduates have been recognized for this honor, which is conferred by the American Association of Community Colleges and recog-

DENNIS KEIM

nizes students from among those attending two-year colleges throughout the nation who have been named to *USA Today*'s Academic All-American Team. The most recent such honoree is Mary Black Tate, a 37-year-old wife and mother of two, who graduated in 1998 with associate's degrees in accounting, general education, secondary education, and elementary education.

Tate embodies a common Calhoun student profile–the older student who is returning to school after several years to upgrade skills or to obtain a degree. "Now the fastest-growing segment of the student population is among those who already have degrees," Carpenter says. "Across the nation, two-year colleges are becoming the largest graduate schools for college-degreed students who want to add skills and learn new technologies. Employers are less concerned about where a degree came from, and more interested in seeing upgraded skills on a résumé."

Fifty Years of Academics

The foundation for Calhoun's long list of student services and academic achievements was first established more than 50 years ago. Since then, Calhoun has served more than 135,000 students, with 70,000 from Huntsville/Madison County, 40,000 from Morgan County, 20,000 from Limestone County, and 5,000 from Lawrence County.

When Carpenter joined Calhoun in 1992, many of the college's technological programs were phasing out due to a lack of student interest. Under his leadership, Calhoun began to build industry partnerships that helped revamp the college's technological programs to reflect the current needs of industry, and rebuilt Calhoun's future in technological education and training.

"We are proud of our good academic program," Carpenter says. "The future is incredibly multifaceted with a tremendous focus on technical training and the infrastructure of the college."

Yet, overriding all the technology Calhoun has to offer its students is its commitment to students, enabling them to create success stories in the classroom, on campus, and in the work environment. Calhoun Community College is preparing high-tech employees for the future by providing state-of-the-art facilities and instruction in an environment that nurtures learning and looks forward to the part it will play in helping to carry the community into the next century.

WITH NEARLY 8,000 STUDENTS, CALHOUN OFFERS A VAST RANGE OF DEGREED PROGRAMS AT ITS DECATUR, ALABAMA, CAMPUS, INCLUDING PROGRAMS OF STUDY IN BUSINESS, FINE ARTS, HEALTH AND PHYSICAL EDUCATION, MATHEMATICS, LANGUAGE ARTS, SOCIAL SCIENCES, AND NATURAL SCIENCES, IN ADDITION TO TECHNICAL PROGRAMS. THE COLLEGE ALSO HAS A CAMPUS IN HUNTSVILLE'S CUMMINGS RESEARCH PARK.

A COMMON CALHOUN STUDENT PROFILE IS THE OLDER STUDENT WHO IS RETURNING TO SCHOOL AFTER SEVERAL YEARS TO UPGRADE SKILLS OR TO OBTAIN A DEGREE. "NOW THE FASTEST-GROWING SEGMENT OF THE STUDENT POPULATION IS AMONG THOSE WHO ALREADY HAVE DEGREES," CARPENTER SAYS. "ACROSS THE NATION, TWO-YEAR COLLEGES ARE BECOMING THE LARGEST GRADUATE SCHOOLS FOR COLLEGE-DEGREED STUDENTS WHO WANT TO ADD SKILLS AND LEARN NEW TECHNOLOGIES. EMPLOYERS ARE LESS CONCERNED ABOUT WHERE A DEGREE CAME FROM, AND MORE INTERESTED IN SEEING UPGRADED SKILLS ON A RÉSUMÉ."

1950-1979

1950	THE UNIVERSITY OF ALABAMA IN HUNTSVILLE
1951	REDSTONE FEDERAL CREDIT UNION
1952	PARKER HANNIFIN CORPORATION
1954	SAINT-GOBAIN INDUSTRIAL CERAMICS
1955	TELEDYNE METALWORKING PRODUCTS
1961	J.F. DRAKE STATE TECHNICAL COLLEGE
1961	TRW, INC.
1962	THE BOEING COMPANY
1963	AVEX ELECTRONICS INC.
1963	THE PORT OF HUNTSVILLE
1964	SOUTHTRUST BANK, N.A.-HUNTSVILLE
1965	CRESTWOOD MEDICAL CENTER
1967	U.S ARMY CORPS OF ENGINEERS, ENGINEERING AND SUPPORT CENTER, HUNTSVILLE
1969	CAMPBELL & SONS OIL CO., INC.
1969	DUNLOP TIRE CORPORATION
1970	U.S. SPACE & ROCKET CENTER
1974	ENGELHARD CORPORATION
1975	HILTON HUNTSVILLE
1975	VON BRAUN CENTER
1979	CAS, INC.

The University of Alabama in Huntsville

IN JUNE 1961, AN UNUSUAL SCENE UNFOLDED AS MEMBERS OF THE ALABAMA LEGISLATURE SAT AND LISTENED AS DR. WERNHER VON BRAUN, DIRECTOR OF NASA'S MARSHALL SPACE FLIGHT CENTER, SPOKE TO THEM ABOUT SPACE TRAVEL AND LANDING A MAN ON THE MOON. AT THAT TIME, IT MUST HAVE SEEMED LIKE A PAGE TORN OUT OF A SCIENCE FICTION NOVEL. HE TOLD THE GROUP THAT THOSE DREAMS WERE POSSIBLE AND COULD BE ACCOMPLISHED IN ALABAMA BY ALABAMIANS, BUT ONE THING WAS MISSING: A STRONG RESEARCH

university. That day, von Braun convinced the legislative body to spend $3 million to help a branch of the University of Alabama evolve into The University of Alabama in Huntsville (UAH), an autonomous university that would control its own destiny, conduct research, and teach exceptional students the skills needed to put a man on the moon and allow travel beyond our solar system.

UAH has since developed into a nationally recognized institution of higher education, valued for its technological research for industry and government agencies, and

THE UNIVERSITY OF ALABAMA IN HUNTSVILLE IS A NATIONALLY RECOGNIZED INSTITUTION OF HIGHER EDUCATION, VALUED FOR ITS TECHNOLOGICAL RESEARCH FOR INDUSTRY AND GOVERNMENT AGENCIES, AND PRIZED FOR THE EXTRAORDINARY EDUCATIONAL OPPORTUNITIES IT PROVIDES ITS STUDENTS.

prized for the extraordinary educational opportunities it provides its students. It is a proud reminder of the synergy between academia, government, and business.

In many ways, UAH complements the research and development needs of local government entities and private industry, and answers the community's need for advanced educational opportunities in science and engineering. Yet, UAH also offers outstanding programs in liberal arts, administrative science, and nursing.

"The research of the university and its Ph.D. programs, with its

concentration in engineering and science, has made us nationally and internationally visible," says UAH President Frank Franz. "We have focused upon building strengths that reflect the needs and interests of the broad-based community that we serve."

UAH's core research strengths are found in propulsion, microgravity, materials, space physics, astrophysics, global climate change and hydrology, optics, and information technology. These areas and the school's other engineering and science programs allow UAH to provide strong support to NASA's Marshall Space Flight Center and nearby U.S. Army laboratories. The university was one of the founding tenants in Cummings Research Park.

In the College of Science, UAH has one of the world's leading authorities in atmospheric science. Professor John Christy chairs a United Nations study on global climate change.

Former UAH student Bernard Dagarin was named Engineer of the Year by *Design News* magazine in 1997 for his design of the Galileo space probe that landed on Jupiter.

The humanities and liberal arts are the heart of the curriculum for every student at UAH. In the College of Liberal Arts, students develop vital creative and interpretive skills, perspective, judgment, and a sophisticated understanding of the world.

UAH's College of Nursing encompasses an intensive medical, scientific, and social sciences education. UAH's curriculum in nursing combines the need for better-educated nurses with the premise that nursing is a caring profession.

In the College of Administrative Science, managing technology is an important focus. UAH has a world-renowned expert in man-

DENNIS KEIM

in providing more student housing and activities.

The university offers more than 100 clubs and organizations on campus, providing a variety of activities outside the classroom, such as intramural and intercollegiate sports, choir and music ensembles, and theater productions. Some of the clubs and organizations include the World Issues Society, Circle K, Society for Ancient Languages, Association for Campus Entertainment, Student Government Association, and professionally oriented clubs and societies in almost every discipline. With six national fraternities and five sororities at UAH, Greek life ranges from social interactions and activities to service projects for local and national charities.

It took a unique community like Huntsville to create a university like UAH. In many ways, the university is a reflection of the educational needs of this high-tech community.

"UAH is the result of the special character of Huntsville," says Franz. "The interaction among the university, federal agencies, and the community is crucial to our success. And the university's success is also crucial to the success of Huntsville."

UAH is a shining star on Huntsville's horizon, expanding the universe of opportunities for both students and the high-technology community that surrounds the university. As the world enters a new millennium, the men and women at UAH continue to look toward the future and provide a vibrant vision locally and nationally.

aging new product development, Professor William Souder, whose book *Managing New Product Innovations* is now in its fifth printing. Souder is currently directing a 17-nation study on product innovation.

The School of Graduate Studies brings together students and faculty scholars whose aims are to pursue advanced research, for both pure knowledge and applications. UAH research activities in both undergraduate and graduate studies give students many opportunities to apply their education in real-life job situations. More than 75 local businesses, industries, and government agencies provide students with hands-on experience and often permanent employment.

While UAH offers a quality education, it also has impressive athletic programs, including a two-time national champion ice hockey

team. Athletics are a highly charged blend of competitiveness and the ideal of the student-athlete. The university is home to 12 NCAA men's and women's sports programs.

Athleticism and scientific research have come together many times to win honors for the university, such as in the four national-award-winning entries submitted by UAH students who used their engineering and athletic skills to design, analyze, construct, and race a canoe made mostly of concrete. UAH students also have won national championships for the engineering, design, construction, and racing of a moon buggy.

Of the more than 6,900 students attending UAH, more than 1,000 live on campus. The demand for additional on-campus housing is increasing along with improvements in the quality of campus life. UAH has expanded its efforts

PEOPLE HELPING PEOPLE—FOR NEARLY 50 YEARS, MEMBERS OF REDSTONE FEDERAL CREDIT UNION (RFCU) HAVE DEPENDED UPON THOSE WORDS. IT IS A SLOGAN AS TRUE FOR MEMBERS TODAY AS IT WAS IN 1951 WHEN 11 FEDERAL EMPLOYEES AT REDSTONE ARSENAL PURCHASED $5 SHARES TO ORGANIZE WHAT IS NOW ONE OF THE LARGEST CREDIT UNIONS IN THE UNITED STATES. ✱ WITH MORE THAN 209,000 MEMBERS TODAY, RFCU USES ITS FINANCIAL STRENGTH TO CONTINUE A LEGACY OF SERVICE

that was established to offer low-cost loans, high-interest savings, and financial planning. Today, this member-owned, not-for-profit co-operative institution provides a variety of savings and lending pro-grams to its members with com-petitive rates and high-tech service.

"Our sole purpose is to assist members in building a financially strong future for themselves," says Gerald E. Toland, RFCU's president. "Our priority is to serve our mem-bers. We pride ourselves in offering professional services with a per-sonal touch and a high-technology financial system."

Growing with Its Members

RFCU has grown alongside the government institutions, organi-zations, and contractors that have located and expanded in Hunts-ville and North Alabama. In fact, RFCU's services are so sought out that they are frequently realized as an employment benefit. "There are many employers who define Redstone Federal as a benefit for their employees," Toland says. "Our superior services have been instrumental to our growth. And, so has the climate of area employ-ees who value and seek our ben-efits and who want to be part of a credit union that serves them."

RFCU's services offer members convenience, stability, and security. Along with its 14 credit union loca-tions in Alabama and Tennessee, the credit union offers its mem-bers access to Online Automated Services and Information Systems (OASIS).

RFCU's automated systems in-clude CALL-24, a 24-hour home teller service, and CLASS, a com-puterized loan application service that allows members to access loan information and rates, calculate payments and schedules, and sub-mit loan applications automatically by phone. OASIS also includes

RFCU's satellite station automated teller machines located throughout the area, as well as the Freedom Check Card with both ATM and purchasing capabilities worldwide. Recently, RFCU began offering members its PC banking service, World Wide Branch On-line (WWBO). WWBO offers a continu-ously growing list of options for members who choose to transact their business from their own PC.

"Convenience is an important factor in our success," Toland says. "We want to do our mem-bers' business better and faster than anyone else, and we want our members to know that we care about their financial needs. OASIS lets our members conduct their financial transactions by phone, on-line, or by other elec-tronic means so that they can do

their business when it is convenient for them."

Providing Many Financial Services

While many RFCU members begin their credit union rela-tionship by opening a savings and checking account, they often realize the true benefits of credit union membership when they apply for a consumer loan. Most consumer loans can be applied for through RFCU's computerized loan applica-tion service.

For members who need an auto loan, RFCU offers its CarSmart pro-gram, which provides pricing infor-mation and helps members make informed decisions concerning vehicle purchases. RFCU also offers on-the-spot financing at area dealerships, AutoPlus services that

RFCU'S SERVICES OFFER MEMBERS CONVE-NIENCE, STABILITY, AND SECURITY. MEMBERS BENEFIT FROM 14 BRANCH LOCATIONS IN ALABAMA AND TENNESSEE. RFCU ALSO OF-FERS SATELLITE STATION AUTOMATED TELLER MACHINES LOCATED THROUGHOUT THE AREA, AS WELL AS THE FREEDOM CHECK CARD WITH BOTH ATM AND PURCHASING CAPABILITIES WORLDWIDE.

locate and purchase any type vehicle at fleet discount prices, and Best Lease services for those who want to purchase a vehicle on a closed-lease plan with an option to purchase at the end of the lease term.

The credit union's real estate lending experts are always available to members who want to invest in a new home. Home mortgages are available through conventional loan programs with fixed, adjustable, or fixed-to-adjustable rates. Land loans, construction loans, and home equity loans are also available.

RFCU also offers special programs for first-time home buyers and for those who need to rebuild credit. "We have put an emphasis on our mortgage services and worked to increase services in this area because it is something our members want," Toland says.

In addition to its standard services, RFCU assists members with investments in individual retirement accounts, money market accounts, share certificates, and U.S. savings bonds. RFCU also offers special services through its Prime Times Club for members age 55 or older and its S.T.A.R. Club for youth members through age 12. "The S.T.A.R. Club gives us a unique opportunity to teach our young members financial responsibility and the value of credit union membership," Toland says.

Building for the Future

RFCU has experienced an annual growth of 7 percent in its membership since 1994, a growth trend that is expected to continue with the ongoing increase in employment in Huntsville and surrounding areas. Assets have increased from $586 million to $900 million in the past six years. Today, RFCU is the largest credit union in the state of Alabama, and has placed among the top 30 credit unions in the country.

To accommodate further membership growth, renovations have been completed at several credit union branches, and new offices and member services are scheduled for the future. "We are continually reviewing and updating the services we offer our members," Toland says. "We want to improve on the services our members want, such as CALL-24, which receives 375,000 to 450,000 calls per month, and the 32 ATMs, which receive more activity than any other institution's ATMs in North Alabama."

More than anything else, Redstone Federal Credit Union is about its members, people who want to help each other on their way to financial strength and security. There's no better way for an institution to gauge its effectiveness than by the success of the people it serves.

▲ DENNIS KEIM

"OUR SOLE PURPOSE IS TO ASSIST MEMBERS IN BUILDING A FINANCIALLY STRONG FUTURE FOR THEMSELVES," SAYS GERALD E. TOLAND, REDSTONE FEDERAL CREDIT UNION'S PRESIDENT. "OUR PRIORITY IS TO SERVE OUR MEMBERS. WE PRIDE OURSELVES IN OFFERING PROFESSIONAL SERVICES WITH A PERSONAL TOUCH AND A HIGH-TECHNOLOGY FINANCIAL SYSTEM."

WHEN PARKER HANNIFIN CORPORATION FIRST ESTABLISHED A PRESENCE IN HUNTSVILLE, ITS CUSTOMERS WERE JUST A FEW MILES AWAY. AT FIRST, THE COMPANY MADE FITTINGS FOR THE MISSILE PROGRAMS AT REDSTONE ARSENAL; THEN BUSINESS SHIFTED TO AEROSPACE FITTINGS FOR THE APOLLO AND SATURN PROGRAMS MANAGED IN HUNTSVILLE AT NASA'S MARSHALL SPACE FLIGHT CENTER. ✳ IN THE INDUSTRY DOWNTURN THAT FOLLOWED THE

completion of these space programs, Parker Hannifin found itself, like many other local companies in the aerospace business, at a crossroads. Parker Hannifin made a strategic decision to move its aerospace manufacturing to California and to fill the Huntsville plant with a new, stainless steel product line transferred from its headquarters in Cleveland, Ohio. It was the high standard of performance set by Huntsville's quality assurance program that saved the plant from closing.

"When Parker Hannifin originally came to Huntsville, it was to be close to its government customers," says David Bush, the company's marketing manager in Huntsville. "But Parker stayed here because of the workforce. The quality assurance program that was used here for the aerospace programs had very high standards, and it was the kind of program that we needed in the manufacturing of stainless steel components."

Quality Products

Today, Parker Hannifin's Huntsville operations design and manufacture tube and pipe fittings,

PARKER HANNIFIN CORPORATION IN HUNTSVILLE IS HEADQUARTERS FOR THE COMPANY'S INSTRUMENTATION CONNECTORS DIVISION, WHICH CONSISTS OF ABOUT 650 EMPLOYEES WORKING AT TWO PLANTS IN HUNTSVILLE AND ONE PLANT IN BOAZ, ALABAMA.

TODAY, PARKER HANNIFIN'S HUNTSVILLE OPERATIONS DESIGN AND MANUFACTURE TUBE AND PIPE FITTINGS AND OTHER COMPONENTS FOR INSTRUMENTATION APPLICATIONS-TECHNOLOGIES THAT CONTROL MOTION, FLOW, AND PRESSURE IN A BROAD SPECTRUM OF USES.

as well as other components for instrumentation applications—technologies that control motion, flow, and pressure in a broad spectrum of uses. The main Huntsville plant is headquarters for the company's Instrumentation Connectors Division, which consists of about 650 employees working at two plants in Huntsville and one plant in Boaz, Alabama.

"We manufacture various fittings and other components in 10 different materials. We have six major product lines with high-volume stainless production in Boaz and high-volume brass production in Huntsville," Bush says. "Our customer base consists of all our traditional markets—chemical, petrochemical, pulp and paper refining, and power. Our customers include General Motors, Air Products and Chemicals, Shell Chemical, and Exxon. Locally, our customers include Champion Paper, SCI Systems, Redstone Arsenal, and the Tennessee Valley Authority."

In addition, a new segment of the Instrumentation Connectors Division spun off from the Huntsville operations in early 1998 to better serve the global semiconductor market. The new plant, located in Huntsville's Chelsea Industrial Park, manufactures ultrahigh-purity fit-

tings for the semiconductor industry.

Growing International Business

Worldwide, Parker Hannifin has about 35,000 employees, 176 manufacturing plants, and 134 administrative and sales offices, company stores, and warehouses around the world. A Fortune 200 company, it is approaching the $5 billion mark in sales, reporting 1997 sales of $4.09 billion, up 14.1 percent from $3.59 billion in 1996.

"We're one of the divisions involved in that growth," Bush says. "U.S. customers who need instrumentation connectors work with Parker Hannifin employees in Huntsville. We've developed from a one product entity at the Huntsville plant to a global division to support sales in the United States, Canada, Asia, ASEAN [the Association of Southeast Asian Nations], Mexico, South America, and Europe."

Parker Hannifin's worldwide success is credited to the company's ability to bring together innovative designs, high-quality manufacturing, competitive pricing, and a broad product line. Adds Bush, "Management within Parker Hannifin is focused on growing the business, treating employees right, and working with customers to give them the products they need."

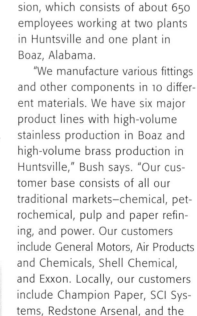

SAINT-GOBAIN INDUSTRIAL CERAMICS IS ONE OF HUNTSVILLE'S BEST-KEPT SECRETS—EVEN THOUGH IT HAS BEEN ONE OF THE CITY'S LARGEST EXPORTERS FOR MORE THAN 40 YEARS. ORIGINALLY ESTABLISHED IN FRANCE IN 1665, SAINT-GOBAIN MANUFACTURES PRODUCTS THAT ARE OF GREAT IMPORTANCE THROUGHOUT THE WORLD. THE INDUSTRIAL CERAMICS AND ABRASIVES PRODUCED IN HUNTSVILLE ARE ESSENTIAL TO MAKING A WIDE VARIETY OF WOOD AND METAL PRODUCTS. ✳ LOCATED BETWEEN THE TENNESSEE

River and the foothills of south Huntsville, this international company may be better known locally as Norton Materials. Today, the company's Huntsville plant is part of a global enterprise that has become a world leader by offering the best quality, the lowest cost, and the most comprehensive service in its market.

Manufacturing Products for International Markets

The raw materials produced at Saint-Gobain's Huntsville plant are shipped all over the world to countries such as India, China, Japan, Brazil, Canada, and the United Kingdom. These materials are for use in a multitude of products made by Saint-Gobain and other companies. For example, the company's abrasive grains are used to manufacture sandpaper and grinding wheels, which have numerous applications in the industrial and commercial metal, timber, glass, electronics, building, do-it-yourself, and auto repair markets. In addition, Saint-Gobain's industrial ceramics—containing the refractory zirconium powder used in the casting of titanium metals and ceramics—are used in the high-technology industry and surface treatment markets.

"Today, Saint-Gobain is the world's largest producer of glass

and ceramic material," says Tom Schuster, manager of the Huntsville plant. "And as a part of the company's industrial ceramics division, we are the world's largest supplier of zirconia abrasives for grinding tools and materials."

Huntsville Production to Grow

In 1954, after the federal government provided grants to encourage the relocation of New York-based abrasive companies, Saint-Gobain's local predecessor became the first industrial manufacturing operation in Huntsville. This well-established company was first attracted to North Alabama for the very same reason it remains here—low-cost energy and close proximity to the zirconium-rich Florida sands.

Saint-Gobain currently employs 150 people at its Huntsville plant, which represents a $40 million investment in the community. The 193,000-square-foot facility includes seven furnaces that produce 20,000 tons of raw materials annually. "Our products are still Norton-based, with 50 percent being abrasives and 50 percent being zirconium," Schuster says. "We have a 12 to 14 percent annual growth rate that is expected to continue as Saint-Gobain acquires new companies that will use our

▶ BOB GATHANY

raw materials and as we expand in the international markets."

The Huntsville community continues to be an asset to Saint-Gobain by providing on-site access to rail lines, a high-quality labor pool, and a port of entry and customs office at the Huntsville International Airport. "Saint-Gobain is committed to the Huntsville facility and continues to invest in this high-tech manufacturing facility," Schuster says. "We are a profitable part of the company, with $60 million of our $1.6 billion abrasive brand sales coming from the Huntsville plant. The work we do here will continue to establish Saint-Gobain's world leadership status in the abrasive market."

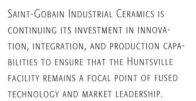

SAINT-GOBAIN INDUSTRIAL CERAMICS IS CONTINUING ITS INVESTMENT IN INNOVATION, INTEGRATION, AND PRODUCTION CAPABILITIES TO ENSURE THAT THE HUNTSVILLE FACILITY REMAINS A FOCAL POINT OF FUSED TECHNOLOGY AND MARKET LEADERSHIP.

NZ"PLUS"™ AND NORTON ABRASIVES® ARE FUSED, CRUSHED, AND SIZED IN A MODERN MANUFACTURING CENTER DEDICATED TO MAKING ONLY THESE SPECIALIZED ABRASIVES (LEFT).

THE HUNTSVILLE FACILITY EARNED ITS ISO 9002 RATING IN 1992. IT IS THE MOST ADVANCED, VERTICALLY INTEGRATED ZIRCONIA FUSION CENTER IN THE WORLD (RIGHT).

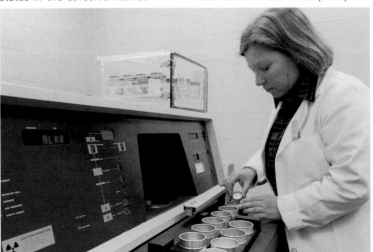

▶▶ BOB GATHANY

A MONG THE MOST RECOGNIZED NAMES IN THE TUNGSTEN INDUSTRY, TELEDYNE ADVANCED MATERIALS, TELEDYNE TUNGSTEN PRODUCTS, AND TELEDYNE FIRTH STERLING HAVE HAD A SIGNIFICANT IMPACT ON NORTH ALABAMA'S ECONOMY. PRODUCING HIGH-QUALITY TUNGSTEN AND TUNGSTEN-CARBIDE POWDERS AND METALS FOR THE AEROSPACE, AUTOMOTIVE, DEFENSE, OFF-ROAD EQUIPMENT, MEDICAL, AND SPORTS INDUSTRIES, THEY ARE PART OF A DYNAMIC GROUP OF COMPANIES THAT HAVE MADE

Teledyne Metalworking Products a technological leader in the manufacture of tungsten products.

Although based in Nashville, Teledyne Metalworking Products traces its Huntsville roots to 1955, and today relies on vertical integration from its North Alabama businesses to supply raw materials as well as finished products. Teledyne Advanced Materials produces pure tungsten powder, tungsten-carbide powders, molybdenum powders, reclaimed tungsten carbide, and ready-to-press grade powders that are sold to Teledyne Tungsten Products and Teledyne Firth Sterling. Tungsten Products uses the powders to manufacture tungsten contact rod, molybdenum and heavy metals, tungsten welding electrodes, spray wire, sheet, and balance weights for aircraft, automobiles, and golf clubs. Firth Sterling uses the powders to manufacture carbide semi-finished inserts, rounds, die and wear, snowplow blanks, and mining blanks. Other customers use the powders to manufacture cutting tools for inserts and for milling, drilling, turning, and threading.

Producing Powders for a Global Market

As one of the world's largest tungsten and tungsten-carbide powder facilities, Advanced Materials and its 260 employees utilize state-of-the-art automated tungsten reduction, carbonization, milling, and spray drying equipment to produce ungraded and graded forms of tungsten and tungsten-carbide powders. Located in a 400,000-square-foot plant in Huntsville, it is also one of the largest recyclers of tungsten-based materials, producing tungsten powders from both virgin and recycled materials. Tungsten powder can be used in a number of important ways: as a base material for producing tung-

sten-carbide powder, as an alloying agent in steel products, as filaments in lighting products, and in various mill applications such as furnace elements and electrodes.

As a result of the company's proprietary automation, low production costs, tungsten-carbide recycling processes, value-added products, and responsive customer support, Advanced Materials sells significant amounts of tungsten-based powders in the global marketplace. "We are a $70 million powder production company with plans of growing to $100 million over the next few years," says John Johnson, vice president of Advanced Materials. "We control about 60 percent of the U.S. market and about 30 percent of the global market. It's a competitive industry, but we plan to continue to grow over the next five years."

Growing Tungsten Product Lines

Tungsten Products manufactures sheets, rods, and machined products that reflect the unique

metallurgical properties of tungsten and molybdenum. The plant's molybdenum is sold in powder form to manufacturers of intermediate products, while its molybdenum wire is marketed for the plasma spray coating of piston rings and gearboxes in the automotive industry. One of the company's major product lines is electrodes for welding equipment, glass furnaces, and high-intensity lamps. Tungsten Products was the first to develop welding electrodes containing radiation-free lanthanum in place of thorium. Also produced are tungsten heavy alloys used in density-critical applications, such as counterweights for fixed-wing aircraft. Tungsten alloys containing nickel, iron, and/or copper are sold under the Densalloy name for a variety of applications in the aerospace and nuclear medicine industries.

In an effort to expand its product scope in the automotive, aerospace, health, sporting, and medical equipment industries, Tungsten Products is adding prod-

ALTHOUGH TELEDYNE METALWORKING PRODUCTS' HOME OFFICE IS IN LaVERGNE, TENNESSEE, IT HAS HUNTSVILLE ROOTS.

uct lines and improving operations. The company has spent more than $5.7 million in start-up costs and capital investments at its newly renovated, 188,000-square-foot facility in Huntsville's Jetplex Industrial Park.

"We are working closely with our customers to design products for new tungsten and molybdenum applications," says Rich Mount, vice president of Tungsten Products. "Our focus on continuous quality improvement, the introduction of cutting-edge products, the expansion of our facilities, and our growing presence in international markets position Tungsten Products as a significant contributor to Teledyne's growth strategy."

Providing Essentials for End Products

From its home base in nearby Grant, Alabama, Firth Sterling has become a recognized leader in supplying sintered tungsten-carbide products in rough and semifinished form. With annual sales of $30 million, the ISO 9002-certified plant has eight production lines operated by 200 employees, and continues to focus on quality improvement and cost reduction

programs. Companies buy Firth Sterling's unfinished tungsten-carbide forms for production of end products that span a multitude of applications and industries—such as metal cutting, die and wear, and earth drilling.

"The majority of what we sell goes to metal-cutting companies," says Tim Malone, Firth Sterling's marketing manager. "We also sell to the woodworking, fastener, and cutting applications industries. Our products are used in deep hole drilling for oil and gas, and in water well drilling. Although our products are involved in these industries, we don't sell to the end user. We sell to other companies that add value for the end user."

Growing in North Alabama

The demand for tungsten and tungsten powders continues to increase as more applications are discovered for the element's wear and heat-resistance properties. New products and applications are being discovered for tungsten-based products in the fields of aerospace, automotive, defense, off-road equipment, earth drilling and exploration, medical, and

DAVID HOGAN, PRESIDENT OF TELEDYNE METALWORKING PRODUCTS (LEFT)

PRODUCT LINES OF TELEDYNE METALWORKING PRODUCTS (RIGHT)

selected sports industries. As a result, Advanced Materials, Tungsten Products, and Firth Sterling are growing and expanding their facilities to take on a higher profile in the tungsten manufacturing industry.

"The support we have received from the community over the years has been very good," Johnson says. "Huntsville and North Alabama continue to provide us with the type of business environment that is conducive to our growth in this area."

A FULLY ACCREDITED, POSTSECONDARY INSTITUTION LOCATED IN HUNTSVILLE, J.F. DRAKE STATE TECHNICAL COLLEGE GRADUATES APPROXIMATELY 300 STUDENTS A YEAR. SOME 800 STUDENTS ATTEND THE SCHOOL TO EXPAND THEIR TRAINING IN A VARIETY OF TECHNICAL PROFESSIONS, INCLUDING PRACTICAL NURSING, DRAFTING AND DESIGN TECHNOLOGY, COSMETOLOGY, INDUSTRIAL ELECTRONICS TECHNOLOGY, AND COMPUTER INFORMATION SYSTEMS TECHNOLOGY. OTHER TWO-YEAR PROGRAMS

include accounting, secretarial and clerical, air-conditioning and heating, automotive, industrial electricity, graphic and printing communication, machine tool, and welding.

Drake State's student body is divided between recent high school graduates needing further education before joining the workforce and older, more mature students wanting to change or enhance their careers. "The average age of our students is about 27," says Dr. Johnny L. Harris, the college's president. "A lot of students either finished or dropped out of high school and then, years later, needed a technical education to get a better job in the workplace.

"Other students are people who are already working in industry, but who want to upgrade their skills," Harris continues. "We have engineers who took a lot of theory courses in college and now want more education on the practical side of their profession. They can get the hands-on education here that they were introduced to in

college. They leave excited about the new skills they have acquired."

Courses Fit Today's Job Market

Drake State has developed curricula designed to provide a highly concentrated and hands-on education that leads to better job opportunities. "A technical college provides students with the opportunity to acquire a technical skill that will make them employable," Harris says. "To do this, we create partnerships with industries that employ people in the skill areas we offer. We have to stay on top of the needs of industry because our job is to graduate students who can and will fill industry needs."

Drake State was founded in 1961 as the Huntsville State Vocational Technical School, offering courses in automotive mechanics, brick masonry, and cosmetology. Electronics was added shortly thereafter. In 1965, the school's name was changed to J.F. Drake Technical Trade School in honor of the late Dr. Joseph Fanning Drake,

who was president of Alabama A&M University for more than 35 years. Then, in 1973, Drake was granted technical college status by the Alabama State Board of Education, and its name was altered to reflect that change.

Today, Drake State employs 34 full-time and 20 part-time faculty members, as well as 30 staff personnel. Part of a statewide network of 32 postsecondary institutions, Drake State operates under the authority of the Alabama State Board of Education. The school is fully accredited by the Commission on Occupational Education.

Drake State's service area includes Madison and Jackson counties, as well as the northern part of Morgan County. The school also offers out-of-state enrollment to seven Tennessee counties. In addition, students who are not within the school's service area can attend Drake State if the technical college in their area does not offer the curriculum they need.

APPROXIMATELY 800 STUDENTS ATTEND J.F. DRAKE STATE TECHNICAL COLLEGE TO EXPAND THEIR TRAINING IN A VARIETY OF TECHNICAL PROFESSIONS, INCLUDING PRACTICAL NURSING, DRAFTING AND DESIGN TECHNOLOGY, COSMETOLOGY, INDUSTRIAL ELECTRONICS TECHNOLOGY, AND COMPUTER INFORMATION SYSTEMS TECHNOLOGY.

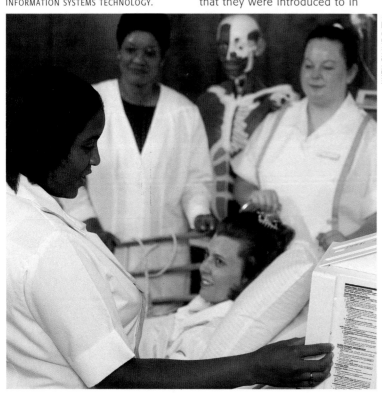

▶ DENNIS KEIM

FULLY ACCREDITED BY THE COMMISSION ON OCCUPATIONAL EDUCATION, DRAKE STATE ENSURES THAT STUDENTS GET THE EDUCATION THEY NEED TO PURSUE THEIR DREAM OF A CHALLENGING VOCATIONAL OR TECHNICAL CAREER.

Drake State was the first two-year college in Alabama to include in its computer information systems curriculum a Microsoft Authorized Academic Training Program certifying students to be Microsoft technical professionals. The college also has a General Motors training center that offers upgrade courses for GM and independent automotive mechanics, an Authorized Intergraph Education Center (drafting and design), and a master Automotive Service Excellence (ASE) certified program.

Meeting Industry Needs

We are constantly reviewing our curriculum to ensure we offer an extensive, technology-driven education to our students," Harris says. "We want to make sure our students have the skills to fill available jobs when they graduate."

To that end, each program of study offered at Drake State is supported by an advisory council consisting of professionals already employed in that field. These councils keep the Drake State staff advised as to the evolving training needs of those professions so courses can be revised and updated to reflect those needs.

"We've spent half a million dollars on our machine tool technology, we plan to add a new telecommunications phase to our electronics curriculum, and we've revamped our entire drafting and design technology curriculum to meet business and industry needs," Harris says.

Secondary School Outreach

While many of Drake's students have already finished high school, there is a growing need for technical education at the high school level. Harris believes technical colleges can fill that need.

"We have a dual enrollment program that permits city and county high school students to enroll at Drake State," Harris says. "It is becoming more and more difficult for city and county school systems to offer technical education because of the expense. We can solve this problem by allowing high school students to obtain their technical training here."

Drake State participates in the Tennessee Valley Tech Prep Consortium with Huntsville City Schools, Madison County Schools, and Scottsboro City Schools to promote technical education during the high school years.

At Drake State, students get the education they need to pursue their dream of a challenging vocational or technical career. Standing by the school's motto, Our Graduates Work, faculty and staff at Drake State are focused on the future as they prepare students to fill the health, business, and technical jobs of the 21st century.

J.F. DRAKE STATE TECHNICAL COLLEGE HAS DEVELOPED CURRICULA DESIGNED TO PROVIDE A HIGHLY CONCENTRATED AND HANDS-ON EDUCATION THAT LEADS TO BETTER JOB OPPORTUNITIES. "A TECHNICAL COLLEGE PROVIDES STUDENTS WITH THE OPPORTUNITY TO ACQUIRE A TECHNICAL SKILL THAT WILL MAKE THEM EMPLOYABLE," SAYS DR. JOHNNY L. HARRIS, THE COLLEGE'S PRESIDENT.

TRW Inc.

T RW HAS ALWAYS AIMED HIGH. BUILDING ON A LEGACY THAT HELPED SEND CHARLES LINDBERGH ACROSS THE ATLANTIC, THIS CLEVELAND, OHIO-BASED COMPANY HAS MADE SIGNIFICANT TECHNOLOGICAL CONTRIBUTIONS TO AIR AND SPACE DEVELOPMENT. BUT IT WAS NOT UNTIL THE LATE 1950S THAT TRW BECAME INVOLVED IN SPACE ENGINEERING AND INTEGRATION WORK, BALLISTIC MISSILES, AND PAYLOAD DEVELOPMENT. BY EMBRACING THESE NEW AREAS OF TECHNOLOGY, THE COMPANY BEGAN BUILDING A FOUNDATION

for the future successes of its Huntsville aerospace operations.

"TRW built the first series of *Pioneer* spacecraft launched into deep space after the *Explorer* in 1958," says Kelley Zelickson, operations manager in Huntsville for TRW Space & Missile Systems. "Our missile technology propelled us into the space game really early. So, when NASA was formed, one of our first steps was to open a field marketing office in Huntsville in 1961. We have had a continuous presence here ever since."

TRW INC. BUILDT THE CHANDRA ADVANCED X-RAY ASTROPHYSICS FACILITY SCIENTIFIC SPACECRAFT IN REDONDO BEACH, CALIFORNIA, FOR THE GEORGE C. MARSHALL SPACE FLIGHT CENTER IN HUNTSVILLE.

Committed to Huntsville Customers

A commitment to technical innovation during the formative years of space exploration helped TRW secure a principal role in NASA's Apollo program. The company built the Lunar Excursion Module's descent engine, allowing TRW employees to claim that "the last 10 miles were on us" during missions to the moon. Other NASA projects during that time included developing and testing Saturn boosters.

In 1972, due to the military's increased reliance on TRW's engi-

IN HUNTSVILLE, TRW IS BUILDING THE BATTLE MANAGEMENT COMMAND, CONTROL, AND COMMUNICATIONS SYSTEM FOR THE NATIONAL MISSILE DEFENSE SYSTEM.

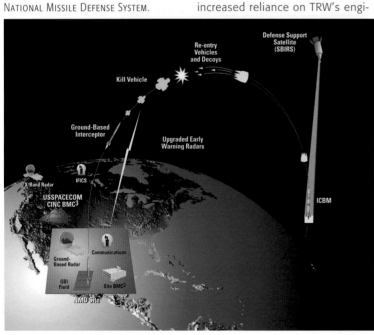

neering and manufacturing expertise, the company established a field engineering office in Huntsville to support U.S. Army software. Additionally, TRW's successful work in army software research and development and in software systems engineering allowed the Huntsville operation to further diversify and develop. The company's steady growth eventually necessitated a new facility in Cummings Research Park, which opened in 1982 and required expansion only five years later.

Today, TRW's 400 local employees are building the Battle Management Command, Control, and Communications Center for the National Missile Defense System. The company is also expanding on its previous work in advanced research, development, and engineering for several government and industrial customers in Huntsville. "The seeds for the work we are doing now were planted in the successes of the late '60s and early '70s," Zelickson says. "Those successes have built for us a high level of expertise in support of government programs that can also be used in other segments of TRW's commercial, space, and defense markets."

Positioned for Growth

W ith 80,000 employees worldwide and operations in 40 countries, TRW reported annual sales in 1998 of approximately $12 billion in the automotive, space, defense, and information systems markets. The company provides innovative, high-tech services in space and defense projects; transforming technologies into high-value products and services for government customers; and marketing products to the commercial sector. In keeping with these goals, the technology developed in support of TRW's Huntsville customers positions the local operation for growth along with the rest of the company.

As the world leader in high energy lasers, TRW is developing the Tactical High Energy Laser for the ASMDC. The company is also developing gel propellant for AMCOM tactical missiles.

"Huntsville has always been a profitable part of our organization," Zelickson says. "It is also very important because of the technological leverage we have developed here. TRW's commitment in Huntsville is to remain a viable and active aerospace company supporting our local customers and our community."

WITH GLOBAL HEADQUARTERS IN HUNTSVILLE AND HUNDREDS OF THOUSANDS OF SQUARE FEET OF DESIGN AND MANUFACTURING FACILITIES THROUGHOUT THE WORLD, AVEX ELECTRONICS INC. IS OFTEN THE COMPANY BEHIND MANY OF THE NAMES RECOGNIZED IN ELECTRONICS. THE AVEX NAME IS NOT SEEN ON ANY COMPUTER, MOBILE TELEPHONE, OR CAMERA IN LOCAL ELECTRONICS STORES, BUT THERE'S A LIKELY CHANCE AVEX HAD A HAND IN MAKING part of it or something like it.

In simplest terms, AVEX provides integrated contract manufacturing services to some of the world's leading electronic, telecommunications, and computer companies. "AVEX acts like the manufacturing arm of these organizations," says David Hester, vice president of global sales. "We offer a wide range of services and technology support, from helping them design their products to getting them shipped to market," says Hester.

AVEX offers a variety of services, including low-volume assembly, engineering and prototype support, through high-volume manufacturing, and production processes. This continuum of service means that AVEX customers enjoy great flexibility and dramatic cost savings in production of their products.

AVEX Leads in Growth

Founded in 1963 as Avco Electronics, the company was purchased in 1987 by the J.M. Huber Corporation, a privately held Fortune 500 company with diversified interests in such fields as engineered materials, engineered woods, and oil and gas.

In addition to Huntsville, other AVEX manufacturing and engineering facilities are located in Pulaski, Tennessee; Csongrád, Hungary; Guadalajara, Mexico; Campinas, Brazil; East Kilbride, Scotland; Cork, Ireland; Katrineholm, Sweden; and the Republic of Singapore. Other international locations are planned over the next several years.

Huntsville is also home to the company's primary design center and research and development operations. New processes are developed and proved in Huntsville and then made available to AVEX locations throughout the world.

Markets Continue to Expand

With an industrywide trend toward increased manufacturing outsourcing, AVEX's future looks secure. "In the last 10 to 15 years, more of the fast-growing technology companies are outsourcing their manufacturing," says Hester. "Many of them would prefer to invest their money in product marketing, research and development, software development, and hardware systems development rather than manufacturing. They concentrate on these areas, while we focus on manufacturing, and as a result, our clients get their product to the market quicker. Being the first to get a product to market has always been important, but the wide range of competitive consumer choices makes this more critical than ever," Hester says.

AVEX continues to respond to customer needs with such offerings as its Total Interactive Manufacturing Environment (TIME), which allows customers to log onto the AVEX Web site to retrieve secure, real-time factory data to monitor the status and quality of their products as they are being produced. "We are one of only two contract manufacturers in the world with this capability," Hester says. "Our Web site acts as a virtual plant for our customers, so they can see where their project is at any given time, as if it were taking place inside their own facility. This helps them make timely decisions on product introductions, availability, anticipated inventory, shipping, and other strategic and tactical issues."

AVEX employees have made their company successful, providing the innovative solutions and high performance achievements that make it possible to offer advanced electronics manufacturing technology and processes to companies worldwide.

DOUG SMOOT

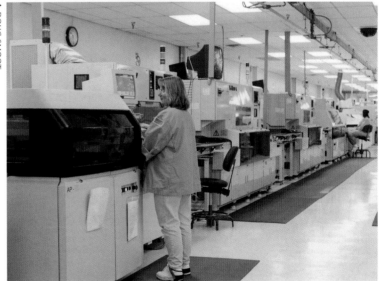

DOUG SMOOT

DOUG SMOOT

CLOCKWISE FROM TOP:
A STANDARD MOUNT ASSEMBLY LINE IS PART OF THE MANUFACTURING TECHNOLOGY THAT ALLOWS AVEX ELECTRONICS INC. TO MEET THE CUSTOMERS' NEEDS.

AVEX IN HUNTSVILLE IS HOME TO THE COMPANY'S PRIMARY DESIGN CENTER AND RESEARCH AND DEVELOPMENT LABORATORIES. HERE AN AVEX WORKER EXAMINES PC BOARD THROUGH RING LIGHT MAGNIFYING GLASS.

THE AVEX CORPORATE HEADQUARTERS ARE LOCATED AT 4807 BRADFORD DRIVE IN HUNTSVILLE.

When The Boeing Company first established a facility in makeshift quarters in Huntsville in 1962, the corporation made an economic pledge to North Alabama. Today, the 690,000-square-foot, four-building Boeing complex is located on a 110-acre site in the Jetplex Industrial Park, contrasting an image of high-tech innovation with the agricultural heritage of the South. Boeing's commitment to being a leading employer in North Alabama was reinforced with the decision to build a new, 1.5 million-square-foot rocket factory in Decatur, positioning the company as one of the area's high-technology front-runners.

Longtime Huntsville Presence

As an integral player in building the nation's space and defense programs, Boeing's Huntsville legacy began in the old Twickenham Hotel, where a handful of engineers developed the first stage of the Saturn V rocket. That project eventually earned the company integration responsibilities for the entire Saturn rocket program. In 1969, Boeing Huntsville participated in several phases of the Apollo program, working with NASA to put a man on the moon. Local employees also designed and built the lunar rovers that transported astronauts across the moon's surface.

The mid-1980s brought new growth for Boeing Huntsville when the company was awarded missile integration and simulation work from the U.S. Army. The company quickly began building a reputation for excellence. Boeing was awarded the contract to build the International Space Station for NASA, and later was selected as the prime contractor for the entire International Space Station industry team.

Between 1984 and 1990, Boeing's local presence expanded again, when the company invested $110 million to build its airport complex. With corporate acquisitions that included the purchase of Rockwell International in 1996 and a merger with McDonnell Douglas in 1997—both of which already maintained local facilities (Rockwell's Rocketdyne in 1956 and McDonnell Douglas in 1958)— Boeing became the largest aerospace company in Alabama.

The Huntsville operations support primarily four customers—NASA's Marshall Space Flight Center, the U.S. Army Aviation and Missile Command, the U.S. Army Space and Strategic Defense Command, and the Defense Intelligence Agency's Missile and Space Intelligence Center. Boeing offers these and other customers expertise in the areas of civil space, space transportation systems, space systems, missile systems, systems engineering and integration, and simulation and training systems.

Leading Space Contractor

In 1987, Boeing Huntsville began the design, development, and production of the heart of NASA's International Space Station: the laboratory and habitation modules, connecting nodes, and environmental and life support system. Now the prime contractor for the multipurpose orbiting Spacelab, one of NASA's most successful long-term programs, Boeing works under contracts valued in excess of $750 million. The company is responsible for more than 40 successful Spacelab missions, with existing contracts and options taking the program into the next century. Employee designs for placement of Spacelab experiments are used by Boeing at Kennedy Space Center to process and install the Spacelab in the shuttle payload bay prior to launch.

In the commercial market, Boeing is the prime contractor on a $350 million project with SPACEHAB, Inc., a company that

The Boeing Company in Huntsville is located on a 110-acre site in the Jetplex Industrial Park.

designs, maintains, integrates, and operates America's first commercially funded space laboratory. A pressurized SPACEHAB module, carried in a shuttle's payload bay, can be configured with a variety of lockers and racks to increase the area available for experiments, which helps ease the backlog of man-tended experiments in scientific, military, and commercial fields. Boeing's role involves designing, fabricating, and integrating the pressurized module facilities, and operating the SPACEHAB fleet of human-habitable laboratory modules. The company's developments in this area have been used to successfully carry scientific experiments on more than a dozen NASA missions.

The Huntsville facility is also responsible for upgrades to the space shuttle main engine, for space shuttle integration, and for the commercially developed Extreme Temperature Translation Furnace designed to fly aboard the shuttle and space station. Developed in cooperation with the University of Alabama in Huntsville, the furnace is capable of operating in a microgravity environment to perform many generalized microgravity materials experiments.

Developing Military Systems

Boeing Huntsville plays a major role in several key Department of Defense programs. In 1998, work began on one of Boeing's major defense programs, a $1.6 billion contract, as the lead system integrator for the National Missile Defense (NMD) program. Managed by the Joint Program office of the Department of Defense Ballistic Missile Defense Organization, the program is intended to defend the country against limited attack by intercontinental ballistic missiles that could be aimed at the United States in the future.

Boeing Huntsville is responsible for developing the weapon system element of the National Missile Defense program. The weapon system includes radar and early-warning

In 1998, Boeing began work as the lead system Integrator for the National Missile Defense program.

Boeing Huntsville develops and manufactures the U.S. Army's Avenger air defense system.

equipment needed to detect and track a threat. The battle management, command, control, and communications system collects, defines, and manages the threat engagement; processes and fuses the information from satellites and radar; and provides vital information to the weapon system, which is launched on demand to destroy attacking missiles in outer space. Boeing is also responsible for system testing, maintaining deployment readiness, and conducting deployment.

In a complementary role, Boeing is a subcontractor for the Joint National Test Facility Research and Development Contract, which involves the development and execution of numerous simulation capabilities for use in war games and defense exercises. Boeing continues to provide simulation support to the U.S. Army Aviation and Missile Command in Huntsville, and has roles in the development of the U.S. Army's Comanche aircraft, Hellfire missile, and helicopter systems.

In 1999, Boeing Huntsville began work on the U.S. Army's Patriot Advanced Capability-3 missile program (PAC-3). An earlier version of the missile was used extensively in the Gulf War. The PAC-3 missile acquires targets with low radar cross sections at increased ranges, hitting a target to ensure complete destruction. Boeing Huntsville's work on the program involves production, assembly, integration, and testing of the PAC-3 seeker.

Boeing Huntsville also develops and manufactures the U.S. Army's Avenger air defense system. This highly mobile, short-range air defense system integrates the Stinger missile in twin launch arms for rapid firing from a Boeing-designed and -produced gyro-stabilized turret. Since 1987, Boeing Huntsville has received contracts for more than 1,000 Avenger units with a total contract value of more than $700 million. The U.S. Army recognized Boeing in 1993 as one of five Contractor Performance Certification Program contractors in the nation. The certification qualified a three-year effort by Boeing, the army, and the Defense Contract Management Command to document contractor performance and customer satisfaction on the Avenger program. As a result, Boeing was awarded an army contract in 1995 for the integration of a Stinger missile launch system on the Bradley Fighting Vehicle, named Bradley Linebacker.

Building Rockets in Decatur

Following an extensive site selection process, Boeing chose Decatur as the home of the Boeing Delta IV Common Booster Core factory. Construction on the 1.5 million-square-foot facility, located on 410 acres in Decatur's Mallard-Fox Creek Industrial Park, began in November 1997.

The factory is designed to manufacture the largest structural component of the Boeing Delta IV family of rockets, the common core booster. The cores are 125 feet in length and 16 feet in diameter—roughly the size of a Boeing wide-body airplane fuselage.

The Delta IV launch vehicles were developed for the U.S. Air Force Evolved Expendable Launch Vehicle program, aimed at reducing space launch costs by at least 25 percent. Much of the engineering work for the program is performed at Boeing's facility in Huntsville. The group includes medium- and heavy-lift vehicles, and three commercial derivatives of the medium-class launch vehicle. The Delta IV vehicles are being offered to commercial launch customers as well as the U.S. government.

Working in the Community

While Boeing is recognized worldwide for its expertise in the areas of engineering, development, management, testing, and manufacturing of space and defense programs, it is also well known in Huntsville for its community spirit. In North Alabama, Boeing contributes more than $1 million annually to local communities, and of that, more than $600,000 annually is in support of health and human services, cultural, civic, and educational activities. Through an employee-funded and -managed program, Boeing also contributes more than $400,000 annually to health and human service agencies in North Alabama. In addition, employees volunteer thousands of hours every year to community projects.

With a long legacy in Huntsville, Boeing and its workforce are committed to being a significant contributor to the nation's space and defense programs, and to being a good corporate neighbor. Like the Boeing airplanes that fly over the Huntsville facility, the company's local presence has left an indelible mark on the economic skyline of Huntsville and North Alabama.

DECATUR IS HOME TO A MANUFACTURING FACILITY FOR BOEING'S DELTA IV ROCKETS (BOTTOM).

BOEING WAS AWARDED THE CONTRACT TO BUILD THE INTERNATIONAL SPACE STATION FOR NASA (TOP).

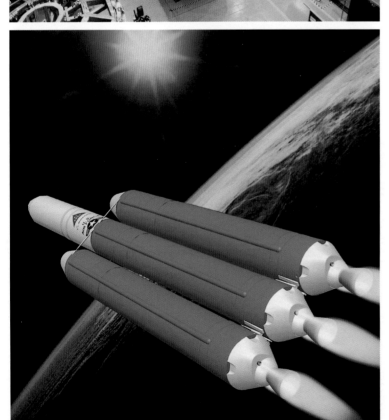

THE SOUTHTRUST FINANCIAL CENTER ON WHITESBURG DRIVE IS MORE THAN JUST A NEW BANKING LOCATION FOR ONE OF ALABAMA'S LARGEST BANKING INSTITUTIONS. IT REPRESENTS SOUTHTRUST'S FUTURE IN THE BANKING INDUSTRY: A FUTURE BUILT ON MAKING BANKING AND FINANCIAL PLANNING EASIER FOR CUSTOMERS WHO WANT COMPLETE FINANCIAL SERVICES LOCATED UNDER ONE ROOF AND WITHIN ONE COMPANY. ✳ LOCATED IN HUNTSVILLE'S NEWEST COMMERCIAL CENTER, THE $10 MILLION,

60,000-square-foot SouthTrust Financial Center represents the bank's strong commitment to offering a wide range of financial services. It is a complete financial center where customers can not only bank, but also obtain services involving trust and asset management, stock and securities management, mortgage lending, private banking, cash management, computer banking, and insurance planning.

Even the location of the new facility is a statement for SouthTrust and its future in Huntsville. The city's southern commercial center gives SouthTrust a strong presence in a prosperous area of Huntsville, while also allowing the bank to maintain its full-service downtown offices. In essence, the new financial center gives SouthTrust the opportunity to better serve its customers in North Alabama and southern Tennessee.

Resources for Growth

While each SouthTrust bank has full autonomy over local operations, each is backed by the financial strength of SouthTrust Corporation, a bank holding company operating more than 600 offices and several bank-related affiliates in Alabama, Florida, Georgia, Mississippi, North Carolina, South Carolina, and Tennessee. With consolidated total assets of $35 billion, SouthTrust Corporation is the 25th-largest bank holding company in the nation and the fifth largest in the Southeast.

"As a superregional bank, we have more resources and products we can offer to customers," says Chairman and President Joe O'Hara. "For business, that means offering very large loans with flexible structure and pricing, as well as sophisticated cash management services. For consumers, that means being able to offer new, innovative products faster and more conveniently than small banks. And, to both types of customers, we offer so many more services beyond traditional banking."

SouthTrust's primary resource is the employees and the team-oriented, seamless delivery they provide their customers. The employees are aggressive, energetic, prepared for change, and totally committed to meeting and exceeding customer expectations in the future. SouthTrust's 150 employees in the Huntsville area also give each customer a quality service guarantee: a guarantee that is backed by money if, for some reason, SouthTrust's delivery of high-quality services breaks down. Such a unique guarantee emphasizes SouthTrust's commitment to complete customer satisfaction.

The SouthTrust Financial Center represents more than the bank's commitment to its customers. It also represents the growth opportunities that SouthTrust has experienced since first opening for business in Huntsville in 1964.

"This area consistently leads the state in the number of jobs created. The growth has given us the opportunity to grow in a business climate which is progressive, friendly, and open to new market growth," says O'Hara, who was raised in Huntsville. "The other side of a growing market is that we are in a very competitive market. In lieu of that competition, we have to differentiate ourselves from our competitors by offering a comprehensive product line, innovation, flexibility, speed, convenience, and quality service through our local decision-making ability."

LOCATED IN HUNTSVILLE'S NEWEST COMMERCIAL CENTER, THE $10 MILLION, 60,000-SQUARE-FOOT SOUTHTRUST FINANCIAL CENTER REPRESENTS SOUTHTRUST BANK, N.A.-HUNTSVILLE'S STRONG COMMITMENT TO OFFERING A WIDE RANGE OF FINANCIAL SERVICES.

POISED TO JET AHEAD OF THE COMPETITION, THE PORT OF HUNTSVILLE IS READY TO MEET ANY MULTIMODAL TRANSPORTATION NEED. COMPRISED OF HUNTSVILLE INTERNATIONAL AIRPORT, THE INTERNATIONAL INTERMODAL CENTER, AND JETPLEX INDUSTRIAL PARK, THIS UNIQUE COMPLEX OFFERS CUSTOMERS A VARIETY OF SERVICES FOUND COLLECTIVELY AT NO OTHER LOCATION IN THE WORLD. THE MULTIMODAL CENTER IS LEADING NOT ONLY HUNTSVILLE, BUT ALSO AN ENTIRE 18-COUNTY SERVICE REGION

into the future of transportation.

"We are unique," says Port of Huntsville Board Chairman Nancy Green-Burg. "To our knowledge, there is no other transportation facility that has passenger service, air cargo, rail cargo with runway access, and an industrial park all located together under the same ownership. Our visionary leadership, from 1963 to the present, has allowed us to provide a vital connection for our customers between the Tennessee Valley and the world. As a result, we are looked upon as a model for other communities looking to enhance their transportation services."

THE PRESENCE OF JETPLEX INDUSTRIAL PARK AND ITS SERVICES EFFECTIVELY POSITIONS THE PORT OF HUNTSVILLE AS A HUB FOR INTERNATIONAL TRADE AND CONTRIBUTES TO THE ECONOMIC COMPETITIVENESS OF THE REGION (TOP).

IN ORDER TO ATTRACT NEW AND EXPANDING BUSINESSES TO A COMMUNITY, TRANSPORTATION INFRASTRUCTURE IS ESSENTIAL. THE PORT OF HUNTSVILLE IS COMMITTED TO PROVIDING THE TENNESSEE VALLEY WITH THE BEST MULTIMODAL TRANSPORTATION RESOURCES POSSIBLE (BOTTOM).

Center of Economic Growth

The Port of Huntsville is a center of vibrant economic growth for the Tennessee Valley, and employs more than 15,000 people with a combined payroll of some $638 million within a two-mile radius of the port itself. As a result of the success of the complex, the Port of Huntsville has created a multiplied regional impact of 28,594 jobs and $971 million in total payroll.

"We are a catalyst for economic growth," says Green-Burg. "Trans-

portation infrastructure is essential for any community in attracting new and expanding businesses. We are committed to providing the Tennessee Valley with the best resources possible in terms of multimodal transportation."

Huntsville International Airport is one of the South's most modern and best equipped international airports. The facility offers passengers many conveniences, including curbside baggage check-in, valet parking, a six-level covered parking facility, nationally recognized concourse concessions, and a special center designed and equipped for business travelers. In addition, visitors can view a series of con-

course murals tracing the history of flight, learn about Huntsville's participation in the nation's space program, or see special displays dedicated to Huntsville's role in the U.S. Army. Passenger air service is provided by American Airlines, COMAIR, Delta Air Lines, Northwest Airlink, US Airways, and US Airways Express.

Opened in 1986, the International Intermodal Center offers cargo customers a multitude of services. The center handles more than 26 million tons of imported goods and 31 million tons of exported goods each year. This inland port facility—built around a 45-ton gantry crane—is a U.S. Customs port of entry and provides a wide range of on-site services for the center, including freight forwarders, customs brokers, logistics companies, U.S. Department of Agriculture (USDA) inspectors, and much more.

The International Intermodal Center is also home to services necessary for receiving, transferring, storing, and distributing air, rail, or highway cargo. Air cargo service is provided by Airborne Express, Cargolux, DHL, Emery Worldwide, Federal Express, Panalpina, and United Parcel Service, and rail service is provided by Norfolk Southern. Due to growth in the air cargo business, the center recently expanded its air cargo apron. More

than 100,000 square feet of warehousing and office space is currently occupied on-site, with the immediate potential to add an additional 100,000 square feet of terminal cargo space.

Located adjacent to Huntsville International Airport, the 2,500-acre Jetplex Industrial Park provides all the necessary ingredients to make the industrial community successful, including U.S. Customs, USDA inspectors, Foreign Trade Zone #83, Alabama Industrial Development Training, and many other intermodal services. Jetplex Industrial Park, home to companies such as Boeing, Chrysler, Futaba, LG Electronics, and Raytheon, offers one-stop service opportunities that enhance business operations in the Tennessee Valley. The presence of Jetplex Industrial Park and its services effectively positions the Port of Huntsville as a hub for international trade and contributes to the economic competitiveness of the region.

Looking toward the Future

The Port of Huntsville continues to grow under a construction and capital expenditures plan that calls for additional expansions at all three if its facilities. This program is just the beginning of plans to develop the complex into one of the world's leading multimodal transportation facilities.

"We are in the midst of a very aggressive land acquisition plan that will take us to more than 8,300 acres," Port of Huntsville Executive Director Richard Tucker says. "Much of the new acreage to the west of the complex is targeted

for aviation growth, which includes additional runways and terminal facilities as determined by demand. This program will make us one of the largest transportation centers, based on land use, in the world."

In addition to runway and terminal expansions, Tucker notes that the master plan calls for additional expansion at both the International Intermodal Center and Jetplex Industrial Park. The expansion will include growth of the intermodal rail spur and truck lanes as well as increased capacity for depot storage and parking. There are also future growth opportunities for additional land at Jetplex Industrial Park.

"What we have accomplished thus far at the Port of Huntsville in terms of expansions and improvements has made us a standout for economic development prospects interested not only in Huntsville, but anywhere in the Tennessee Valley," Tucker adds. "We plan to improve and grow continuously

in order to meet and exceed the demands of our customers. We will continue to help attract new companies to the Tennessee Valley region by providing the finest in multimodal transportation opportunities."

The Port of Huntsville has a clear vision for the 21st century: to transport the world to its customers and its customers to the world.

HUNTSVILLE INTERNATIONAL AIRPORT IS ONE OF THE SOUTH'S MOST MODERN AND BEST EQUIPPED INTERNATIONAL AIRPORTS. THE FACILITY OFFERS PASSENGERS MANY CONVENIENCES, INCLUDING CURBSIDE BAGGAGE CHECK-IN, VALET PARKING, A SIX-LEVEL COVERED PARKING FACILITY, NATIONALLY RECOGNIZED CONCOURSE CONCESSIONS, AND A SPECIAL CENTER DESIGNED AND EQUIPPED FOR BUSINESS TRAVELERS.

OPENED IN 1986, THE INTERNATIONAL INTERMODAL CENTER OFFERS CARGO CUSTOMERS A MULTITUDE OF SERVICES. THE CENTER HANDLES MORE THAN 26 MILLION TONS OF IMPORTED GOODS AND 31 MILLION TONS OF EXPORTED GOODS EACH YEAR.

Crestwood Medical Center

S ONE OF ALABAMA'S LEADING HEALTH CARE INSTITUTIONS, CRESTWOOD MEDICAL CENTER OFFERS HIGH-TECH, COMPREHENSIVE SERVICES TO A COMMUNITY OF PATIENTS WHO DEMAND THE BEST FROM A CONCERNED, CARING, AND HIGHLY SKILLED STAFF OF MEDICAL PERSONNEL. PUTTING PERSONAL SERVICE FIRST AND COMBINING THE HUMAN VALUES OF COMPASSION AND RESPECT WITH THE MOST ADVANCED MEDICAL TECHNOLOGY AND PROCEDURES IS THE CRESTWOOD WAY. ✳ "WHAT WE OFFER IS A MORE PERSON-

LOCATED IN SOUTHEAST HUNTSVILLE, CRESTWOOD MEDICAL CENTER IS A FULLY ACCREDITED, 120-BED HOSPITAL OFFERING CONVENIENT ACCESS TO ITS MAIN FACILITIES AND TWO MEDICAL OFFICE BUILDINGS FOR RESIDENTS OF NORTH ALABAMA AND SOUTH TENNESSEE. CRESTWOOD'S 415 ON-STAFF PHYSICIANS—REPRESENTING 39 SPECIALTIES—ARE ASSISTED BY 450 FULL-TIME EMPLOYEES (TOP RIGHT).

CRESTWOOD OFFERS HIGH-TECH, COMPREHEN-SIVE SERVICES TO A COMMUNITY OF PATIENTS WHO DEMAND THE BEST FROM A CONCERNED, CARING, AND HIGHLY SKILLED STAFF OF MEDI-CAL PERSONNEL. "WHAT WE OFFER IS A MORE PERSONALIZED SERVICE," SAYS TOM WIESE, CHIEF EXECUTIVE OFFICER OF CRESTWOOD MEDICAL CENTER. "WE ARE ABLE TO GIVE PATIENTS AND THEIR FAMILIES THE COMPAS-SIONATE CARE AND PERSONAL ATTENTION THEY NEED WHILE IN THE HOSPITAL."

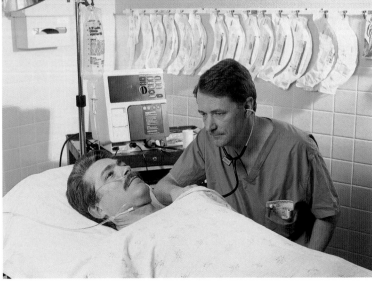

alized service," says Tom Wiese, chief executive officer of Crestwood Medical Center. "We're not as large as other medical centers, but we have the same technical capabilities of larger centers, particularly in the areas of surgery and diagnostics. And because of our smaller size, we are able to give patients and their families the compassionate care and personal attention they need while in the hospital."

Located in southeast Huntsville, this fully accredited, 120-bed hospital offers convenient access to its main facilities and two medical office buildings for residents of North Alabama and south Tennessee. Crestwood's 415 on-staff physicians—representing 39 specialties—are assisted by 450 full-time employees. Together, they offer a wide range of services, including comprehensive diagnostic imaging and laboratory services, inpatient and outpatient surgery, physical therapy, adolescent and adult behavioral health services, and emergency medical care.

Growing with Patient Needs

In 1965, a group of doctors established Crestwood so that the community would have a choice

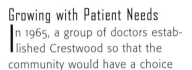

for medical services in Huntsville. The hospital was privately owned until 1982, when it was purchased by Columbia/HCA. While Crestwood has had exceptional growth in services, it has never lost focus on its mission: to provide an alternative, friendly environment for health care. The hospital has recently added an oncology program that augments the Center for Cancer Care, opened the state's first birthing center, and added services to meet demands in the areas of cardiology, orthopedics, outpatient care, and emergency care. The medical center is in the process of expanding, renovating, and relocating several departments, including emergency, special procedures, business office, and the main lobby entrance. At the end of the first quarter of 2000, the community will have a choice of where to have babies delivered when Crestwood begins offering full obstetrical services.

Crestwood provides three inpatient units—surgery, medical, and critical care. Outpatient services include ambulatory surgery and special procedures such as endoscopy, pain management, and laser surgery. Diagnostic services include mammography, computerized axial tomography, magnetic resonance imaging, ultrasound, nuclear medi-

cine, cardiac catheterization, and cardiopulmonary care. Crestwood also provides specialized services in the fields of behavioral health, sleep disorders, and physical therapy. In addition, the hospital operates the Madison Medical Center in Madison and the North Madison County Family Practice Clinic in Hazel Green.

"We are working to pinpoint areas that are underserved in Madison County and then develop a plan to serve those areas," Wiese says. "They may include communities that actually need on-site medical facilities or they may need medical specialties that we can provide from our main hospital. We are working to fulfill the medical needs of the people of Madison County."

Besides providing the best in personal care for its patients, Crestwood is also a good corporate neighbor. The facility reaches out to the community through health fairs and wellness initiatives such as the Senior Friends program, which provides not only medical care, but also social programs for senior members. However, it is in the hospital environment where the employees of Crestwood Medical Center really make a difference as they focus on seeing the person in every patient.

ELEBRATING 30 YEARS AS A SUCCESSFUL, DIVERSIFIED PETROLEUM BUSINESS, CAMPBELL & SONS OIL COMPANY CONTINUES A FAMILY TRADITION STARTED BY FOUNDER CLAUDE CAMPBELL. BEFORE BECOMING A TEXACO DISTRIBUTOR, CAMPBELL PUMPED GAS AND CHANGED OIL FOR CUSTOMERS AT HIS GAS STATION ON DRAKE AVENUE. WITH A COMMITMENT TO HONEST BUSINESS PRINCIPLES, A DEDICATION TO HARD WORK, ATTENTION TO CUSTOMER AND EMPLOYEE NEEDS, AND A FOCUS ON GROWING HIS BUSINESS,

Campbell eventually expanded into selling and distributing gasoline on a consignment basis. His success did not go unnoticed by Texaco, and he was offered a distributorship in Huntsville in 1969.

Business with a Handshake

Once known as C.H. Campbell Oil Company, Campbell & Sons is today the number one seller of gasoline in the Huntsville/Madison County area, and the fifth-largest branded gasoline jobber in the state. Campbell & Sons distributes 130,000 gallons of gasoline each day. The company distributes 48 million gallons of gasoline and diesel fuel annually to customers throughout North Alabama through Texaco and Conoco retail facilities and two sub-jobberships.

Campbell's work ethic, management style, and business savvy are today carried on by his three sons, all of whom were required to start in the family business on the bottom rung before climbing the ladder to management positions and, eventually, ownership. Campbell's oldest son, LaBronn, entered the business in 1975. Tony joined the company in 1977, and Alan followed suit in 1984. All three brothers took over management positions in the company before their father's retirement in 1988.

"We still do business with a handshake," says Tony Campbell. "We stand by our word, and we stand together. In all our expansion plans, if even one brother is against a business venture, then we are all against it. LaBronn, Alan, and I manage this company as a team."

Growing the Petroleum Business

Campbell & Sons has experienced constant growth throughout its history, with significant activity dur-

ing the 1990s. The company's 20 employees provide gasoline and other petroleum products throughout Dekalb, Jackson, Jefferson, Lawrence, Limestone, Madison, Marshall, and Morgan counties to 74 Texaco- and Conoco-branded gasoline convenience stores, 35 of which are owned by Campbell & Sons. In addition, Campbell & Sons Lubricants, based in Decatur, supplies customers across North Alabama with motor oils, industrial lubricants, and greases. Lubeco, another subsidiary company, manages and operates Texaco Xpress Lube Centers in North Alabama, Georgia, and Tennessee.

"A lot of our growth can be attributed to the strong brand recognition that customers have with the Texaco name," Tony Campbell says. "But our growth is also a product of our dedication to providing the best service and

the highest-quality product to our customers at a fair price, and to identifying business opportunities that expand our services in the market."

Since 1994, Campbell & Sons has invested $15 million in the growth and expansion of the company and, as a result, has seen its sales double. "We are proud of our success in Huntsville and North Alabama," Tony Campbell says. "And we will continue to provide our customers with the best product at the best price in locations that are safe, clean, and convenient."

CELEBRATING 30 YEARS AS A SUCCESSFUL, DIVERSIFIED PETROLEUM BUSINESS, CAMPBELL & SONS OIL COMPANY CONTINUES A FAMILY TRADITION STARTED BY FOUNDER CLAUDE CAMPBELL AND CARRIED ON BY HIS SONS (FROM LEFT), ALAN CAMPBELL, TONY D. CAMPBELL, AND LABRONN CAMPBELL.

CAMPBELL & SONS OWNS 35 TEXACO- AND CONOCO-BRANDED GASOLINE CONVENIENCE STORES TRHOUGHOUT DEKALB, JACKSON, JEFFERSON, LAWRENCE, LIMESTONE, MADISON, MARSHALL, AND MORGAN COUNTIES IN ALABAMA. "WE ARE PROUD OF OUR SUCCESS IN HUNTSVILLE AND NORTH ALABAMA," TONY CAMPBELL SAYS. "AND WE WILL CONTINUE TO PROVIDE OUR CUSTOMERS WITH THE BEST PRODUCT AT THE BEST PRICE IN LOCATIONS THAT ARE SAFE, CLEAN, AND CONVENIENT."

IN 1967, THE U.S. ARMY CORPS OF ENGINEERS BEGAN A 30-YEAR LEGACY IN HUNTSVILLE AS AN IMPORTANT CONTRIBUTOR TO THE NATIONAL DEFENSE THROUGH ITS SPECIALIZED ENGINEERING AND TECHNICAL EXPERTISE. THEN KNOWN AS THE HUNTSVILLE DIVISION, THE GROUP BEGAN WITH THE DESIGN AND CONSTRUCTION OF THE NATION'S BALLISTIC MISSILE DEFENSE SYSTEM. THE ORGANIZATION WAS ESTABLISHED TO MANAGE THE DESIGN AND CONSTRUCTION OF THE RADAR, LAUNCH, AND OTHER SITE FACILITIES NEEDED TO PROTECT

U.S. ARMY

CLOCKWISE FROM TOP:

THE U.S. ARMY CORPS OF ENGINEERS, ENGINEERING AND SUPPORT CENTER, HUNTSVILLE'S WORK FOR THE NATIONAL MISSILE DEFENSE PROGRAM HAS INCLUDED PROJECT MANAGEMENT OF THE DESIGN AND CONSTRUCTION OF THE GROUND-BASED RADAR PROTOTYPE FACILITY ON KWAJALEIN ATOLL IN THE SOUTH PACIFIC.

A COMPLEX DESIGN OF STEEL REINFORCING BARS AND 20-INCH-THICK, CONCRETE BLAST CONTAINMENT WALLS FORM THE BARRIER BETWEEN THE DESTRUCTION OF CHEMICAL WEAPONS AND THE PUBLIC.

THE HUNTSVILLE CENTER IS THE LIFE CYCLE PROJECT MANAGER FOR THE DESIGN, CONSTRUCTION, EQUIPMENT ACQUISITION, AND INSTALLATION FOR THE FACILITIES THAT WILL DESTROY THE NATION'S STOCKPILE OF AGING, TOXIC CHEMICAL WEAPONS.

the country from foreign missile attack. Although the nation's initial ballistic missile defense program gradually diminished in the 1970s, the Corps of Engineers in Huntsville has continued to play a role in this important national defense program. Over the past few years, the Hunstville Corps has expanded its expertise beyond ballistic missile defense to support a variety of national military programs.

Today, the agency is known as the U.S. Army Corps of Engineers, Engineering and Support Center, Huntsville. Supporting more than 500 funded projects, the Center's 600 employees work with an annual budget that exceeds $500 million. Although a government agency, the Center operates like a private business. Government customers buy its services and products based on quality, customer satisfaction, and competitive cost.

The Huntsville Center's missions involve programs that are broad in scope; require integrated facilities that cross geographical boundaries; require commonality, standardization, multiple-size adaptation, or technology transfer; require a centralized management structure for the effective control of program

development, coordination, and execution; or require services not normally provided by other Corps of Engineers' elements.

High-Technology Support

The Huntsville Center serves as the Corps of Engineers' National Missile Defense Program Manager for the new millennium. In doing so, it continues its long-standing commitment to the nation to support the testing and deployment of a missile defense program.

However, the Huntsville Center's primary focus is now centered on

the destruction of the nation's aging chemical weapons stockpile. The Center is the U.S. Army's Life Cycle Project Manager for the facilities that will destroy these toxic chemical munitions. The Huntsville Center is responsible for the facility design, construction, equipment acquisition, and installation for the eight chemical demilitarization facilities planned for the United States. The Center manages construction of incineration facilities at sites in Anniston, Pine Bluff, and Umatilla, as well as sites in Newport, Indiana, and Aberdeen, Maryland. The

LINDA JAMES / U.S. ARMY CORPS OF ENGINEERS

ROBERT DIMICHELE / U.S. ARMY CORPS OF ENGINEERS

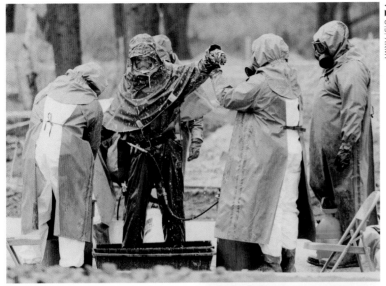

Center's design work in this program has earned special recognition from the Department of Defense for advanced engineering in the disposal of toxic chemicals. In addition, the Center is the design and construction manager for the first chemical weapons destruction facility in the Russian Federation.

The Center's munitions expertise includes a national public safety program to detect and dispose of unexploded ordnance found at closing or formerly used defense sites around the country. The Center's experts dispose of unexploded ordnance that poses an imminent and substantial endangerment to public health or the environment. Based on technical capabilities, experience in conventional weapons effects, and the attendant methodologies to mitigate explosives effects, the Huntsville Center has earned the designation as the Corps of Engineers' Center of Expertise for Unexploded Ordnance.

The Center also serves as the Center of Expertise for Ranges and Training Land Management. It provides the U.S. Army, the National Guard Bureau, and the U.S. Marine Corps with technical support and design guidance in the standardization of training ranges so that the firing of military munitions can be done as safely and effectively as possible.

Expertise for Military Programs

The Huntsville Center's innovative and cost-effective technical skills support a wide array of ser-

vices for government facilities. For example, the Center has a program to maintain, repair, and renew medical facilities cheaper, better, and faster than traditional government methods. It manages a nationwide program to save money and reduce energy usage, and, as a result, has saved American taxpayers millions of dollars while providing private enterprise opportunities for growth. This energy program has received two federal Hammer awards for innovation in American government from the vice president. In addition, the Center develops and maintains the standard engineering designs for many of the facilities commonly found on military installations such as conforming storage facilities, child development centers, fire stations, and physical fitness centers.

Innovation and specialized expertise have led the Center into

the forefront of electronic security and utility monitoring systems. Huntsville Center's reputation in this field extends far beyond support to military installations. Its customers include the White House, the Federal Bureau of Investigation, the Bureau of the Mint, and the Smithsonian Institution.

For more than 30 years, the Huntsville Center has used its specialized engineering and technical expertise, as well as its contracting, project management, and construction experience, to provide unique services to the nation. Concerned about efficiency and cost-effectiveness of government business practices, the Huntsville Center is dedicated to continuous improvement. In fact, the organization has been recognized by the President's Quality Award Program as one of the top-performing agencies in all the federal government.

CLOCKWISE FROM TOP LEFT:
A BATH IN BLEACH IS NECESSARY TO DECONTAMINATE ORDNANCE EXPERTS AFTER THEY RECOVER CHEMICAL WARFARE MATERIAL FROM FORMERLY USED DEFENSE SITES.

THE HUNTSVILLE CENTER'S SPECIALIZED PROJECT MANAGEMENT, ENGINEERING, AND CONTRACTING EXPERTISE ALLOWS THE CENTER TO PERFORM WORK FOR MILITARY MEDICAL FACILITIES CHEAPER, BETTER, AND FASTER THAN TRADITIONAL GOVERNMENT METHODS.

THE HUNTSVILLE CENTER REMOVES THE PUBLIC SAFETY HAZARD OF UNEXPLODED ORDNANCE, A LEGACY THAT SOMETIMES REMAINS AT FORMERLY USED DEFENSE SITES AROUND THE COUNTRY.

THE HUNTSVILLE CENTER EARNED A HAMMER AWARD IN GOVERNMENT REINVENTION FROM VICE PRESIDENT AL GORE FOR ITS INNOVATIVE ENERGY SAVINGS PROGRAM AT FORT POLK, LOUISIANA.

Dunlop Tire Corporation

OR MORE THAN 100 YEARS, DUNLOP TIRE CORPORATION HAS KEPT ITS BUSINESS STRATEGY FOCUSED ON MEETING THE NEEDS OF ITS CUSTOMERS. THE COMPANY'S SUCCESS HAS BEEN BASED ON THE PERFORMANCE OF ITS TIRES SINCE 1888, WHEN FOUNDING FATHER JOHN BOYD DUNLOP, A SCOTTISH VETERINARY SURGEON LIVING IN IRELAND, INVENTED THE AIR-INFLATED TIRE FOR USE FIRST WITH THE BICYCLE AND THEN WITH THE AUTOMOBILE. ✳ DUNLOP, NOW A SUBSIDIARY OF SUMITOMO RUBBER INDUSTRIES

of Japan, established its largest U.S. operation in Huntsville in 1969. The Buffalo-based company maintains a 1.2 million-square-foot facility in Lowe Industrial Park, representing an investment of more than $250 million and employing more than 1,700 people to design, develop, test, and manufacture tires for passenger cars and light trucks.

"Dunlop is one of three tire manufacturers that have made Alabama the third-largest tire-making state in the nation," says Mark Sieverding, manager of the Huntsville plant. "There are two Dunlop tire manufacturing plants in the United States, and the Huntsville plant does the majority of the company's U.S. manufacturing."

Responsive to Customers

In 1989, Dunlop established a competitive edge in the marketplace by adding a $10 million, state-of-the-art test facility and track to the Huntsville operation. Here, employees can test tires for wet and dry handling, noise vibration, and other technical design elements. "The test facility helps us to be more responsive to our customers during new product development," Sieverding says. "We can shorten the cycle of de-velopment, prototype manufacturing, and testing because we have immediate access to a test track. The facility and the business philosophy behind it make Dunlop and Sumitomo unique in the industry."

To capitalize on its enhanced capabilities in Huntsville, Dunlop relocated its car tire design group to the plant in 1988, thus creating a complete development, manufacturing, and test facility. Since then, the company's reputation has continued to grow in the highly competitive tire manufacturing industry, particularly with original equipment customers.

"Our competitive elements reflect the quality of our products, service to our customers, technology, and the ability to respond to original equipment needs," Sieverding says. "Although more tires are sold in the replacement market than in the original equipment market, the latter is essential to providing our company with market exposure because a high percentage of consumers replace tires with the vehicle's original tire brand. Original equipment business also provides us with manufacturing stability."

FOR MORE THAN 100 YEARS, DUNLOP TIRE CORPORATION HAS FOCUSED ITS BUSINESS STRATEGY ON MEETING THE NEEDS OF CUSTOMERS. IN 1969, DUNLOP ESTABLISHED ITS LARGEST U.S. OPERATION IN HUNTSVILLE. THE FACILITY IS A 1.2 MILLION-SQUARE-FOOT PLANT LOCATED IN LOWE INDUSTRIAL PARK (TOP).

TODAY, THE DUNLOP HUNTSVILLE MANUFACTURING FACILITY HAS BECOME A MAJOR PLAYER IN THE WORLDWIDE TIRE INDUSTRY. THE FOUR-CREW OPERATION NEVER STOPS—SEVEN DAYS A WEEK, 24 HOURS A DAY—PRODUCING QUALITY AUTOMOTIVE TIRES (BOTTOM LEFT AND RIGHT).

DENNIS KEIM

DENNIS KEIM

DENNIS KEIM

Dunlop maintains a close working relationship with car manufacturers during the design phase of a new tire, incorporating the manufacturer's specifications for size, speed performance, speed rating, handling characteristics, noise characteristics, rolling resistance, and appearance. "Car manufacturers are a demanding market because they are looking for the best overall package that they can offer when selling a car. Tires are a very important and visible part of that package," Sieverding says. "We concentrate on offering performance, appearance, and value in the products we design for car manufacturers. But, ultimately, our growth in Huntsville and as a company overall is dependent on the performance of our tires."

The Huntsville plant's ability to meet customer needs and to give world-class service was demonstrated when Dunlop Huntsville-produced tires were selected as the primary equipment tire for the Mercedes M-Class made in Vance, Alabama. Honda, Toyota, Nissan, Mazda, Infiniti, Lexus, and Isuzu are just some of the other manufacturers whose autos come equipped with Dunlop tires.

A Worldwide Presence

When Sumitomo became Dunlop's majority shareholder in 1986, the Japanese company was actually reestablishing a rela-

tionship that had developed around the beginning of the 20th century. It all started in 1889, when Dunlop founded the Pneumatic Tire and Booth Bicycle Company in Ireland. After the business began producing automobile tires in 1900, he changed the name to Dunlop Rubber Company. In 1909, Dunlop opened a manufacturing plant in Japan.

The company's first American-made tire rolled off its Buffalo assembly line in 1923. When the Huntsville plant opened more than four decades later, the role of Dunlop's U.S. operations significantly strengthened within the larger international organization. With headquarters in Great Britain and a presence in 19 countries, Dunlop had established itself as the first worldwide tire company.

During the years that followed, Sumitomo acquired a majority interest in Dunlop's Japanese unit. When Dunlop's British operations began a downhill slide in the 1970s and 1980s, amid devastated European tire markets, Sumitomo purchased the company's European factories, as well as the Dunlop World Technical Center in the United Kingdom. The Japanese company also became majority shareholder of Dunlop's American operations, bringing the entire worldwide organization under a stable and financially strong common ownership.

Pursuing Safety and Quality

At Dunlop, success has been no accident. The company's emphasis on performance accountability at all levels, conformance to internal and external customer-driven requirements, a systems approach to problem solving, measurement of the right things involved in the manufacturing process, and quality education and training at all levels has fueled its recent prosperity.

As a prime manufacturing location, Huntsville has further ensured Dunlop's success and future growth by providing a favorable business environment and an available workforce. Additionally, the railroad line located adjacent to the Huntsville facility, the International Intermodal Center at the nearby Huntsville International Airport, and proximity to major interstate highways ensure easy distribution of the company's products across North America.

Every time a Dunlop tire meets the road, employees prove their commitment to providing tires that are manufactured with performance and durability in mind. "We at Huntsville believe that the only route to world-class performance is through the pursuit of safety and quality in all our manufacturing operations," Sieverding says. "And all of our decisions are consistent with this belief."

THERE IS A GREAT DEMAND FOR DUNLOP'S TIRES. HONDA, TOYOTA, NISSAN, MAZDA, INFINITI, LEXUS, AND ISUZU ARE JUST SOME OF THE MANUFACTURERS WHOSE AUTOMOBILES COME EQUIPPED WITH STATE-OF-THE-ART DUNLOP TIRES (LEFT).

EVERY TIME A DUNLOP TIRE MEETS THE ROAD, THE FIRM'S HUNTSVILLE EMPLOYEES PROVE THEIR COMMITMENT TO PROVIDING TIRES THAT ARE MANUFACTURED WITH PERFORMANCE AND DURABILITY IN MIND (RIGHT).

To many people, the U.S. Space & Rocket Center is a tourist attraction, introducing visitors of all ages to the excitement and fun of space exploration. But beyond such thrilling exhibits as Space Shot, Mission to Mars, Journey to Jupiter, and Shuttle to Tomorrow is a driving sense of purpose to teach the space experience, share the adventures of science, and show the realities of space challenges. ▼ The U.S. Space & Rocket Center

Visitors to the U.S. Space & Rocket Center can feel like an astronaut for a day and experience the excitement of space exploration in exhibits that demonstrate the realities of space challenges (top right).

Founded in 1970, the U.S. Space & Rocket Center today boasts more than 1,500 historical space artifacts, several exhibits and attractions, an IMAX® theater, U.S. Space Camp®, and Aviation Challenge®. The hands-on, innovative space science museum strives to teach, entertain, challenge, and encourage its 400,000 annual visitors to support and participate in the nation's efforts to explore space.

was founded in 1970 largely due to the efforts of German-born rocket scientist Dr. Wernher von Braun, who, as the first director of NASA's Marshall Space Flight Center, sought $2 million from the Alabama legislature for construction of the Space & Rocket Center's museum. Today, boasting more than 1,500 historical space artifacts, several exhibits and attractions, an IMAX® theater, U.S. SPACE CAMP®, and AVIATION CHALLENGE®, the hands-on, innovative space science museum strives to teach, entertain, challenge, and encourage its 400,000 annual visitors to support and participate in the nation's efforts to explore space.

"We are the number one paid tourist attraction in the state," says Ralph Gipson, the center's interim executive director. "Surveys have shown that 70 percent of our visitors are from out-of-state areas. We need to expand the center to accommodate the growing interest in space exploration and to provide the types of facilities that will increase our attractiveness with both tourists and students interested in space."

Continuing von Braun's Dream

To continue its founder's vision, the U.S. Space & Rocket Center

is entering a new phase of development with a 15-year, $100 million master plan that will quadruple the size of the center and possibly double attendance records. With funding solicited from local, state, and federal governments; private foundations; and corporations, the renovated center will revolve around the theme A Space Walk into the Future, with four zoned areas—the Arrival Zone, Museum Zone, Base Camp Zone, and Education/Tech Zone—unified within the center's 335-acre campus and connected by a monorail that travels the entire campus.

"The idea behind the master plan is to build on the legacy that launched America into the space age," Gipson says. "That same legacy launched this center, and we hope to further promote the idea of space exploration through new exhibits and attractions that help to strengthen America's interest and commitment to space, and that, on a more personal level, encourage a lifelong interest in space and science."

The U.S. Space & Rocket Center has a significant impact on the local economy, employing 850 in its peak season and generating $64.8 million in annual expenditures,

according to a University of Alabama in Huntsville study. "We are hoping that our economic impact—both past and future—will make our master plan a worthwhile project for government and private enterprises to support," Gipson says.

As details of the master plan are finalized, the U.S. Space & Rocket Center continues to offer and build on attractions and educational programs that have made it a popular destination for visitors. From experiencing the G forces of a shuttle launch to living and working on a space outpost, a visit to the U.S. Space & Rocket Center is truly a first-class ticket to space.

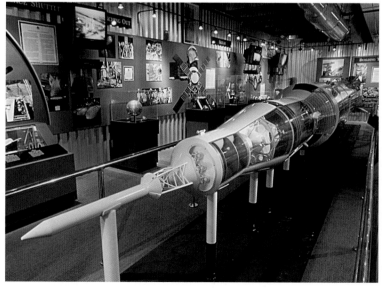

HOSPITALITY IS FIRST-CLASS, SOUTHERN-STYLE AT THE HILTON HUNTSVILLE, THE CITY'S ONLY DOWNTOWN HOTEL. FROM THE INTERIOR DECOR OF ITS LOBBY AND MEETING ROOMS TO ITS BUSINESS AND TOURISM AMENITIES, THE HOTEL REPRESENTS ALL THE HOSPITABLE ATTRIBUTES ASSOCIATED WITH HUNTSVILLE'S IMAGE AS A LEADING BUSINESS AND TOURISM CENTER. ✳ LOCATED WITHIN WALKING DISTANCE OF THE VON BRAUN CENTER, THE HUNTSVILLE MUSEUM OF ART, THE TWICKENHAM

Historic District, and the city's financial and legal center, the Hilton Huntsville caters to two distinct groups of clientele—business travelers and leisure visitors. Added to that mix are the local residents and professionals who make the Hilton's restaurant a frequent choice for luncheon dining and business meetings.

Opened in 1975 by a group of local investors as a 194-room hotel, the Hilton Huntsville earned a reputation as a site for small hotel conventions and meetings after a 1979 expansion. That expansion added 93 hotel rooms, a second ballroom, and a reception room, located in a separate wing of the hotel from the original ballroom. With two distinct convention sites, the Hilton is able to host two conventions at the same time.

"We are downtown Huntsville's hotel, and we take our role as a representative of the city and its hospitality quite seriously," says Bob Rogers, general manager. "In everything we do, we want our visitors to see us as a hospitable,

friendly hotel with amenities to satisfy the needs of any traveler."

Accommodating a Variety of Visitors

The Hilton Huntsville has 277 rooms and more than 14,000 square feet of meeting and convention space, accommodating more than 100,000 visitors a year. Approximately 50 percent of the hotel's annual rooms business consists of conventions and meetings, and the remaining 50 percent are business and leisure travelers.

In 1984, HJH Associates of Alabama purchased the Hilton Huntsville. It then underwent an extensive remodeling of its common areas, including the lobby, restaurant, and lounge. "HJH gave it a traditional look in nature," Rogers says. "It's comfortable, not glitzy. It has a classical, traditional look that is truly southern."

Lofton's, the hotel's restaurant, has a reputation for serving a variety of exquisite selections, making it one of Huntsville's most notable dining establishments. The Hilton's

chefs create daily specials in several European and American styles, including fresh seafood flown in from the Gulf of Mexico.

"We have a real strong culinary staff here that can do just about anything," Rogers says. "We are now working in the off-site catering market, where we are pursuing opportunities to serve Huntsville's social and civic groups at their special functions."

The Hilton is one of the first hotels in the city to offer a business center, complete with two computers that offer Internet access, telephones, and facsimile and copier machines. There is also a fitness center, an outdoor swimming pool and Jacuzzi, and an executive level of hotel rooms with extra amenities such as two phone lines, complimentary continental breakfast, and complimentary hors d'oeuvres each evening in the private lounge area.

Whether traveling on business or for fun, the Hilton Huntsville offers its visitors a combination of luxury, convenience, and value in the best of southern traditions.

OPENED IN 1975 BY A GROUP OF LOCAL INVESTORS, THE HILTON HUNTSVILLE HAS 277 ROOMS AND MORE THAN 14,000 SQUARE FEET OF MEETING AND CONVENTION SPACE, ACCOMMODATING MORE THAN 100,000 VISITORS A YEAR. LOCATED WITHIN WALKING DISTANCE OF THE VON BRAUN CENTER, THE HUNTSVILLE MUSEUM OF ART, THE TWICKENHAM HISTORIC DISTRICT, AND THE CITY'S FINANCIAL AND LEGAL CENTER, THE HILTON HUNTSVILLE CATERS TO TWO DISTINCT GROUPS OF CLIENTELE—BUSINESS TRAVELERS AND LEISURE VISITORS.

TECHNOLOGICAL INSIGHT AND ENVIRONMENTAL CONCERN HAVE MADE ENGELHARD CORPORATION THE WORLD'S LEADING MANUFACTURER OF AUTOMOTIVE EXHAUST AND INDUSTRIAL EMISSION CONTROL CATALYSTS. AS PART OF THE CORPORATION'S ENVIRONMENTAL TECHNOLOGIES GROUP, ENGELHARD IN HUNTSVILLE IS RECOGNIZED AS A LEADER IN AIR QUALITY TECHNOLOGY AND AS A MANUFACTURER OF UNIQUE PRODUCTS THAT CHANGE THE QUALITY OF AIR, MAKING IT CLEANER,

safer, and more comfortable for people all around the world.

A pioneer in the manufacturing of catalytic converters, Engelhard's Huntsville facility develops and manufactures automobile exhaust catalysts and catalysts for motorcycles, lawn mowers, diesel trucks, and airplanes. Huntsville is also the location for the company's production of silver nitrate for use in the X-ray and photography industry, silver oxide for use in light-sensitive glass and battery applications, and silver powder for use in rear-window defrosters and electrical contacts. In all its product lines, Engelhard is committed to delivering breakthrough innovations that improve customer products, expand or create new markets, and make the world a better place to live.

Bringing Technology to Huntsville

Founded as a U.S. company by Charles Engelhard Sr. in 1902, Engelhard has grown through a long history of acquisitions, mergers, and reorganizations that have

reflected the changing needs of its customers. Today, it is a world leader in the development, production, and marketing of specialty chemical products and engineered materials. Based in Iselin, New Jersey, Engelhard has annual sales of more than $4 billion and about 6,400 employees.

As the location for Engelhard's largest catalytic converter facility, Huntsville provides a business environment that has proved beneficial in supporting the com-

pany's substantial growth. When Engelhard was searching for a site for its catalysts operations in the early 1970s, Huntsville had many characteristics in its favor—affordable land, state-offered recruiting incentives, a positive labor relations environment, low taxes, moderate climate, and good location near customers. But, above all those things, Engelhard's top asset in Huntsville continues to be the well-educated, highly motivated, and dedicated workforce that has helped build the company's catalyst market share to the number one position in the world.

In 1974, Engelhard opened its Huntsville facility in Lowe Industrial Park near the Huntsville International Airport. Ford Motor Company was its only customer, and Engelhard had developed and patented Ford's automobile exhaust catalysts. Since then, the Huntsville facility has grown to 450 employees who manufacture catalysts not only for Ford, but also for General Motors, Honda, Nissan, Mercedes-Benz, Cummins, BMW, Volvo, Mazda, and others. Silver chemicals manufacturing was added in 1977, and today, customers include Fuji, DuPont, Polaroid, and Sterling. Industrial emission control catalysts were added in 1982, and aeronau-

IN 1974, ENGELHARD CORPORATION OPENED ITS HUNTSVILLE FACILITY. IT IS GROWN INTO A FOUR-BUILDING COMPLEX LOCATED ON 30 OF THE 100 ACRES OWNED BY ENGELHARD.

WHEN IT COMES TO EMPLOYEES, ENGELHARD STRESSES SAFETY ON THE JOB. THE HUNTSVILLE FACILITY HAS RECEIVED THE ENGELHARD PRESIDENT'S SAFETY AWARD, AN AWARD OF MERIT FROM THE NATIONAL SAFETY COUNCIL, AND AN AWARD OF ACHIEVEMENT FROM THE CHEMICAL MANUFACTURERS ASSOCIATION. THE FACILITY HAS BEEN RATED AMONG THE WORLD'S LEADERS FOR SAFETY AND ENVIRONMENTAL ACHIEVEMENT.

DENNIS KEIM

tical catalyst production was added in 1984 to serve Boeing, the former McDonnell Douglas, and Airbus. A process development lab and a testing laboratory for the simulation of auto exhaust systems were added in 1986, and diesel catalyst production was added in 1992.

Hub of Global Technology

The company's four-building complex, located on 30 of the 100 acres owned by Engelhard in Lowe Industrial Park, has undergone two major expansions since its early days. A large plant expansion was completed in 1996 and another expansion is ongoing, each providing additional space to expand production.

Within Engelhard's Environmental Technologies Group, the Huntsville facility serves as the hub for the company's Global Technology Transfer effort, which works to develop new business using the company's innovative technology.

Recognized as a Leader

When it comes to employees, Engelhard stresses safety on the job. The Huntsville facility, which has gone more than 10 years without a lost workday, has received the Engelhard president's safety award, an award of merit from the National Safety Council,

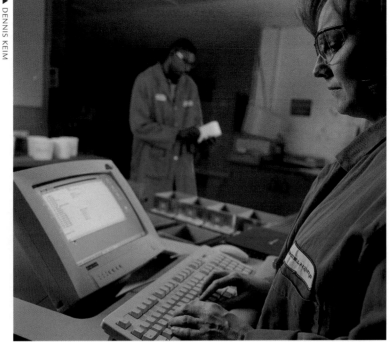

and an award of achievement from the Chemical Manufacturers Association. The facility has been rated among the world's leaders for safety and environmental achievement.

Engelhard's customers have also recognized the Huntsville facility's commitment to safety and quality. The firm was the first automobile supplier to receive Ford's Total Quality Excellence Award, and it has received top awards from BMW, Honda, Cummins, and Corning. Engelhard received ozone converter certifications from the Federal Aviation Administration, Boeing, Airbus, the former

McDonnell Douglas, the former Daimler-Benz, and Gulfstream. The site has also achieved both ISO and QS 9002 certifications for its quality systems.

Engelhard's dedication to improving the environment continues to be the overriding factor in the products it develops and manufactures. In fact, the Fortune 150 company has received an award from the United Nations for the invention of the catalytic converter and its impact on the world. Today, the Huntsville facility remains a technology leader in all its markets by producing breakthrough products, services, and results; incorporating excellence into all its products; building a culture of commitment, quality, and flexibility among its employees; and impressing, rather than merely satisfying, customers and partners.

Working to Change the Nature of Things is Engelhard's worldwide commitment to its customers, a commitment reflected in the way employees of Engelhard in Huntsville deliver value to customers through innovative, environmentally friendly products, as well as in the application of Engelhard's technologies and experience to achieve total solutions for customers. It is this commitment that has made Engelhard the world's fastest-growing clean air company.

WORKING TO CHANGE THE NATURE OF THINGS IS ENGELHARD'S WORLDWIDE COMMITMENT TO ITS CUSTOMERS, A COMMITMENT REFLECTED IN THE WAY EMPLOYEES OF ENGELHARD IN HUNTSVILLE DELIVER VALUE TO CUSTOMERS THROUGH INNOVATIVE, ENVIRONMENTALLY FRIENDLY PRODUCTS, AS WELL AS IN THE APPLICATION OF ENGELHARD'S TECHNOLOGIES AND EXPERIENCE TO ACHIEVE TOTAL SOLUTIONS FOR CUSTOMERS.

TODAY, THE HUNTSVILLE FACILITY REMAINS A TECHNOLOGY LEADER IN ALL ITS MARKETS BY PRODUCING BREAKTHROUGH PRODUCTS, SERVICES, AND RESULTS; INCORPORATING EXCELLENCE INTO ALL ITS PRODUCTS; BUILDING A CULTURE OF COMMITMENT, QUALITY, AND FLEXIBILITY AMONG ITS EMPLOYEES; AND IMPRESSING, RATHER THAN MERELY SATISFYING, CUSTOMERS AND PARTNERS.

GETTING READY FOR COMPANY IS A DAILY PART OF DOING BUSINESS AT HUNTSVILLE'S VON BRAUN CENTER. WHETHER IT'S A HOCKEY GAME, BROADWAY PRODUCTION, ROCK CONCERT, BANQUET GATHERING, NATIONAL CONVENTION, OR SYMPHONY ORCHESTRA, THE CENTER'S STAFF MAKE IT THEIR BUSINESS TO HANDLE EVERY DETAIL FOR THEIR PERFORMING GUESTS AND VISITING TICKET HOLDERS. ✳ SINCE 1975, THE VON BRAUN CENTER, NAMED FOR ROCKET PIONEER WERNHER VON BRAUN, HAS BEEN

at the heart of the city's entertainment, civic, and cultural events. Located in historic downtown Huntsville, this showpiece civic and convention center is designed to meet the needs of both large and small gatherings of people for the arts, sports, professional conventions, and community events.

"We are a multipurpose center built to meet the demands of local, regional, and national groups in need of meeting and convention space and to comply with the needs of a community that wants the best in entertainment and sports choices," says Executive Director Ron Evans. "We have an impact on the city's economy by bringing in millions of dollars in annual income from conventions and sports and entertainment events. In addition, the Von Braun Center enhances the quality of life for residents in Huntsville and the North Alabama area."

Growing with Community Needs

Originally built to support the demand for meeting space from local groups, the Von Braun Center has grown with the North Alabama community it serves. Driven by local civic needs, the East Hall and the elegant North Hall were later expanded to provide an additional 48,000 square feet of flexible

exhibit, meeting, and banquet space. In 1997, the need for more convention space to allow the center to successfully compete for large-scale national and international conventions necessitated the $26 million South Hall addition. The new South Hall provides 100,000 square feet of continuous space, including a main hall containing 82,000 square feet of column-free exhibit space, a lobby, and a pre-function area.

"Most communities build or expand convention facilities to create market demand," Evans says. "We are fortunate that we already had the demand for more space before we broke ground for the South Hall. The expansion allowed us to hold on to some of our most significant local customers, such as the Intergraph Users Group, the Technical and Business Exhibition/Symposium, and the North Alabama Industrial Show. Our larger facilities have also made us a more attractive destination on the national and international convention circuit."

Today, the Von Braun Center is one of the largest venues of its kind in the Southeast. It offers 170,000 square feet of exhibit space, including the Arena; the South, North, and East halls; the Concert Hall; and the Playhouse. The Arena, with concert seating for 10,000 and hockey rink seating for 6,582, is home to two championship hockey teams: the Chargers of the University of Alabama in Huntsville and the Huntsville Channel Cats of the Central Hockey League. It also hosts rodeo events and the circus. The Concert Hall seats 2,153 guests in continental style for cultural performances as well as lectures and multimedia presentations. The Playhouse offers in-the-round, thrust, or proscenium staging, with seating for up to 502.

With such a diverse offering of facilities and space, the Von Braun Center is capable of hosting a variety of events any time of the year. But most important, the staff of this Huntsville landmark are always ready for company.

CLOCKWISE FROM TOP RIGHT:
THE CENTER'S NEWLY CONSTRUCTED SOUTH HALL PROVIDES 100,000 SQUARE FEET OF EXHIBIT SPACE FOR TRADE SHOWS AND CONVENTIONS.

ELTON JOHN PERFORMED A SELLOUT CONCERT AT THE VON BRAUN CENTER.

THE NASHVILLE PREDATORS PLAYED THEIR OPENING PRESEASON NHL GAME IN THE ARENA.

THE BROADWAY THEATRE LEAGUE HAS BEEN ENTERTAINING HUNTSVILLE AUDIENCES AT THE VON BRAUN CENTER FOR THE PAST 40 YEARS.

◀ KEVIN MAZUR

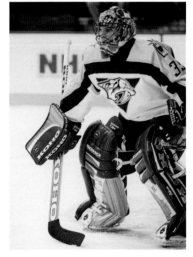

AFTER A WORKDAY FILLED WITH ENGINEERING, SYSTEMS ANALYSIS, SIMULATION, SOFTWARE DEVELOPMENT, COST PLANNING, LOGISTICS, OPERATIONAL ANALYSIS, AND OTHER HIGH-TECH DUTIES, IT IS NOT UNUSUAL TO FIND EMPLOYEES OF CAS, INC. DISCUSSING THE FINANCIAL NEEDS OF CHARITABLE AGENCIES IN HUNTSVILLE. THOUGH CAS IS A GOVERNMENT CONTRACTOR WELL KNOWN FOR ITS EXPERTISE IN SYSTEMS ENGINEERING AND TECHNICAL ASSISTANCE SUPPORT FOR

numerous government weapons systems, the company is also recognized for a humanitarian philosophy that has made it one of Huntsville's leading charitable contributors.

With an annual budget of about $100,000, the organization known as CAS Cares, Inc. looks to employees in determining what agencies can best use a contribution. "It's a very touching experience for the employees," says company CEO William H. Stender. "Each quarter, they choose a charity to receive a $10,000 grant. In addition, smaller awards are given to other charities. It's our way of working together to give back to a community that has given us the opportunities we enjoy today."

Focused on Weapons Systems Analyses

Founded in 1979 by Stender and company president Fred Clark, CAS is a major Department of Defense weapons systems analysis contractor. With 400 employees in its Huntsville headquarters, the company is recognized as one of the best-managed small businesses in Alabama. CAS provides material development, combat development, test and evaluation, and operational user customers with complete engineering, analytical, and automation services solutions. The company's capabilities include providing system engineering and analysis support for air and missile missile defense; aviation and land combat missile systems; and related surveillance, battle management, command, control, communications, and computer systems.

Government contracting sales reach about $60 million annually, with a customer list that includes the U.S. Army Aviation and Missile Command's Patriot missile system and NASA's tethered satellite pro-

gram at the Marshall Space Flight Center. In order to support its other customers, CAS employs another 150 people strategically located at offices in El Paso, Newport News, and Washington D.C. The company also works on a global scale in support of the Patriot international program, which involves the governments of Germany, the Netherlands, Japan, Italy, Saudi Arabia, and Kuwait.

Always focused on its corporate goal of "opening doors through systems analysis," CAS provides expert support in such areas as software/simulation development and use, threat analysis, test and evaluation, logistics, program management, prototype development, systems integration, and information and data management services. The company's technical staff offers

the full spectrum of life-cycle systems support required to develop, acquire, field, employ, and maintain the complex weapons systems used today by Department of Defense organizations, allied nations, and NASA. Says Stender, "We work in an extremely synergistic environment that is healthy for our business and our customers."

Despite CAS, Inc.'s high-tech orientation, its personal touch extends beyond charitable, employee-raised contributions and into the day-to-day management of complex government contracts. "There are three principles on which this company was founded—the customer, the employee, and ethics," Stender says. "We are a customer- and employee-oriented organization that believes in ethics in business."

CLOCKWISE FROM TOP:
CAS, INC. EMPLOYEES GO THE EXTRA MILE TO SUPPORT MILITARY EXERCISES ALL OVER THE WORLD.

EMPLOYEES AT CAS GIVE BACK TO THE COMMUNITY WITH THE ORGANIZATION CAS CARES, INC., DONATING THOUSANDS OF DOLLARS TO LOCAL CHARITIES.

FOUNDED IN 1979 BY WILLIAM H. STENDER AND COMPANY PRESIDENT FRED CLARK, CAS IS A MAJOR DEPARTMENT OF DEFENSE WEAPONS SYSTEMS ANALYSIS CONTRACTOR WITH HEADQUARTERS IN HUNTSVILLE.

1980-1999

1980	COLSA CORPORATION
1981	CYBEX COMPUTER PRODUCTS CORPORATION
1981	EXECUTIVE LODGE SUITE HOTEL
1981	LG ELECTRONICS ALABAMA, INC.
1983	RISE REAL ESTATE, INC.
1984	COLONIAL BANK
1984	EER SYSTEMS INC.
1985	ADTRAN, INC.
1985	UWOHALI INCORPORATED
1986	COMCAST CABLEVISION OF HUNTSVILLE
1986	MADISON RESEARCH CORPORATION
1986	SIGMATECH, INC.
1986	VMIC
1987	QUANTUM RESEARCH INTERNATIONAL, INC.
1987	RUSS RUSSELL COMMERCIAL REAL ESTATE
1987	SUMMA TECHNOLOGY, INC.
1987	TIME DOMAIN
1988	QUALITY RESEARCH, INC.
1988	TEC-MASTERS, INC.
1989	COLONIAL PROPERTIES TRUST
1989	COMPUTER SYSTEMS TECHNOLOGY, INC.
1989	MEVATEC CORPORATION
1993	MAGNETEK, INC.
1993	TRIAD PROPERTIES CORPORATION
1994	WOLVERINE TUBE, INC.
1997	POWERTEL, INC.
1997	QUANTUM TECHNOLOGIES, INC.
1998	HERITAGE BANK OF HUNTSVILLE
1998	SOUTHERN BANK OF COMMERCE

IT'S NOT ENOUGH FOR COLSA CORPORATION TO BE KNOWN AS ONE OF HUNTSVILLE'S LEADING HIGH-TECHNOLOGY COMPANIES. SINCE ITS EARLY DAYS AS A SMALL GOVERNMENT CONTRACTOR BUSINESS, THIS HISPANIC-OWNED COMPANY HAS PROVIDED QUALITY SERVICE TO ITS CUSTOMERS AND HAS TAKEN AN ACTIVE ROLE IN ITS HOMETOWN COMMUNITY. ✳ ESTABLISHED IN 1980 BY COFOUNDERS FRANCISCO AND CARMEN COLLAZO, COLSA HAS REMAINED STEADFAST IN ITS COMMITMENT TO ONE GOAL: TO SERVE THE COMPANY'S CLIENTS

with dedication and excellence. Today, with nearly 500 employees and annual revenues of more than $70 million, COLSA continues to provide high-quality, advanced technical assistance and engineering services to its clients, including U.S. government agencies, foreign governments, and commercial customers.

COLSA's primary focus is in the areas of missile systems technology and computer systems for government and commercial use. The company excels in four key areas of service: information systems, commercial services, systems engineering, and testing and evaluation. It offers customers diversified experience and extensive academic training, with 70 percent of its employees holding advanced degrees.

"COLSA employees approach each project with the same thing in mind–providing the best value to each customer, the best solution for each problem, and the most innovative products that technology will allow," says Frank L. Collazo, executive vice president of Collazo Enterprises, Inc., COLSA's parent company.

"Our employees make up an effective team that has the support of a dynamic management structure and the most up-to-date technical tools," Collazo continues.

"That combination ensures that our customers receive the responsive service and superior products they deserve."

Committed to the Community

One of Huntsville's best corporate neighbors, COLSA shares its professional successes with the community through several corporate initiatives and employee programs. In addition to its support of several community agencies, COLSA encourages entrepreneurship by offering managerial and financial assistance to other small, minority-owned firms and by providing college scholarships to students in Huntsville and Puerto Rico, where the Collazos' lived before immigrating to the United States. Recognized for its philanthropy, COLSA has

been named one of the top 500 Hispanic-owned businesses in the nation by *Hispanic Business* magazine, as well as regional and national Small Business Prime Contractor of the Year by the Small Business Administration.

"The business that we have been able to build in Huntsville has given us a way to give back to the community," says Collazo. "Because of this community, COLSA has been successful. We want to share that success with the community."

Winning Service and Products

Headquartered in Cummings Research Park, COLSA has maintained business activities in Texas, Virginia, Colorado, Puerto Rico, and the Middle East. Other companies have also been established as part of Collazo Enterprises, including COLSA International, which supports engineering programs in Saudi Arabia; FJC Growth Capital Corporation, which offers venture capital opportunities to small and disadvantaged businesses; and FCA Properties, Inc., which provides property management and facilities maintainence, and manages nearly $15 million in real estate.

"We have diversified our business base. But our focus remains on being a world-class provider of innovative technical products and services," Collazo says. "And in everything we do, our focus is on customer satisfaction."

COLSA CORPORATION'S ADVANCED RESEARCH CENTER IN HUNTSVILLE

COLSA'S CORPORATE HEADQUARTERS IS LOCATED IN CUMMINGS RESEARCH PARK.

AS THE LARGEST LOCALLY OWNED REAL ESTATE COMPANY IN NORTH ALABAMA, RISE REAL ESTATE IS WELL KNOWN AS A "HOUSE SOLD WORD" AMONG RESIDENTS IN BOTH CITY AND RURAL NEIGHBORHOODS. BUT RAPID GROWTH IN THE NUMBER OF AGENTS LICENSED WITH THE FIRM AND THE NUMBER OF PROPERTIES IT HAS LISTED AND SOLD HAS NOT DETERRED THE MANAGEMENT AND AGENTS OF RISE REAL ESTATE FROM REMAINING FOCUSED ON PROVIDING EACH CUSTOMER/CLIENT

with the personal service he or she deserves. In fact, success for this company comes from its agents' determination to serve customers and clients in the most trustworthy, knowledgeable, and professional manner possible. And, more often than not, that success relies on teamwork among Rise agents.

"In October 1997, we had 38 agents. Today, we have more than 140 agents," says Tommy Adams, owner and broker of the company. "Through all that growth, we've developed a reputation for having a lot of teamwork among the agents. It's that teamwork that makes this company a success. And it's that teamwork that has made us grow into the real estate company that we are today. We have more listings than anyone else in our market and we have more listings sold than anyone else in our market."

Fourth Largest in the State

Rise Real Estate ranks as the fourth-largest real estate agency in Alabama, with three offices in Huntsville, one in Madison, and one in Ardmore. It is also the largest-selling company in North Alabama, with about $180 million in annual sales.

Rise is a member of RELO, a national referral network, that gives the company the opportunity to market its services to employees involved in corporate relocations. Once a referral is made to Rise, an agent will provide the customer with in-depth information about schools, neighborhoods, shopping, culture, sports, and other quality-of-life aspects that make Huntsville attractive to new residents. Rise provides the same service to families leaving Huntsville for other states or foreign countries.

Every Rise agent conducts business in a personal and caring way. Professional training is encouraged, and many of the company's agents have designations as graduates of the Realtors Institute (GRI), as certified residential specialists (CRS), and as certified residential brokers (CRB).

Personal Service a Goal

We're a service company, and we couldn't have grown without the personal service the agents give to their customers and clients. That service is our strength," Adams says. "We also believe strongly in continuing education for our agents, because it is education that keeps them knowledgeable about changes in the real estate industry that could affect their customers and clients.

"This is one of the best real estate markets in the state," Adams says. "The three- to five-year turnover in the government contracting industry, combined with a high average income, makes Huntsville a market that offers plenty of opportunity for investment growth."

With a dedication to customer/client service, agent education, and teamwork, Rise Real Estate is sure to reach its goals, and will continue to be a vital part of the Huntsville community for many years to come.

WELL KNOWN IN HUNTSVILLE FOR DEDICATION TO CUSTOMER SERVICE, AGENT EDUCATION, AND TEAMWORK, RISE REAL ESTATE IS THE FOURTH-LARGEST REAL ESTATE AGENCY IN ALABAMA.

CYBEX COMPUTER PRODUCTS CORPORATION IS ONE OF THE COUNTRY'S FASTEST-GROWING COMPUTER HARDWARE MANUFACTURERS. ESTABLISHED IN 1981, THIS INNOVATIVE DEVELOPER OF COMPUTER SWITCHING AND EXTENSION PRODUCTS GOT ITS START IN THE SOFTWARE BUSINESS. LIKE THE SWITCHING PRODUCTS THAT HAVE MADE CYBEX A LEADER IN THE DEVELOPMENT OF COMPUTER NETWORKS, THE COMPANY MADE ITS OWN PRODUCT SWITCH IN 1984 TO BEST REALIZE ITS GROWTH POTENTIAL.

CYBEX COMPUTER PRODUCTS CORPORATION EMPLOYS MORE THAN 200 PEOPLE AT ITS HUNTSVILLE LOCATION AND MORE THAN 300 PEOPLE WORLDWIDE (RIGHT).

IN 1998, CYBEX COMPLETED CONSTRUCTION OF A NEW, 126,000-SQUARE-FOOT FACILITY IN CUMMINGS RESEARCH PARK IN HUNTSVILLE (BELOW).

"This company was an entrepreneurial start-up involving a couple of programmers who wanted to do engineering consulting work for the commercial and defense markets," says Stephen Thornton, president, CEO, and chairman of the board. "Cybex was a service company involved in software development, but in the mid-'80s, we were contracted to install a personal computer network for NASA's space station testbed. After that, we set out to develop and sell hardware products, as opposed to only providing engineering and software services for office automation."

That shift in product focus was a good move for Cybex and its employees. Today, the company has made a name for itself with a line of computer products designed to meet the challenges of complex computer configurations. As a result, Cybex has been recognized as one of *Business Week*'s hottest 100 growth companies and one of *Forbes'* best 200 small businesses.

"Cybex will continue to grow by further penetrating its current markets, pinpointing and expanding into emerging markets, and continuing with international expansions," Thornton says. "The ongoing growth in PC and server deployment continues to create opportunites for us."

Specializing in Innovative Products

Cybex first entered the computer hardware market with an extender product, which lets users remotely control personal computers with a keyboard and monitor. Today, the extender is part of the company's popular KVM (keyboard/video/mouse) family of switching system products.

"More than 80 percent of our business involves KVM switch, ex-

tension, and expansion products for use in the computer industry," Thornton says. "We develop, manufacture, and market products for computers that boost, split, or switch the signals between a computer system's central processing unit and the keyboards, monitors, and mice. Our high-end switch products are designed to work on IBM-compatible computers, Apple Macintosh, Sun, and certain Hewlett-Packard, IBM, and Silicon Graphics workstations."

The company's KVM switch products are used on network computers, and allow the user to control multiple computers with a single keyboard, video monitor, and mouse. One Cybex product–the AutoBoot Commander 4xp–allows the control of thousands of servers from multiple user consoles. This capability increases user productivity while providing substantial savings in reduced computer components and energy costs.

In addition, Cybex's KVM extension products allow a computer's central processing unit (CPU) to be separated from the keyboard, video monitor, and mouse by up to 600 feet. This capability is used to increase space for the user by

moving the CPU to a remote location or to increase security by moving the unit off the user's desk to a secure location. The KVM extension can also increase safety by removing the CPU from hazardous locations, such as manufacturing areas, to a more protected environment.

The KVM expansion products offered by Cybex allow multiple keyboards, monitors, and mice to be connected to a single computer. This application is used in classrooms where teachers and students must view the same material on individual screens, and in situations where the user needs access to a computer from multiple locations. Expansion products are designed to work off of a single central processing unit, eliminating the need for special network software or multiple software licenses.

Networking around the Globe

Cybex is a leader in its industry, with a 35 percent market share that is translated into revenues of more than $82 million a year. The company's growth has benefited from accelerated sales of new products, increased demand in Europe, and expanding distribution channels. In 1995, Cybex became a publicly traded company in order to strengthen its overseas position and to more aggressively pursue its U.S. markets.

Located in a $10.5 million facility in Cummings Research Park, the company's Huntsville headquarters is also the center for its North and South American sales, while operations in Ireland and Germany market Cybex products in Europe. The company employs 200 people in Huntsville, with another 60 at manufacturing plants in Shannon, Ireland, and 45 in Steinhagen, Germany.

"Huntsville has been a good place to expand our company because it has the technology base that we need to continue our growth," Thornton says. "And Cummings Research Park has been a good location for us because of its reputation as being one of the best and largest research parks in the world. That sends a message about our company that we are a part of a strong research and development environment."

With growth expected to continue well into the 21st century, Cybex is on the rise as one of the nation's leading computer hardware companies. "Our overall strategy is products, places, and partners," Thornton says. "We develop the products that bring different computer sites together and make us a partner with our customers in building their computer networks. Cybex is developing products that give customers the ability to network across the office, across the building, and across the world."

IT IS NOT UNUSUAL FOR YVONNE BOYINGTON AND THE STAFF AT EXECUTIVE LODGE SUITE HOTEL TO STRIKE UP FRIENDSHIPS WITH NEWCOMERS TO HUNTSVILLE/MADISON COUNTY. AFTER ALL, THE HOTEL IS OFTEN THE FIRST PLACE OF RESIDENCE FOR THE FAMILIES OF EMPLOYEES WHO COME TO HUNTSVILLE AS CORPORATE AND GOVERNMENT TRANSFERS. AND, WHETHER GUESTS STAY A FEW DAYS, WEEKS, OR MONTHS, THE STAFF AT EXECUTIVE LODGE IS COMMITTED TO MAKING THEM FEEL AT HOME. ✳ WITH A VARIETY OF SUITE

THE STAFF AT THE EXECUTIVE LODGE SUITE HOTEL WANT ALL THEIR RESIDENTS— WHETHER STAYING OVERNIGHT OR FOR SEVERAL MONTHS—TO FEEL THE EXECUTIVE LODGE IS THEIR HOME AWAY FROM HOME (TOP).

WITH 208 SUITES ON A HILLTOP OVERLOOKING CUMMINGS RESEARCH PARK AND 105 SUITES OFF SPARKMAN DRIVE, THE EXECUTIVE LODGE IS THE LARGEST LOCALLY OWNED SUITE HOTEL IN THE SOUTHEAST REGION (BOTTOM).

sizes and amenities to fit the lifestyles of newcomers, the Executive Lodge offers living arrangements that can take the stress out of a major family relocation. "It is a wonderful opportunity to work with family relocations because they stay with us here, and then they become part of the community," says Boyington, the hotel's general manager. "It is nice to know that we can help make their first days and weeks in Huntsville a pleasant time for them."

Home Away from Home

While the staff at the Executive Lodge works to make sure all short-term and long-term guests are comfortable, it is convenience, amenities, and suite size, along with the beauty and charm of the hotel's facilities, that first draw business and leisure travelers and relocating families to the hotel. In many ways, the Executive Lodge does, indeed, become a home away from home during their stay.

The Executive Lodge offers its guests travel convenience, as it is located near the U.S. Army Aviation & Missile Command and NASA's Marshall Space Flight Center at Redstone Arsenal, Cummings Research Park, The University of Alabama in Huntsville (UAH), U.S. Space & Rocket Center, Von Braun Center, and Huntsville International Airport. With the interchanges of University Drive, Sparkman Drive, and Interstate 565 nearby, the hotel is in the center of a major shopping and restaurant district that includes North Alabama's largest mall, Madison Square Mall.

The hotel's amenities include swimming pools, night security, health club privileges, laundry facilities, videocassette recorder and movie rentals, a private park, free local phone calls, fully equipped kitchens, airport transportation, and complimentary deluxe continental breakfast. There are also computer dataports and modems available to guests, and each room has an independent phone system complete with voice mail.

A Suite for All Needs

But it is the suites themselves that make the Executive Lodge stand out from the other hotel offerings in Huntsville. Ranging from the studio suite at 480 square

feet up to the 1,400-square-foot, three-bedroom suite, the accommodations offer all the amenities of home.

"Our fully furnished corporate apartments are popular with a lot of corporate and government relocations," Boyington says. "And, though we do go out of our way to make a family's stay here comfortable and stress-free, I think it's the size of our suites that makes us unique. Even our smallest room is double the size of a traditional hotel room."

The Executive Lodge offers dry-cleaning and valet services, as well as providing an on-site laundry room, along with washers and dryers in the two- and three-bedroom suites. "We have a lot of apartment amenities that families moving to Huntsville are looking for and that many standard hotels do not offer," Boyington says. "We have a lot of repeat business from the companies and government agencies we work with because of the suite sizes and the amenities we offer."

Largest Locally Owned Hotel

With 208 suites on a hilltop overlooking Cummings Research Park and 105 suites off Sparkman Drive, the Executive Lodge is the largest locally owned suite hotel in the Southeast region. It is also the only hotel in Huntsville with two separate, yet distinct locations. In 1989, the Executive Lodge expanded to include the suites and office on Sparkman Drive. Improvements continue, with the hotel just completing a $1 million renovation that updated both the exterior and interior areas of the suites.

The Executive Lodge also offers meeting space for groups of up to 750 people, and often reserves blocks of rooms through the Huntsville/Madison County Convention & Visitors Bureau for use by conventiongoers traveling to Huntsville.

"Besides the employee transfers that stay with us, we also have school groups from the U.S. Space & Rocket Center, UAH athletic teams, and teams playing the Huntsville Stars baseball team," Boyington says. "We also work

closely with Realtors whose clients have to move somewhere temporarily, when they have sold their house but haven't purchased a new home yet."

Though the Executive Lodge is locally owned, it has been able to remain competitive in a market that also offers travelers several nationally owned hotel chains to choose from. "Through the years, we've made an impact as far as being a real player in the city's hotel industry," Boyington says. "The trend in the hotel business is for extended-stay hotels, and we fit that description, while also providing competitive prices and excellent service to guests. We at the Executive Lodge work by the saying that 'There is less to fear from outside competition than

there is from inside inefficiency, discourtesy, and bad service.'" Boyington and the staff at the Executive Lodge want all of their residents—whether staying overnight or for several months—to feel the Executive Lodge is their home away from home. The hotel offers information about the accommodations it has to offer at its Internet site at www.executivelodge.com.

"I want guests to feel that we're small enough to know them by name, but big enough to give them the service they need and deserve," Boyington says. "Repeat business is something that every hotel should strive for, and I believe that if we give our guests the service they expect and deserve, then they will come back and they will tell others about us."

THE HOTEL'S AMENITIES INCLUDE SWIMMING POOLS, NIGHT SECURITY, HEALTH CLUB PRIVILEGES, LAUNDRY FACILITIES, VIDEOCASSETTE RECORDER AND MOVIE RENTALS, A PRIVATE PARK, FREE LOCAL PHONE CALLS, FULLY EQUIPPED KITCHENS, AIRPORT TRANSPORTATION, AND COMPLIMENTARY DELUXE CONTINENTAL BREAKFAST.

AS KOREA'S PIONEER CONSUMER ELECTRONICS COMPANY, LG ELECTRONICS INC. MADE A COMMITMENT TO EXPAND INTO THE MOST TECHNOLOGICALLY ADVANCED COUNTRY IN THE WORLD. IN THE LATE 1970S, THE SOUTH KOREAN CONGLOMERATE—THEN KNOWN AS THE LUCKY-GOLDSTAR GROUP—DECIDED TO BUILD THE FIRST KOREAN MANUFACTURING COMPLEX IN THE UNITED STATES TO MEET THE NEEDS OF THE CONSUMER MARKETS FOR GOLDSTAR TELEVISIONS AND MICROWAVE

ovens in North, South, and Central America.

In 1981, after months of study, analysis, and on-site investigations, Huntsville emerged as the ideal choice for Korea's first overseas manufacturing complex—formerly called GoldStar of America. Huntsville was chosen as LG Electronics' first U.S. site for several reasons: the city offered a foreign trade zone and U.S. customs port of entry, and it boasted an excellent quality and quantity of local parts vendors. Several city and state incentives were offered as well, such as the construction of a railroad spur to the plant site, employee training programs, site preparation, and assistance in securing industrial revenue bonds.

"We originally established our company in Huntsville for the manufacturing of televisions, microwave ovens, and videotapes. However, our electronics manufacturing has been transferred from this facility, and we are now a centralized customer service center for North America.

Service is extremely important to LG Electronics in order to remain competitive in the electronics business," says Kevin Kim, president of Huntsville operations.

Shifting to Customer Service

Although LG Electronics Alabama has been successful in all work performed at its Huntsville complex, this American venture has evolved from a business focused primarily on manufacturing to one centered on providing the best service in the electronics industry.

Currently, the business focus is on being a total solution provider for supply chain management, including customer service, international procurement, technical support, warranty service, and parts supply, as well as manufacturing. In the late 1980s and early 1990s, the Huntsville operation was converted to a service business as television and microwave oven manufacturing was relocated. Only videotape manufacturing remained, with production lines that currently manufacture 30 million videotapes annually.

"The competition caused us to shift our manufacturing elsewhere so that we could keep our costs down," Kim says. "Now we can concentrate on expanding our service role, but future plans do call for us to bring additional manufacturing to the Huntsville facility. Instead of televisions and microwave ovens, we will produce high-technology products, such as computer monitors, CD-ROMs, cellular telephones, and configuration for notebook PCs. We will also concentrate on providing worldwide company access to sophisticated development and test facilities for home appliances in Huntsville."

In 1995, the Lucky-GoldStar Group and all GoldStar manufacturing operations were renamed LG Group and LG Electronics, a

LG ELECTRONICS ALABAMA, INC. IS LOCATED IN HUNTSVILLE INTERNATIONAL AIRPORT'S JETPLEX INDUSTRIAL PARK.

"OUR GOAL IS TO SHOW OUR CUSTOMERS THAT IN EVERYTHING WE DO, WE WORK TO CREATE VALUE FOR THE CUSTOMER," SAYS PRESIDENT KEVIN KIM.

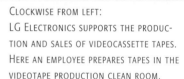

brand name that has quickly become associated with premium quality and superior design worldwide. Today, LG Electronics Alabama is home to the company's U.S. and Canadian customer service call center, parts distribution, technical support, and new product development and engineering. The company also supports the production and sales of magnetic tape products, including videocassette tapes, the purchase and resale of various consumer electronic products and information systems products, and the American procurement of parts and materials. Housed in a four-building, 430,000-squarefoot service and manufacturing complex in Huntsville International Airport's Jetplex Industrial Park, the company's 190 employees create value for the electronics customer by providing after-the-sale service.

With operations in 47 countries and more than 33,800 employees worldwide, LG Electronics has global sales of more than $9.7 billion annually. The demand for the company's information and communication products, such as CD-ROM drives, computer monitors, and cellular phones, is high in the United States, Japan, and Europe. In markets such as Asia, the Middle East, Africa, and Latin America, LG Electronics has concentrated on expanding appliance sales for such products as microwave ovens, refrigerators, washing machines, and air conditioners. The company is also positioning itself to be a top three supplier of such consumer products as televisions, videocassette recorders, and computer equip-

ment in high-growth-potential markets like China and India.

Setting the Standard for Service

Continuing the company's 40-year legacy as the leading Korean electronics manufacturer in the world, LG Electronics Alabama serves as an example of U.S. business success for other Korean companies. "The experience we have gained in operating a manufacturing facility overseas has helped our company and other Korean companies with the transition into the American consumer market," Kim says. "We have benefited from the technology and new business development that we have been involved in at our Huntsville facility. Now, we want to focus on improving our service sector. LG Electronics Alabama in Huntsville will set the standard of service for other

Korean companies that are doing business overseas."

In this move from manufacturing to service, LG Electronics Alabama has shifted its strategy from building a low-end consumer market share to a focus on high-end-value products. "By servicing all of LG Electronics' appliances, computer systems, and telecommunications products through a U.S. and Canadian network of 2,600 authorized servicers, as well as maintaining our production lines for videotape and continuing to provide design engineering and logistics management services, we have become the company's U.S. hub for logistics, service, and research," says Kim. "The addition of new products will introduce LG Electronics to new customers. Our goal is to show our customers that in everything we do, we work to create value for the customer."

Clockwise from left:
LG ELECTRONICS SUPPORTS THE PRODUCTION AND SALES OF VIDEOCASSETTE TAPES. HERE AN EMPLOYEE PREPARES TAPES IN THE VIDEOTAPE PRODUCTION CLEAN ROOM.

AT LG ELECTRONICS' CUSTOMER SERVICE CALL CENTER, EMPLOYEES ARE FOCUSED ON PROVIDING THE BEST SERVICE IN THE ELECTRONICS INDUSTRY.

ALL EMPLOYEES ARE HELPING SET THE STANDARD FOR SERVICE AT LG ELECTRONICS. SHOWN HERE IS THE CELLULAR PHONE REPAIR CENTER.

SINCE ITS INCEPTION IN 1981, COLONIAL BANK HAS GROWN INTO AN $10 BILLION, MULTISTATE BANK HOLDING COMPANY BY SUCCESSFULLY REDEFINING THE CONCEPT OF COMMUNITY BANKING. FROM ITS HEADQUARTERS IN MONTGOMERY, THE GROWING COLONIAL COMMUNITY CONTINUES TO THRIVE ON THE BASIS OF SUPERIOR PERSONALIZED SERVICE, ADVANCED PRODUCTS, AND THE FULL EMPOWERMENT OF LOCALLY AUTONOMOUS MANAGEMENT. WITH AN EYE TO THE FUTURE, COLONIAL BANK

maintains an established corporate commitment to disciplined growth and a fundamental belief that banking is and will remain a "people" business.

Colonial conducts business throughout Alabama, Florida, Georgia, Nevada, Tennessee, and Texas, and offers mortgage lending services in 45 states. Alabama and Florida are the largest markets, with $4.5 billion in assets in Alabama and $2.5 billion in Florida. A principal part of Colonial's growth, as well as its community strategy, included the introduction in 1998 of two new lines of business: Colonial Preferred Services (a Private Client Group) and International Banking. These two complementary areas have allowed Colonial to fully integrate its corporate philosophy of providing locally needed services.

"I believe we are successful because our service and market-

ing strategies are built around the communities in which our offices are located," says Linda Green, president and CEO of Colonial Bank's Huntsville Region. That community touch, combined with Colonial's "we can do" attitude, gives it a strong presence in the seven counties and nine cities it serves within the Huntsville region. Though one of the state's fastest-growing banks when it entered the Huntsville market in 1984 with the purchase of the Bank of Huntsville, Colonial, with its home-town-bank business philosophy and community-oriented services, has achieved a perfect fit in the Huntsville community.

Building a Higher Profile

Colonial Bank is seeking an even higher profile in the growing Huntsville market with its $12 million office building and parking

garage currently under construction in downtown Huntsville.

"This new building is an exciting opportunity for us," Green says. "It not only consolidates our region's banking and mortgage business in Huntsville, but it also gives us a higher profile in the city's financial center. It is a good economic opportunity for Huntsville, as it continues to build the downtown business district."

Colonial Bank also is committed to its growing communities, providing support for numerous activities that improve the quality of life. As with its banking services, each bank is given the ability to respond to needs unique to its community.

"Community involvement is critical to what we do, whether in a small town or a large city," Green says. "We're involved in the community because we want to make a difference."

SINCE ITS INCEPTION IN 1981, COLONIAL BANK HAS GROWN INTO AN $10 BILLION, MULTISTATE BANK, CONDUCTING BUSINESS THROUGHOUT ALABAMA, FLORIDA, GEORGIA, NEVADA, TENNESSEE, AND TEXAS, AND OFFERING MORTGAGE LENDING SERVICES IN 45 STATES.

IN MANY WAYS, HUNTSVILLE HAS BECOME A HOTBED OF OPPORTUNITIES FOR THE TECHNICAL SERVICES GROUP OF EER SYSTEMS INC. NOT ONLY ARE THE COMPANY'S AREA EMPLOYEES WORKING TO PROVIDE QUALITY TECHNICAL SUPPORT TO THE U.S. ARMY IN HUNTSVILLE, THEY ARE ALSO DEVELOPING A REPUTATION WITHIN THE COMPANY FOR PROVIDING TOP-NOTCH TECHNICAL EXPERTISE TO OTHER EER SYSTEMS PROJECTS. AND CHANGES IN THE LOCAL MISSION OF THE ARMY ARE making it possible for the $75 million company to further expand and diversify technical knowledge across the board. Such opportunities continue to maintain Huntsville as a significant market for EER Systems.

Offering Technical Expertise

About 250 of EER Systems' 800 employees work for its Technical Services Group. The company was established as a Virginia corporation in 1979, specializing in engineering and economics research. During the early 1980s, opportunities to provide engineering services to the U.S. Army brought EER Systems to Huntsville. "As the company's headquarters for its Technical Services Group, we are the largest group within the company," says Frank Bettinger, vice president of the Huntsville-based group. "We contribute 30 percent of the company's annual revenues."

"In the early days, we tended to gravitate toward systems engineering technical assistance and program management contracts," says Mike Gamino, director of advanced programs for the Huntsville group. "We had many of those kinds of small support contracts, which eventually parlayed us into competing for and winning a $162.5 million battlefield automated systems engineering contract to support the U.S. Army Aviation & Missile Command's Software Engineering Directorate in Huntsville."

Though the majority of EER Systems' local employees work on this contract, which will extend through 2001, the Huntsville group also provides engineering, cost analysis, and training systems support to various army, air force, and NASA customers throughout the United States.

Growing as a Team Player

In all the work we do in Huntsville, our technical strength is built on a strong belief in teamwork among our employees, customers, and subcontractors," Bettinger says. "EER Systems has a seamless team philosophy where customer priorities always rise to the top."

As a team player, EER Systems is involved in supporting customers for other groups within the company, such as the Aircraft Systems Group, which has done pioneer work for the navy in upgrading the avionics of large helicopter systems and in developing aircraft training systems. EER Systems' Huntsville operation hopes to take advantage of that technology by using it to win contracts with the U.S. Army Aviation & Missile Command's aviation activities now taking place in Huntsville.

EER Systems' support of local federal operations may also increase with the awarding of a U.S. General Services Administration Seat Management contract that puts the company among eight contractors approved for outsourcing of desktop computing as a non-owned service or information utility in support of any government agency. The contract, one of the largest technology contracts awarded in 1998, could be worth a total of $9 billion over 10 years to the eight contractors.

"Being in Huntsville has been very worthwhile for our company," Bettinger says. "It is a very competitive market, but it also offers an exceptionally skilled workforce for us to draw from in supporting our contracts. Huntsville is a classic high-tech city where we think EER Systems has a bright future."

EER SYSTEMS INC.'S BATTLEFIELD SYSTEMS ENGINEERING DIVISION UTILIZES SYSTEMS-LEVEL TEST BEDS (A UH-60K HELICOPTER IS SHOWN HERE) IN SOFTWARE TESTING (TOP).

EER SYSTEMS' TECHNICAL SERVICES GROUP IS CENTRALLY LOCATED IN THE RESEARCH PARK AREA (BOTTOM).

ADTRAN'S SUCCESS STORY FOLLOWS A PLOTLINE THAT IS AS BASIC AS BUSINESS 101: INTRODUCE THE RIGHT PRODUCT TO THE RIGHT CUSTOMER AT THE RIGHT TIME TO PRODUCE CORPORATE REVENUES AND GROWTH. BUT THIS DECEIVINGLY SIMPLE EQUATION ONLY TELLS PART OF THE STORY FOR THIS HUNTSVILLE-BASED DEVELOPER OF INNOVATIVE, COST-SAVING NETWORK ACCESS PRODUCTS. ✳ "WE STARTED THE COMPANY FROM A TECHNOLOGY STANDPOINT OF DEVELOPING PRODUCTS THAT WOULD TURN THE LOCAL

loop between telephone companies and their customers from analog to digital," says Mark Smith, chairman and CEO of ADTRAN, Inc. "Our success in the market required, however, not just a technology or capability of doing something, but also a business climate in industry where we could position our technology to sell it."

That business climate was created by AT&T's federally mandated divestiture of the Regional Bell Operating Companies (RBOCs), which also barred the companies from manufacturing equipment. The divestiture opened a window of opportunity for companies like ADTRAN to supply network equipment to the regional companies, as well as to more than 1,300 independent telephone companies in the United States. That opportunity became even more attractive to companies that could also transfer their technology into the corporate sector, where users of telecommunications services needed the speed, flexibility, and reliability offered by emerging digital transmission technology.

Providing Digital Solutions

Incorporated in 1985, ADTRAN took advantage of these market opportunities by designing, developing, and manufacturing advanced transmission products for high-speed digital communications. Three years after introducing its first product, ADTRAN held a leading position in the telephone company equipment market. In the early 1990s, the company began adapting telephone company equipment technology for application in the customer premises equipment market, where it now also holds a leading position.

Today, more than 500 ADTRAN products support major digital technologies, making it one of the leading suppliers in all three of its markets—telephone companies, corporate end users, and original equipment manufacturers. The company, which has achieved annual sales approaching $300 million and which is listed as a Nasdaq 100 Index stock, employs 1,100 people at its complex in Cummings Research Park West.

"What we have attempted to do from day one is to use tech-

nology to bring the cost of digital communications down," Smith says. "By using technology to lower the cost of communicating, we have been able to enjoy the growth associated with expansion in different commercial areas."

Tapping into Growing Markets

Supplying telephone companies with data transmission technologies remains ADTRAN's most significant market, accounting for about 65 percent of its total revenues. That focus is expected to continue as ADTRAN taps further into a market of 160 million copper wire local loops in the United States and more than 500 million worldwide, all of which must be converted to meet the need for fast, flexible digital communication services.

At the same time, technology will constantly change, providing additional opportunities for the company. "Our success absolutely depends on developing products that will allow network service providers to increase the level of business or reduce costs," Smith says. "We need to continuously develop and improve products while maintaining quality, price-to-performance value and customer support."

WITH NEARLY 300 ENGINEERS DEDICATED TO CREATING NEW PRODUCT LINES AND IMPROVING EXISTING PRODUCTS, ADTRAN, INC. IS UNIQUELY POSITIONED TO SUPPLY BOTH NETWORK SERVICE PROVIDERS AND END USERS A BROAD PRODUCT LINE TO COVER ALL THEIR NETWORKING NEEDS (TOP).

AT ITS CORPORATE HEADQUARTERS IN CUMMINGS RESEARCH PARK WEST, ADTRAN DESIGNS, DEVELOPS, AND MANUFACTURES HIGH-SPEED DIGITAL TELECOMMUNICATIONS EQUIPMENT (BOTTOM).

BUILT ON A FOUNDATION OF RESOURCEFULNESS, INDEPENDENCE, HONESTY, FAIR DEALING, AND RESPECT FOR EACH PERSON, UWOHALI (CHEROKEE FOR EAGLE) HAS ESTABLISHED A FIRM COMMITMENT OF QUALITY TO ITS CUSTOMERS, EMPLOYEES, AND THE COMMUNITY. THE COMPANY'S PHILOSOPHY OF COMBINING A STRONG TECHNOLOGY-ORIENTED BASE WITH INNOVATIVE MANAGEMENT ALLOWS THE EAGLE TO FLY HIGH. ✳ ESTABLISHED IN 1985, UWOHALI INCORPORATED IS A PRODUCT OF

Huntsville, a community with the right stuff. The city's direct role in the early space exploration years of the 60s has created an environment where both technical expertise and vision live hand-in-hand.

Founded and owned by American Indian W. Diane Weston, Uwohali is a multifaceted, technology-oriented business. Known for delivering the right product on time and within budget, Uwohali has a 100 percent contractual completion rate. As a result, the company has been the recipient of many awards, and was named Southeast Prime Contractor of the Year for 1995 by the Small Business Administration.

The company's focus is on satisfying the customer's needs with the highest quality products, services, and innovation. Uwohali provides active leadership in solving today's challenging problems, reducing costs, improving performance, and extending the service life of weapon systems, complex electronic components, and mechanical systems. Much of Uwohali's success stems from viewing customers as partners and striving to make their objectives, expectations, and priorities its own.

The company's daily mission statement sums up its attitude, "Let integrity, responsiveness and competency show in everything we do."

The People

A company is only as strong as the quality of its people, and Uwohali prides itself on its people. Uwohali employees provide a wide variety of expertise and technical backgrounds to ensure decades of experience in scientific and engineering analysis; logistics information and data management; electrical, mechanical and chemical engineering; and contract administration. The company offers vast experience in communications,

command and control, modeling and simulation, configuration management, integrated logistics support, systems engineering, electronics design and engineering, and procurement.

The highly motivated and empowered workforce at Uwohali challenges the status quo to provide innovative solutions to continuously improve quality.

The Products

Although Uwohali was established with a single contract valued at $7,000, today the company is a leader in systems engineering and analysis, electronic component obsolescence management (ECOM), integrated logistics support (ILS) and manpower and personnel integration (MANPRINT) service, electronic manufacturing, and life cycle sustainment.

Uwohali's wide variety of customers include the U.S. Army Aviation and Missile Command, NASA's Marshall Space Flight and Kennedy Space Centers, the U.S. Army Corps of Engineers, and numerous commercial companies. These customers not only demand the best products and services, but they deserve them.

The Community

Uwohali's involvement in the professional community is well established through the actions of

founder W. Diane Weston. She has worked on the NASA Industry Process Action Team and on the International Space Station Advisory Committee for the NASA Advisory Council. Weston was a participant in the Joint Civilian Orientation Conference for the Department of Defense, and is a member of the Defense Advisory Committee on Women in the Services. Additionally, Weston is the cofounder and past president of the Women's Economic Development Council.

In a few short years, Uwohali has built a reputation for excellence based on honesty, trust, and customer commitment. The company approaches every contract, every project, and every business relationship with the fair-mindedness of its Cherokee heritage. It is a business philosophy that has made this company and its founder a success.

U. S. SECRETARY OF DEFENSE WILLIAM S. COHEN AND UWOHALI FOUNDER AND CEO W. DIANE WESTON (TOP)

ESTABLISHED IN HUNTSVILLE IN 1985, UWOHALI HAS BECOME ONE OF HUNTSVILLE'S SMALL-BUSINESS RISING STARS. BUILT ON A FOUNDATION OF RESOURCEFULNESS, INDEPENDENCE, HONESTY, FAIR DEALING, AND RESPECT FOR THE DIGNITY OF EACH PERSON, UWOHALI HAS ESTABLISHED A FIRM COMMITMENT OF QUALITY TO ITS CUSTOMERS, ITS EMPLOYEES, AND THE COMMUNITY (BOTTOM).

SINCE 1986, COMCAST CABLEVISION OF HUNTSVILLE HAS PROVIDED TELEVISION'S BEST ENTERTAINMENT TO HUNTSVILLE RESIDENTS. USING ITS HIGH-TECH CAPABILITIES AND EXPERTISE IN THE CABLE INDUSTRY, THE COMPANY ALSO PROVIDES INFORMATION, EDUCATION, AND COMMUNITY SERVICE PROGRAMS, MAKING HUNTSVILLE A BETTER PLACE TO LIVE AND WORK. THE COMPANY'S HUNTSVILLE OFFICE IS ALSO THE CABLE OPERATIONS HEADQUARTERS FOR TUSCALOOSA AND FLORENCE, ALABAMA, AS

well as for Tupelo and Corinth, Mississippi.

Comcast-Huntsville is owned by Comcast Corporation, the nation's fourth-largest cable operator, which provides service to 5.5 million subscribers in 850 communities in 21 states, and is headquartered in Philadelphia.

Focused on Huntsville

Comcast-Huntsville provides its 43,000 customers with a wide variety of community broadcasting, including live telecasts of the Huntsville city council and school board meetings, which Comcast pioneered, along with a 24-hour local weather radar channel. Comcast also broadcasts local high school football and basketball games, graduation ceremonies, city election forums, the annual Von Braun Exploration Forum, and all of NASA's space shuttle launches.

"We focus much of our energy on finding ways to give back to the Huntsville community," says Len Rozek, manager of Comcast-Huntsville and area vice president

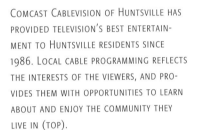

COMCAST CABLEVISION OF HUNTSVILLE HAS PROVIDED TELEVISION'S BEST ENTERTAINMENT TO HUNTSVILLE RESIDENTS SINCE 1986. LOCAL CABLE PROGRAMMING REFLECTS THE INTERESTS OF THE VIEWERS, AND PROVIDES THEM WITH OPPORTUNITIES TO LEARN ABOUT AND ENJOY THE COMMUNITY THEY LIVE IN (TOP).

PROVIDING 43,000 CUSTOMERS WITH A VARIETY OF POPULAR CHANNELS, COMCAST ALSO BROADCASTS EXCLUSIVE CONCERT AND COMEDY SPECIALS, MOVIE MARATHONS, AND UNIQUE CHANNELS SUCH AS FOX NEWS CHANNEL, THE TRAVEL CHANNEL, THE NASHVILLE NETWORK, AND BLACK ENTERTAINMENT TELEVISION (BOTTOM).

DENNIS KEIM

of Comcast Cablevision. "We want our local cable programming to reflect the interests of our viewers, as well as to provide them with opportunities to learn about and enjoy the community they live in.

"Comcast offers customers a high quality of expertise in cable communication and broadcasting," Rozek adds. "This gives us the ability to develop unique programs for the communities we serve."

That means not only providing cable programming that fits Huntsville customers, such as *NASA Select*, *Sci-Fi*, and *Fox Sports South*, but also producing such local programs as a family-oriented weekly program called *The P.E.N. (Partnership Educational Network) Show* for the Partnership for a Drug-Free Community, Inc., *People's Law School*, and *Comcast Cooking Show*. In addition, Comcast-Huntsville provides free cable service in all city schools and offers additional local telecasts of *Cable in the Classroom*.

"We do a multitude of local programming, in addition to offering such popular channels as CNN, the Discovery Channel, Nickelodeon,

ESPN, Turner Classic Movies, the History Channel, and Animal Planet," says Rozek. "We also add variety by broadcasting exclusive concert and comedy specials, movie marathons, and unique channels such as Fox News Channel, the Travel Channel, the Nashville Network, and Black Entertainment Television."

Comcast-Huntsville actively solicits subscriber comments via phone or through the Internet at www.inyourtown.com. Its 100 local employees use customer input to further develop a quality mix of cable programming, and to provide customers with maximum video and audio quality. The company offers stereo telecasts of traditional cable channels such as TBS, VH1, TNN, and TNT, along with digital music services. Future plans for Huntsville service include cable modems, digital video, high-speed data services, and multiplexing.

With intelligent and innovative programming and easy customer access, Comcast stays connected to its customers, living up to its motto: Comcast . . . Everything You Connect With!

FOCUS ON THE GOAL, PLAY AS A TEAM, AND PLAN FOR ALL THE CONTINGENCIES. THESE THREE LEADERSHIP PRINCIPLES HAVE PROVIDED THE FOUNDATION FOR THE EMERGENCE OF MADISON RESEARCH CORPORATION (MRC) AS ONE OF HUNTSVILLE'S PREMIER TECHNOLOGY COMPANIES. JOHN STALLWORTH, THE COMPANY'S COFOUNDER, PRESIDENT, AND CHIEF EXECUTIVE OFFICER, AND HIS BUSINESS PARTNER DECIDED THAT BUSINESS AND ENGINEERING SKILLS COULD COMPLEMENT EACH OTHER TO BUILD THE GROUNDWORK FOR A SUCCESSFUL

enterprise in Huntsville's high-tech environment. In July 1986, Madison Research was incorporated, and the company received its first contract a year later.

Madison Research began to realize significant growth in the 1990s, following its certification as an 8(a) company under the Small Business Administration's Small and Disadvantaged Business Program. The company branched out from its corporate headquarters in Huntsville's Cummings Research Park to include offices and employees in South Carolina, Tennessee, Georgia, Florida, New Mexico, and Washington, D.C. Throughout MRC's expansion, the employee base has grown from three to more than 250 today. The company's revenue growth averaged 28 percent in the first five years of operation, and is now growing in excess of 40 percent a year. The success Madison Research has experienced has also brought regional and national recognition to the firm. In 1997, the company was selected by the Chamber of Commerce of Huntsville/Madison County as Small Business of the Year in Technology Services. *Inc.* magazine ranked MRC as one of the 500 fastest-growing companies in the nation, and the firm's CEO was selected as Alabama's and the Southeast Region's Minority Businessman of the Year by the Small Business Administration.

Focusing on High Technology

To ensure that products and services for customers are on the cutting edge of technology, MRC reorganized into five broad business areas to group similar and complementary services. This breakdown allows each business-area leader to focus on identifying industry trends and refining and developing the company's core capabilities. The five business

areas are Information Systems, Software Engineering, Systems Sustainment, Systems Acquisition, and Administrative Support Services.

Madison Research strives to provide innovative solutions for customers' needs and requirements. Customers include a wide range of government and military contracts, as well as a host of other large and small engineering and information technology companies in the private sector.

Employees Make a Winning Team

Madison Research employees are dedicated to the motto Quality People Doing a Quality Job. The company encourages every employee to submit ideas to enhance MRC's products and services, and ensure quality in all aspects of work. "Our employees are highly skilled, experienced, and qualified professionals who can offer customer services in a

variety of technology areas," says Stallworth. Because the employees are the true experts at their jobs, they are involved at every level of decision making.

With the company's commitment to innovation and quality, MRC has received numerous letters of commendation and recognition for both the company and its employees. Madison Research has been recognized by many customers for its ability to make the transition into larger contracts with little or no interruption in the services provided. A NASA customer states, "This is one company you can count on to provide the right skills for a top-quality job at very reasonable costs. They are professionals."

"Our diversification—along with competitive pricing, high performance standards, and delivery of quality products and services—makes us ideally suited to satisfy a broad range of customer requirements," says Stallworth.

FOCUS ON THE GOAL, PLAY AS A TEAM, AND PLAN FOR ALL THE CONTINGENCIES. THESE THREE LEADERSHIP PRINCIPLES HAVE PROVIDED THE FOUNDATION FOR THE EMERGENCE OF MADISON RESEARCH CORPORATION AS ONE OF HUNTSVILLE'S PREMIER TECHNOLOGY COMPANIES. THE COMPANY'S OFFICERS INCLUDE (FROM LEFT) GLEN GLASNER, FLO STALLWORTH, SAM LIBERATORE, AND JOHN STALLWORTH.

Sigmatech, Inc.

SIGMATECH, INC. WAS FOUNDED IN HUNTSVILLE ON JULY 14, 1986, BY DR. GURMEJ S. SANDHU, A FIRST-GENERATION U.S. IMMIGRANT, UNIVERSITY OF ALABAMA IN HUNTSVILLE GRADUATE, AND HUNTSVILLE RESIDENT FOR A QUARTER OF A CENTURY. TODAY, AS SIGMATECH'S CHIEF EXECUTIVE OFFICER, SANDHU SHARES HIS ENTREPRENEURIAL DREAM WITH THE COMPANY'S 200 EMPLOYEES. NOW A SUCCESSFUL SMALL BUSINESS SERVING A VARIETY OF GOVERNMENT AND COMMERCIAL CUSTOMERS, SIGMATECH IS AN EMPLOYEE-OWNED

"WE HAVE ESTABLISHED OUR COMPANY AS A LEADER IN THE APPLICATION OF CUTTING-EDGE TECHNOLOGIES, AND INNOVATIVE SUPPORT FOR GOVERNMENT AND COMMERCIAL CUSTOMERS," SAYS DR. GURMEJ S. SANDHU, SIGMATECH, INC.'S CHIEF EXECUTIVE OFFICER (TOP RIGHT).

FOUNDED IN 1986 IN HUNTSVILLE, SIGMATECH IS AN EMPLOYEE-OWNED AND -OPERATED COMPANY FOCUSED ON BRINGING NEW AND EXISTING TECHNOLOGIES TOGETHER TO IDENTIFY INNOVATIVE, COST-EFFICIENT SOLUTIONS TO CHALLENGING TECHNICAL ISSUES (BOTTOM).

company. "We all stay more motivated because we share in the success of our company," Sandhu says.

Success Is in the Name

Sigmatech is immersed in Huntsville's high-tech arena; even the name Sigmatech—meaning the summation of technologies—emphasizes the company's forte: integrating existing and emerging technologies to develop 21st-century electronic and information system products. "We have established our company as a leader in the application of cutting-edge tech-

nologies and innovative support for government and commercial customers," Sandhu says.

In 1986, Sandhu used his experience with sensor and seeker technology to win a series of Small Business Innovative Research contracts from the U.S. government. Those contracts—ranging from $50,000 to $500,000 in value—were the beginning for Sigmatech. Today, the company's multimillion-dollar technology programs include electronics; signal processing; simulation; interactive software; virtual reality; 2-D and 3-D graphics and animation; guidance, dynamics, and control; information systems; software development; and data management.

Technology Expertise

Sigmatech's experience in the government sector includes system engineering and battle integration center support for the U.S. Army's Space and Missile Defense Command and the Army Program Executive Office for Air and Missile Defense, sensor and seeker technologies support to U.S. Army Aviation and Missile Command, and human engineering and propulsion technology support for NASA. Sigmatech also supports such Department of Defense agencies as the Air Force and the National Guard Bureau, and assists in resolving technology transfer issues and supporting logistics engineering efforts for the U.S. Army Aviation and Missile Command's foreign military sales programs.

In the commercial market, Sigmatech provides world-class interactive multimedia training support for corporate clients, such as Mercedes-Benz, Toyota, Honda, and ADTRAN. The company also partners with Calhoun Community College to develop interactive media technical training in support of industrial development

throughout the Tennessee Valley. These customized training courses, delivered via CD-ROM or network, enable technicians to follow best practice procedures to achieve maximum productivity and safety in the work environment.

Sigmatech also offers a variety of exceptional multimedia services in the areas of corporate presentations, kiosk and Web site development, and distance learning architecture.

"Our work in the commercial sector is very strong, and we believe it will grow to be about 50 percent of our business base," Sandhu says. "We have established ourselves as a premier interactive multimedia company."

Sigmatech's strength lies in the experience and expertise of its employees and in how they are organized into expert teams to respond to customer needs. Corporate engineers and scientists act as a think tank within their areas of responsibility to develop innovative solutions for complex problems.

In its many highly diversified areas of work, Sigmatech constantly demonstrates a knowledge of how to bring existing and new technologies together to identify innovative, cost-efficient solutions to challenging technical issues.

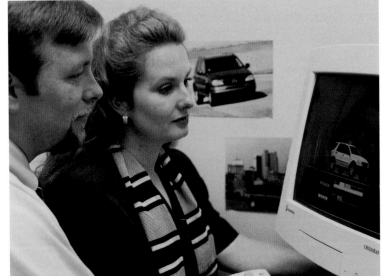

Based in Huntsville, VMIC is a software and hardware company that has built its foundation on close customer teamwork and strategic alliances. For more than 12 years, employees have worked to ensure the company's success by building on the cornerstones of high ethical values and world-class customer service. As a result, VMIC has experienced tremendous growth and today earns nearly $36 million in annual sales. ✳ Originally established

as a division of SAIC, the company was purchased in a 1986 leveraged buyout by Carroll E. Williams, VMIC's founder, president, and chief executive officer. With a business plan that included product manufacturing, VMIC developed a mix of both government and commercial customers. Now totaling more than 2,000, the firm's customers include General Motors, Reynolds Aluminum, Kodak, Tuscaloosa Steel, Boeing, Siemens, Chrysler, and others.

"Our success—today and in the future—is in the hands of our customers," says Williams. "We differentiate ourselves from our competition by making customer satisfaction the driving force behind everything we do. Our employees are focused on friendly communications, while remaining dedicated to providing products that our customers need to be successful and profitable."

Solutions as well as Products

VMIC is focused on continued growth, offering an extensive product line designed around open hardware and software solutions for international markets. VMIC's I/O systems solutions are based on providing configurations for complete systems shipped with chassis, power supplies, I/O boards, computer processing units, expansion links, and software. This package provides the user with an out-of-the-box computing solution that is preconfigured, loaded, and factory tested.

The company's 266 employees are involved in the research and development, production, and marketing of products that have applications in data acquisition and control, simulation and training, robotics, communications, plant monitoring, telecommunications, industrial automation, testing and measurement, environmental monitoring, and general computing.

"We develop, sell, and market our own products," Williams says. "VMIC is a multifaceted company involved in providing computer solutions for several different markets, such as automotive, aeronautical, and industrial automation. Our strategy is to continue to dominate the markets where we have had tremendous success while diversifying through major investments in new markets and new products."

Global Presence

VMIC has a long history of working with large, well-known contractors on projects that often span several countries. To support its international operations, VMIC has established a worldwide organization of sales representatives, distributors, and system integrators in 50 foreign countries. This global presence is necessary to support the company's rapidly expanding product line and the unique applications of its customers. With corporate headquarters in Huntsville, VMIC has direct sales personnel in Texas, Georgia, North Carolina, South Carolina, and Paris, France.

While VMIC reaches out with its products to companies all over the world, Huntsville continues to be an ideal location for this high-technology leader. "This community is very supportive of technology companies," Williams says. "We have built a successful business in a location known for its innovation and synergy that will ensure VMIC's capabilities to provide solutions today that will work in tomorrow's application environments."

"WE DEVELOP, SELL, AND MARKET OUR OWN PRODUCTS," SAYS CARROLL E. WILLIAMS, VMIC'S FOUNDER, PRESIDENT, AND CHIEF EXECUTIVE. "VMIC IS A MULTIFACETED COMPANY INVOLVED IN PROVIDING COMPUTER SOLUTIONS FOR SEVERAL DIFFERENT MARKETS, SUCH AS AUTOMOTIVE, AERONAUTICAL, AND INDUSTRIAL AUTOMATION."

VMIC IS FOCUSED ON CONTINUED GROWTH, OFFERING AN EXTENSIVE PRODUCT LINE DESIGNED AROUND OPEN HARDWARE AND SOFTWARE SOLUTIONS FOR NATIONAL AND INTERNATIONAL MARKETS (BOTTOM LEFT).

VMIC'S EMPLOYEES ARE INVOLVED IN THE RESEARCH AND DEVELOPMENT, PRODUCTION, AND MARKETING OF PRODUCTS THAT HAVE APPLICATIONS IN DATA ACQUISITION AND CONTROL, SIMULATION AND TRAINING, ROBOTICS, COMMUNICATIONS, PLANT MONITORING, TELECOMMUNICATIONS, INDUSTRIAL AUTOMATION, TESTING AND MEASUREMENT, ENVIRONMENTAL MONITORING, AND GENERAL COMPUTING (BOTTOM RIGHT).

Quantum Research International, Inc.

SPECIALIZING IN BEING ON THE CUTTING EDGE OF TECHNOLOGY, QUANTUM RESEARCH INTERNATIONAL, INC. AND ITS SUBSIDIARY, QUANTUM TECHNOLOGIES, HAVE PROVIDED CUSTOMERS WITH STATE-OF-THE-ART PRODUCTS AND SERVICES SINCE 1987. THE HUNTSVILLE-BASED COMPANY OFFERS THE TECHNICAL EXPERTISE THAT SUPPORTS THE NEEDS OF GOVERNMENT DEFENSE AGENCIES AND THE ENTIRE DEFENSE INDUSTRY. ✳ SYSTEMS DESIGN AND ANALYSIS, TECHNOLOGY ASSESSMENTS, MODELING AND

simulation, and operational and technical expertise with weapons systems—all are technical capabilities that Quantum provides in its support of military programs for both U.S. and allied governments. From the beginning, Quantum has lived up to its slogan: Where Vision Becomes Reality.

Excelling with Technology

With a primary focus on government defense programs, Quantum performs more than half its work from its local facility in Cummings Research Park. Additional offices are located in Arlington and Fairfax, Virginia; El Paso and Killeen, Texas; and Bel Air, Maryland. Quantum also maintains personnel sites in Fort Leavenworth, Kansas; Fort Huachuca, Arizona; Fort Monroe, Virgina; and Fort Shafter, Hawaii—all strategically located near government customers.

Quantum provides analysis services in several areas: com-

mand, control, communications, computers, and intelligence (C41) technologies; information warfare; air and missile defense operational assessments; modeling and simulation; systems engineering and technical assistance; and technology applications. Government customers include the Ballistic Missile Defense Organization, Defense Advanced Research Project Agency, Defense Modeling and Simulation Office, Land Information Warfare Activity, Army Digitization Office, Army Research Laboratory, Aviation and Missile Command, Air Defense Artillery School, Operational Test and Evaluation Command, Navy Surface Warfare Center, and several international customers, including NATO and the governments of Germany and the United Kingdom.

The pursuit of Quantum's additional business area, technology applications, resulted in the formation of a subsidiary company, Quantum Technologies, in 1997.

Focused on Customer Requirements

In 1987, D. Frank Pitts, Quantum president and chief executive officer, pursued his goal to establish a business that would provide technology analysis services and products to U.S. and allied governments. Since then, Quantum has posted a cumulative sales growth exceeding 40 percent per year. With many of its customers located in Huntsville, Quantum has found the city to be an excellent high-technology location from which to build its business base.

A Commitment to High Quality

Quantum's steady growth has resulted from a commitment to high-quality, responsive service to customers. Quantum provides independent, objective assessments of operational and system requirements, as well as cost-versus-performance trade-off analyses. The company focuses on key performance, survivability, and affordability drivers to understand total system capabilities.

Success for Quantum Research has brought recognition not only from customers, but also from the local, state, and national business communities. The company has been a finalist several times in the Small Business of the Year competition sponsored by the Chamber of Commerce of Huntsville/Madison County, and it has received *Business Alabama*'s Rising Star Award. Quantum has also been included in *Inc.* magazine's list of the 500 fastest-growing private companies in the United States.

Given Quantum's high degree of business success and its numerous industry accolades, it's no surprise that this Huntsville company is a place "where vision becomes reality."

CLOCKWISE FROM TOP RIGHT: QUANTUM RESEARCH INTERNATIONAL, INC. PROVIDES AIR AND MISSILE DEFENSE SERVICES RANGING FROM NEW TECHNOLOGY ASSESSMENTS TO WORLD-WIDE MISSILE FIRING SUPPORT.

QUANTUM'S HEADQUARTERS IN HUNTSVILLE

D. FRANK PITTS, QUANTUM PRESIDENT AND CHIEF EXECUTIVE OFFICER

STUDIO K PHOTOGRAPHY

BOB GATHANY

FORMED IN APRIL 1997, QUANTUM TECHNOLOGIES, INC. (QTI) HAS MADE SOUND, VIDEO, AND VIDEOCONFERENCING COME ALIVE FOR COURTROOMS, BOARDROOMS, CHURCHES, AND CONVENTION CENTERS ACROSS THE COUNTRY. A WHOLLY OWNED SUBSIDIARY OF QUANTUM RESEARCH INTERNATIONAL, QTI HAS QUICKLY BLAZED INTO THE NATIONWIDE AUDIO AND VIDEO DESIGN AND INSTALLATION SCENE. IT'S DIVERSELY TALENTED STAFF EXCELS IN THE AREAS OF ACOUSTICAL ANALYSIS, DESIGN, ASSEMBLY, INTEGRATION,

installation, and training. From microphones to multipoint videoconferencing, Quantum is creating the new total audio/video solution standard.

Quantum Technologies has delivered and installed complete systems for hundreds of federal courtrooms across the country. While most jobs are performed outside of Huntsville, locally Quantum has designed or installed systems for numerous industries and churches, the South Hall of the Von Braun Center, and the new Huntsville Museum of Art.

Acoustical Analysis

For existing rooms that need an acoustical face-lift, as well as for new facilities that require optimal sound quality, Quantum engineers use state-of-the-art, computerized analysis tools to determine the best acoustic solution. EASE software is used to generate three-dimensional acoustical models for analyzing the audio and acoustical characteristics of a room. On-site measurements are made with a TEF (time-energy-frequency delay) spectrometry analyzer. Quantum then recommends acoustical solutions and provides the customer with digitally created images of the proposed changes.

Design

In the design arena, Quantum Technologies' engineers create electronic circuit designs, schematics, and printed circuit boards for customized applications. They also employ AutoCAD workstations to produce mechanical, fabrication, and conduit schedule drawings. Most unique is Quantum's comprehensive system design approach, whereby Quantum engineers create complete audio and video system designs, which are then implemented in-house by Quantum

technicians. In their 20,000-square-foot Huntsville Cummings Research Park assembly and test facility, Quantum technicians can simultaneously assemble, integrate, and test system control racks and other custom components for several jobs according to their respective engineering designs.

System Integration

Quantum specialists work with architects and design consultants to integrate complex system requirements. Imagine a judge presiding in a courtroom and before him sits a 10- by 10-inch color touch screen that can be used to control courtroom lighting, sound, video, and multiple site teleconferencing, as well as controlling the preview of electronic evidence or data, all from one control panel. These features are typical of the easy-to-use, fully integrated systems that Quantum develops for its customers.

Installation and Training

Another unique aspect of Quantum Technologies is its crew of skilled and experienced installation teams. The teams travel across the nation to install and integrate custom-designed system racks and equipment into a fully functional, user-friendly system.

After installation, Quantum provides user training, complete operation and maintenance manuals, and warranty service on all system components.

Sight and Sound Come Alive

Multimedia communication technologies are the wave of the future, and Quantum is at the forefront of this rapidly changing environment. With its extensive professional audio and video experience, Quantum Technologies is shaping the future of integrated audio, video, and videoconferencing systems.

QUANTUM TECHNOLOGIES' ENGINEERS AND TECHNICIANS CREATE AND PRODUCE QUALITY AUDIO AND VIDEO SYSTEM DESIGNS AND INSTALLATIONS.

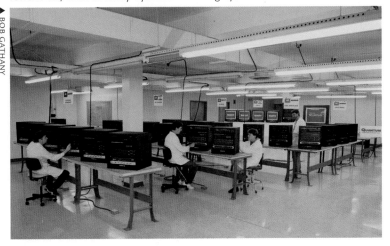

QUANTUM TECHNOLOGIES IS THE RECOGNIZED NATIONAL LEADER IN FEDERAL COURTROOM AUDIO/VIDEO TECHNOLOGY.

SUMMA Technology, Inc.

IN A CITY KNOWN FOR THE HIGH-TECH ENGINEERING SERVICES OF ITS AEROSPACE INDUSTRY, HUNTSVILLE'S SUMMA TECHNOLOGY, INC. HAS ESTABLISHED ITSELF IN A CLASS ALL ITS OWN. BY COMBINING ENGINEERING EXPERTISE WITH HIGH-QUALITY PRECISION MANUFACTURING, SUMMA HAS GROWN FROM ITS 1987 FOUNDING TO BECOME A GLOBAL LEADER IN THE DESIGN, MANUFACTURE, AND SUPPORT OF COMMERCIAL AND MILITARY AIRCRAFT, SPACE VEHICLES, AND DEFENSE SYSTEMS. ✳ WITH 400,000 SQUARE FEET OF

manufacturing space in three locations, this growth-oriented company has established a competitive edge in the marketplace. One of few Huntsville companies with manufacturing expertise, SUMMA provides customers with services beyond the usual research and development, as well as engineering design.

"What makes us unique in Huntsville and in the Southeast is our manufacturing capability," says President and Chief Executive Officer E.C. "Pony" Lee. "We are a world-class manufacturing facility sitting in this very large cauldron of high-technology activity. Our competitive edge is our infrastructure and the experience of our employees."

Excelling in High-Tech Manufacturing

SUMMA's large-scale resources include manufacturing and design facilities in Huntsville and in Fayetteville, Tennessee, as well as robotic welding capabilities in Cullman, Alabama. This combination of services has won the company numerous high-tech commercial and military aircraft contracts. As a result, SUMMA manufactures more than 1,300 different machined parts for each Gulfstream IV aircraft made by Gulfstream Aerospace, around 600 link assemblies for the U.S. Army's CH-47 Chinook helicopter, and more than 20 ground support equipment items for the U.S. Air Force's C-17 aircraft.

"Many of our contracts are in support of other aerospace companies," Lee says. "In essence, we do contract manufacturing for them, but what makes us different is that we also have design and development capability."

NASA has been another major source of business for SUMMA. Contracts in support of space ex-

ploration include manufacturing more than 30 hatch plates for NASA's space station modules, precision machining many large aluminum-lithium panels for the space shuttle's superlightweight external tank, and machining and fabricating space station end structure rings.

SUMMA's engineering expertise also led to NASA contracts for the development of a two-stage launch vehicle and a low-cost rocket engine for small payloads, as well as launch defense contracts to provide logistic support services; computer software development, system test, and operator and maintenance training; and diagnostic test equipment test program sets.

Growing with Huntsville

In 1992, SUMMA further solidified its presence in the Huntsville market with the purchase of a facility at Cummings Research Park

from Pratt & Whitney. This added manufacturing resource led to rapid growth for the company. In the first 10 months of business, sales reached about $15 million. Today, SUMMA is a $75 million company with more than 500 employees and a business mix of 50 percent defense, 25 percent space, and 25 percent commercial work.

"Practically overnight, the purchase of the Huntsville facility gave us the capabilities and resources of a large aerospace company with the flexibility and responsiveness of the small business that we are," Lee says.

"We have been successful because we produce the highest-quality product at the lowest price. Somebody else may be able to do that for one part, but SUMMA offers consistency in quality and low price for everything manufactured with our equipment and by our experienced employees," says Lee.

HIGH-TECHNOLOGY ENGINEERING AND MANUFACTURING ARE SUMMA'S TRADEMARK.

LOCATED IN HUNTSVILLE'S CUMMINGS RESEARCH PARK, ACROSS FROM THE UNIVERSITY OF ALABAMA, SUMMA TECHNOLOGY, INC. IS RIGHT IN THE MIDDLE OF ALABAMBA'S HIGH TECHNOLOGY EXPLOSION.

MR. E.C. "PONY" LEE IS THE FOUNDER, PRESIDENT, AND CEO OF SUMMA.

COMMERCIAL REAL ESTATE IS A WAY OF LIFE FOR RUSS RUSSELL, OWNER AND BROKER OF RUSS RUSSELL COMMERCIAL REAL ESTATE. A HUNTSVILLE NATIVE, RUSSELL HAS ALWAYS KNOWN THAT WITH THE FAST GROWING BUSINESS ENVIRONMENT OF HIS HOMETOWN, HE WOULD FIND HIS OPPORTUNITY IN THE COMMERCIAL REAL ESTATE MARKET. ✳ SINCE FOUNDING HIS BUSINESS, RUSSELL HAS INTRODUCED THE CITY'S COMMERCIAL REAL ESTATE MARKET TO A NEW LEVEL OF EXCELLENCE. HE BECAME

Huntsville's first Certified Commercial Investment Member (CCIM), a designation conferred by the Commercial Investment Real Estate Institute, an affiliate of the National Association of Realtors. He was also Huntsville's first Certified Exchange Adviser (CEA), a designation obtained through the American Institute of Real Estate Exchangers.

Both designations reflect hours of dedicated study of real estate disciplines, and exemplify the real estate industry's highest professional and ethical standards. Both equip commercial real estate professionals like Russell with the knowledge needed to assist their clients in building a profitable investment portfolio.

"Huntsville's commercial real estate market is full of challenging opportunities, and if commercial real estate professionals are going to take advantage of those opportunities, they need the experience and education to meet the challenges of a fast growing, ever changing marketplace," says Russell.

Dedicated to Growth

Russell, whose family has been involved in the commercial real estate business since 1959, grew up learning about the challenges and opportunities of real estate. Deciding to pursue the career as a young man, Russell earned his real estate degree from the University of Alabama in 1984. He gained experience in the commercial real estate market first as a qualifying broker for Century 21 Accent Realty, and then as an associate broker in charge of Accent's commercial real estate department.

In 1987, Russell began Russ Russell Commercial Real Estate, a company specializing in commercial and investment brokerage business, leasing, tax-deferred exchanges, and build-to-suits. The company has grown to more than $10 million in annual real estate sales.

Although "Russells Another" Sold signs are the most visible part of Russell's commercial real estate business, his clients see the true results of his education and experience at the bottom line of their investment statements. "In all the work that I do with clients, I work to minimize risk through building a balanced real estate portfolio, maximizing potential yields, and building personal wealth," Russell says. "At first glance, my business may only appear to market and sell commercial real estate. But we do much more than that for clients who want to build their investment portfolio."

Russell is confident that Huntsville will continue to provide the opportunities for his business to grow. "This is the best place in Alabama to do business," he says. "Our infrastructure is fantastic. Redstone Arsenal, Cummings Research Park, the University of Alabama in Huntsville, and the Chamber of Commerce's Economic Development Department have all been part of a very good team that has made Huntsville's commercial real estate market full of business opportunities."

COMMERCIAL REAL ESTATE IS A WAY OF LIFE FOR HUNTSVILLE NATIVE RUSS RUSSELL, OWNER AND BROKER OF RUSS RUSSELL COMMERCIAL REAL ESTATE. RUSSELL IS HUNTSVILLE'S FIRST CERTIFIED COMMERCIAL INVESTMENT MEMBER (CCIM), A DESIGNATION CONFERRED BY THE COMMERCIAL INVESTMENT REAL ESTATE INSTITUTE, AN AFFILIATE OF THE NATIONAL ASSOCIATION OF REALTORS. HE IS ALSO HUNTSVILLE'S FIRST CERTIFIED EXCHANGE ADVISER (CEA), A DESIGNATION OBTAINED THROUGH THE AMERICAN INSTITUTE OF REAL ESTATE EXCHANGERS.

TIME DOMAIN IS ONE OF HUNTSVILLE'S NEWEST AND MOST PROMISING ENTREPRENEURIAL ENTERPRISES. ESTABLISHED IN 1987, THE COMPANY IS ON THE VERGE OF RESHAPING TODAY'S COMMUNICATIONS WITH THE DISCOVERY OF A WIRELESS MEDIUM THAT ALLOWS HIGH-SPEED, LOW-POWER, COVERT COMMUNICATIONS, AS WELL AS HIGH-DEFINITION, LOW-POWER IMAGING RADAR. TIME DOMAIN'S HIGH-TECHNOLOGY INNOVATION PROMISES TO TAKE WIRELESS MARKETS TO A NEW DIMENSION AND

transform the communications industry.

"Our mission is to convert the technology we have into one of the world's essential technologies," says Peggy L. Sammon, a senior vice president at Time Domain. "We are growing this technology so that it becomes as pervasive as the world's current wireless technology. Although growth rates are extremely hard to predict, we strongly believe that this technology has the ability to revolutionize wireless communications, and in doing that, our company will become one of Huntsville's next major technology-based employers."

Revolutionizing Wireless Communications

Larry W. Fullerton, company founder and chief technical

officer, discovered and patented Time Domain's breakthrough technology—known as Digital Pulse Wireless (Time Modulated Ultra-Wideband). Currently, wireless communications rely on conventional signals that are highly visible electronically because their power is packed into a narrow slice of radio spectrum. Fullerton's Digital Pulse technology transmits millions

of coded pulses per second at emissions indistinguishable from the noise floor and across an ultrawide band, yielding a virtually undetectable, high-performance, extremely high-speed communication link.

Despite a variety of promising applications, Time Domain has focused the price and performance advantages of Digital Pulse Wireless in areas where present technology is incapable of meeting defined market demands. These applications include short-range, high-performance wireless LANs (local area networks) for home and office environments, military and law enforcement covert communications, real-time geopositioning and navigation, groundpenetrating radar, and real-time, high-definition surveillance and inspection radar.

RALPH PETROFF (LEFT), PRESIDENT AND CEO, AND LARRY W. FULLERTON, FOUNDER OF TIME DOMAIN, REVIEW THE COMPANY'S FIRST CHIP, PICOTIMER™, A KEY BUILDING BLOCK OF DIGITAL PULSE WIRELESS.

THE PROFESSIONAL STAFF AT TIME DOMAIN INCLUDES ELECTRONIC ENGINEERS, COMMUNICATION ENGINEERS, PHYSICISTS, MATHEMATICIANS, AND CHIP DESIGNERS.

"We are now getting this technology out of the lab and into product prototypes for government and commercial applications," Sammon says. "The wireless technology that we can offer on a chip promises to introduce a magnitude of improvements in three main areas: wireless communication, geopositioning, and radar imaging."

Many of the expansion constraints that today's wireless communication systems are facing can be solved using Digital Pulse Wireless. The technology will dramatically increase the amount of wireless information that can be sent while lowering the amount of power needed to send the information.

In the field of geopositioning, existing technology can be unavailable because of obstructions from other objects—such as trees and buildings.

"Our system sends out little pulses marked in time that can pinpoint an object within a few inches," Sammon says. "All we need to locate an object are three receivers, so there aren't the satellite problems associated with shadowing, trees, and other structures getting in the way. Digital Pulse is applicable both for law enforcement and for asset tracking. You can even put chips on cattle and farm equipment, and then track your animals or your vehicles."

With the radar-imaging field, Time Domain's technology can provide accurate, high-definition, through-object imaging. "The markets for our radar technology are tremendous, and include through-wall imaging and ground-penetrating radar," Sammon says.

Becoming a Worldwide Standard

Presently, Time Domain is adapting its Digital Pulse Wireless technology for use in military applications. The company holds 10 broad-based U.S. patents for the technology, as well as 32 foreign patents. "Once Digital Pulse Wireless becomes a new standard in the industry, the company's growth potential will be enormous," Sammon says.

"In 1998, our expenses are being financed largely through the sale of equity," Sammon continues. "But once this technology becomes commercial, we will support our licensees with system-level technology for their integration."

In 1996, Sammon, a member of the Petroff Venture Group, Ltd.— a Huntsville-based firm comprised of several founders of ADS Environmental Services, Inc., a high-tech electronics and engineering company—realized the potential of Fullerton's technology, and brought capital and management to Time Domain.

All employees are stock option holders in Time Domain. Today, a staff of 50 employees makes up the Time Domain team. With varied expertise in the fields of electronics, physics, optics, chip design, software, and mathematics, these employees are engineering Digital Pulse technology for the marketplace. "All of us who work for Time Domain are in this together; we have a stake in adapting this technology to address our customer needs. There is a start-up feeling here that is exciting, and all employees are encouraged to participate fully as owners in the mission of Time Domain," says Sammon.

At Huntsville-based Quality Research, Inc., employees are treated as entrepreneurs for this high-technology computing and engineering firm. In fact, they are the key to diversification of the company's services and customer base, as well as an important part of the successful government contracting work that has made Quality Research one of the fastest-growing companies in the country. Following this business strategy,

Dr. Dusit "Dusty" Charern, founder and chief executive officer, has evolved Quality Research into an employee-owned and -managed company.

"At Quality Research, a young entrepreneurial society has been organized to groom the company's new generation of leaders," says Charern. "They develop their own vision, own mission, own strategy, and own execution plan that could possibly lead to the creation of a new subsidiary for Quality Research. We encourage our entrepreneurs to come up with new ideas and then grow it into a company."

Quality in Everyday Business

Since Charern started the business in 1988, the focus has been on providing quality services to government contractors. The company's first assignment was a simulation and modeling contract for the Guidance and Control

Directorate at the U.S. Army Aviation and Missile Command. In early 1992, Quality Research was accepted into the Small Business Administration 8(a) program for small and disadvantaged businesses. By 1998, the company was awarded a seven-year, $75 million contract from the U.S. Army Strategic Missile Defense Command to provide information-management services to government workers.

In day-to-day operations, Quality Research has a strong commitment to project and customer satisfaction. For this reason, the company's motto is Winning with Quality. The company credits customer referrals and successful contract completion for making it a $22.2 million operation in 1998.

"We believe that meeting the needs of our customers, partners, and employees is fundamental in fulfilling our vision of growth and stability," Charern says. "We are

winning because quality is our main objective."

As a result, Quality Research has been named Small Business of the Year in the technology services category of the annual Small Business Awards program sponsored by the Chamber of Commerce of Huntsville/Madison County. The company has also been named twice in *Inc.* magazine's list of the 500 fastest-growing private companies in America.

Today, Quality Research has offices in Huntsville; Anniston; Atlanta; Columbus, Georgia; St. Petersburg; New Cumberland, Pennsylvania; Washington, D.C.; and Colorado Springs. Customers include the U.S. Army, the U.S. Air Force, NASA, and various law enforcement agencies.

A Core of Expertise

Although Quality Research has diversified its technical capabilities, Charern has led successful efforts to develop core competencies in three areas: engineering and analysis, modeling and simulation, and information technology. Its numerous government contracts rely on employee expertise in the areas of engineering, computer science, strategic defense, software development, mathematics, physics, and information systems.

Quality Research is on the cutting edge in the development of military modeling and simulation systems, primarily because the army and other government agencies are interested in the cost-savings factor of the technology. "We can simulate all types of military systems in a battlefield environment so that the customer can determine the value added by new equipment or new designs of existing equipment," says Abner Lee, senior vice president of modeling and simulation. "Beyond this capability, we can provide on one

Quality Research, Inc. is headquartered in Huntsville's Corporate Research Park.

computer a distributive computing environment where computers at several different locations can interact with each other in the same battlefield environment."

The company's systems allow the government a unique opportunity to test and analyze ground vehicles, missiles, aircraft, and other equipment under computer-generated battlefield conditions. "You don't have to bend metal or build a prototype," Lee explains. "You can use the equipment by building it into a computer modeling and simulation system. Some of the technology even allows you to have a bird's-eye view of the battlefield. We are one of the few companies with the state-of-the-art technology to do this type of work."

Diversifying High Technology

Although Quality Research continues to focus on established high-technology services, it is also expanding the use of its expertise into nontraditional areas. The company provides training support for the nation's law enforcement officials, assists the army in evaluating future technology needs, and develops training courses for the military.

"The areas in which we use our expertise are broad and diverse," says Tom Watkins, senior vice president of engineering and analysis. "You can't put us in a niche because we perform various tasks to support our customers, much of which goes beyond providing technology support."

With the expertise Quality Research has developed in the training field, the company hopes to expand into the commercial sector, providing training in the fields of protection and individual security. "As the company has grown, we have developed credibility in many areas," Watkins says. "The technology that we use to build modeling and simulation systems has also laid the foundation for relationships that we need to grow into other fields of expertise. Now, we can provide training and support for the modeling and simulation systems we have developed, and

this has allowed us to explore new opportunities."

Looking to the future, Quality Research and its employees are building on opportunities to ex-

pand the company's expertise even further. According to Charern, it's all about Winning with Quality every day with every customer.

QUALITY RESEARCH IS PROVIDING STATE-OF-THE-ART TRAINING FOR CUSTOMERS AND EMPLOYEES IN INFORMATION TECHNOLOGY AND SPECIALIZED SUBJECT MATTERS (TOP).

QUALITY RESEARCH'S EXECUTIVE STAFF (FROM LEFT) ABNER LEE, SR. VICE PRESIDENT MODELING AND SIMULATION; DR. DUSTY CHARERN, FOUNDER AND CEO; TERRY JENNINGS, CHIEF ADMINSTRATION OFFICER. (LEFT TO RIGHT BACK ROW) TOM WATKINS, SR. VICE PRESIDENT ENGINEERING AND ANALYSIS; JEFF RAGAN, VICE PRESIDENT BUSINESS DEVELOPMENT; TED BAUDENDISTEL, CHIEF FINANCIAL OFFICER (BOTTOM).

To Dr. Marvin Carroll, founder and president of Tec-Masters, Inc. (TMI), technology is just a way of getting things done. At first glance, Tec-Masters looks like a high-technology company providing engineering support. The company's products can be found everywhere from military systems and the space shuttle to the dashboards of cars. But, equally important to the company's success is imagination. When technology meets imagination,

RALPH JOHNSON (STANDING), EXECUTIVE VICE PRESIDENT OF TEC-MASTERS, INC., TOURING THE COMPANY'S MULTIMEDIA FACILITY WITH DON RAY (SEATED), MULTIMEDIA PROGRAMS DIRECTOR (RIGHT)

DR. MARVIN CARROLL, PRESIDENT AND CEO, STARTED TEC-MASTERS AFTER A 30-YEAR CAREER IN WEAPON SYSTEMS RESEARCH, DEVELOPMENT, AND ACQUISITION WITH THE U.S. ARMY. CARROLL HOLDS A B.S. IN ELECTRICAL ENGINEERING FROM HOWARD UNIVERSITY AND A DOCTORATE IN PUBLIC ADMINISTRATION (LEFT).

energy and invention follow. It is this atmosphere that makes Tec-Masters world class.

"We describe ourselves as the company where technology meets imagination," says Carroll. "My job is to maintain an environment where people have the flexibility and the motivation to look at things from different angles, because that is where the real creative breakthroughs come. Sometimes, these breakthroughs can be an idea for a new line of business or an innovative way to solve a perplexing problem. But make no mistake, imagination makes it happen."

Tec-Masters' work environment attracts the kind of talent that has made it one of the fastest-growing companies in the United States. The company was recognized by *Technology Transfer Business* as the third-fastest-growing company in the nation during a five-year period between 1990 and 1994. It also ranked 147th among *Inc.* magazine's top 500 fastest-growing private companies in 1996.

Carroll holds a B.S. in electrical engineering from Howard University and a doctorate in public administration. He started Tec-Masters in 1988, after a 30 year career in weapon systems research, development, and acquisition with the U.S. Army. Since then, things have changed substantially at Tec-Masters. Carroll remembers going all over town shopping for used furniture and office equipment. Recently, the founder became the last person in the company to replace his secondhand desk.

Positive Attitude

Although the overwhelming majority of Tec-Masters' 325 employees are engineers, they think like entrepreneurs. "The spirit of imagination applied to the marketplace, as well as the needs of our customers, opens new worlds of opportunities," says Carroll. One of the most common phrases heard around the office is "We can do that."

Tec-Masters is best known for its Department of Defense work, which includes systems engineering and integration, software development, battlefield simulations, test and evaluation, precision navigation, training, and much more. However, the company has also found that the same combination of imagination and technology can make it a leader in developing products for commercial business customers and even consumers.

As a leader in developing global positioning systems (GPS) technology, which uses satellites to determine the position of a vehicle, Tec-Masters found a natural market for navigation systems in automobiles. Tec-Masters is one of two nationwide distributors of the Carin navigation system.

"If you're driving in a strange part of town, the Carin system tells you exactly where you are and guides you to your destination turn by turn. If you miss a turn, it recalculates your route and keeps you on your way. You don't even have to look down or look at a map, because the onboard com-

A PROTOTYPE OF THE AUTO PC NAVIGATION SYSTEM

puter knows where you are and reads out your directions over a speaker. It is virtually impossible to get lost," says Carroll.

Tec-Masters is also pioneering the growing field of inventory and property control applications. In addition to systems using traditional bar codes, the company is now using state-of-the-art "smart buttons"—small memory chips that store data about items to which they are attached for even better inventory management and control systems.

Another area of commercial opportunities is growing out of the firm's government work in training and computer simulations. "Our experience in training and in computer simulations naturally led to development of a first-rate multimedia division, which can do anything from a simple video to interactive distance learning programs," says Carroll. "There is a great deal of business demand for these types of services."

A Bright Future

Tec-Masters' engineers are hard at work on projects that could make major changes in the way people live and work. One of the most exciting innovations is the auto PC. "In the future, a single

unit will integrate stereo, CD, navigation, climate controls, Internet access, video, and applications we haven't even thought about yet," says Carroll. Tec-Masters is one of the first companies in the nation to begin working on the product, using a special version of Microsoft Windows being developed just for cars. Tec-Masters is currently developing a system for one of the largest automotive equipment manufacturers in the country.

The company is also developing a prototype for a bus of the future for the Department of Transportation. Integrating the latest technologies, the prototype

DAVE MOBLEY (SEATED), DIRECTOR OF ADVANCED TECHNOLOGY & SPACE PROGRAMS, RECEIVES A DEMONSTRATION OF THE AUTO-MATED MANAGEMENT INVENTORY SYSTEM FROM ARNOLD KNOTT.

will be rolled out in 2000, according to Carroll.

"The advances being made today will affect all of us by making us more informed, more efficient, safer, and more comfortable in everything we do. But the really exciting prospects are yet to come, the possibilities that have yet to be imagined," says Carroll.

In that kind of future, Carroll likes Tec-Masters' prospects. "After all, we're the place where technology meets imagination. Imagination lets us see the possibilities. It lets us find solutions that others might miss. That enables us to put our technology to work in the best possible direction," says Carroll.

COLONIAL PROPERTIES TRUST IS ONE OF THE LARGEST DIVERSIFIED REAL ESTATE INVESTMENT TRUSTS IN THE NATION, SERVING MARKETS IN ALABAMA, GEORGIA, TENNESSEE, MISSISSIPPI, FLORIDA, NORTH CAROLINA, SOUTH CAROLINA, TEXAS, AND VIRGINIA. WITH A TOTAL MARKET CAPITALIZATION OF MORE THAN $2 BILLION, THIS PUBLICLY TRADED COMPANY HAS AMASSED REAL ESTATE HOLDINGS THAT INCLUDE MORE THAN 15,300 APARTMENT UNITS, 13.5 MILLION SQUARE FEET OF RETAIL SHOPPING

space, and 2.7 million square feet of office space.

In 1989, Colonial Properties emerged on the Huntsville commercial real estate market in a big way. The company's first commercial venture was the city's largest and most modern downtown office building, the 11-story AmSouth Center. Its construction marked the beginning of Colonial's aggressive expansion into Huntsville.

First-Class Properties Managed Locally

Although based in Birmingham, Colonial develops, acquires, manages, leases, and offers third-party brokerage services for multi-family apartments, retail centers, and office buildings in Huntsville. Within the local office building market, Colonial has a variety of product types, including both research and development buildings and executive space serving such tenants as AmSouth Bank; Bradley, Arant, Rose & White; EER Systems, Inc.; and MEVATEC Corp.

"Our most noticeable presence in Huntsville is our office developments," says Kyle Collins, Colonial's market officer. "We manage and own nearly 1 million square feet of office space consisting of the AmSouth Center, Lakeside Office

Park, Perimeter Corporate Park, Progress Center, and Colonial Center at Research Park."

From Colonial's initial entry in the market, its employees have remained focused on providing first-class office property and first-class service. "Even though we have assets across the Southeast, our Huntsville properties are handled by local property managers," Collins says. "Since 1989, the office building market in Huntsville has been one of our strongest areas and has contributed significantly to the company's overall holdings. "

Service Puts Colonial on Top

All of our customers are important. We believe in providing

BRIAN ROBBINS

them with better services than any of our competitors," Collins says. "Our growth is measured not only by the number of holdings we have, but also by the number of clients we support on a daily basis. The reason a company locates in a particular building comes down to the service they receive, and that's what separates Colonial from the rest. We take care of the people once their companies are in our office space."

That philosophy has helped Colonial maintain above market occupancy rate in its properties. The company works to deliver a full range of services for tenants with two things in mind: providing comfortable surroundings and ensuring a pleasant leasing experience.

"We see Huntsville as the premier market in Alabama," Collins says. "With the close proximity of NASA and the Department of Defense, as well as the diversification of the local economy, Huntsville will continue to provide us with opportunities to develop and acquire more properties. We are the number one commercial real estate and development company in Huntsville, and that's a distinction we want to maintain."

CLOCKWISE FROM TOP:
IN 1989, COLONIAL PROPERTIES' FIRST COMMERCIAL VENTURE WAS HUNTSVILLE'S LARGEST AND MOST MODERN DOWNTOWN OFFICE BUILDING, THE 11-STORY AMSOUTH CENTER.

COLONIAL PROPERTIES MANAGES AND OWNS PREMIER OFFICE SPACE IN HUNTSVILLE, SUCH AS PERIMETER CORPORATE PARK.

ANOTHER SIGNIFICANT BUILDING IN COLONIAL PROPERTIES' OFFICE SPACE IS THE LAKESIDE OFFICE PARK.

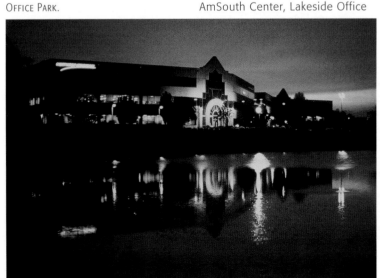

ESTABLISHED IN 1989 BY BUSINESS ASSOCIATES WITH HIGHLY TECHNICAL BACKGROUNDS, COMPUTER SYSTEMS TECHNOLOGY, INC. (CST) IS A REFLECTION OF HUNTSVILLE'S REPUTATION AS A SUPPORTIVE BUSINESS COMMUNITY, THE OPPORTUNITIES PRESENTED BY THE GROWING MARKET FOR INFORMATION TECHNOLOGY, AND THE FIRM'S FOUNDERS' DETERMINATION TO SUCCEED. ✳ "HUNTSVILLE IS THE KIND OF COMMUNITY THAT SUPPORTS SMALL BUSINESSES AND GIVES THEM OPPORTUNITIES TO THRIVE, IN BOTH

government and commercial sectors," says Bobby Bradley, CST's president and CEO, who started the company with Jay Newkirk, vice president of partnership/business development. "The information technology market was our key to growth. We knew we could capitalize on the opportunities in the market to achieve success and reach the goals that we had, while providing opportunities for our customers and employees to reach their goals for success," Bradley says.

CST provides information technology and systems engineering support, with a focus on hardware and software sales, hardware support and maintenance, information technology and support services, program and acquisition support, environmental engineering, and logistics support. The company's 350 employees provide integrated information solutions to government agencies, prime contractors, and commercial enterprises.

Exceeding Customer Expectations

Sixty percent of CST's business is in Huntsville, and the com-

pany also maintains offices in Baton Rouge, Louisiana; Louisville, Kentucky; Memphis; Nashville; Tullahoma, Tennessee; Kings Bay, Georgia; and Washington, D.C. CST has annual revenues in excess of $36 million, and a customer base that includes such government agencies as the U.S. Army's Aviation and Missile Command, Corps of Engineers, and Space and Missile Defense Command; NASA's Marshall Space Flight Center; the General Services Administration; and such private industry clients as Boeing, Lockheed Martin, Computer Sciences Corporation, and ADTRAN.

"We work to develop partnerships with our customers. That's our goal, and we do it by exceeding our customers' expectations with quality products delivered on time and on budget," Bradley says. "We've got to be able to deliver excellent products that meet our customers' needs."

To achieve this goal, CST is organized along two distinct business lines: the Federal Systems Division, which draws from the company's experience as a federal government contractor to respond to the unique requirements of government organizations; and the

MicroSystems Division, which is a leading supplier of computer hardware and software products, and other information technology services to commercial customers. The company's subsidiary, CST TelCom, provides telecommunications services to government agencies, prime contractors, communication systems providers, and corporations.

"To compete successfully, you have to be cost competitive and technically competent," Bradley says. "Your partners must see you as value added. Our employees are vital to making CST a value added partner in all our working relationships. CST supports employee efforts to grow in their technical competencies, because that kind of growth is valuable to both the employee and the company."

CST's success in developing partnerships with customers was recognized in 1996 and 1998 with the SBA's Administrator's Award of Excellence, and in 1998, when Bradley won the Small Business Executive of the Year award from the Chamber of Commerce of Huntsville/Madison County. For the future, CST plans to continue building partnerships with private industry, and federal and state governments, working to achieve success as Your Information Technology Partner.

"WE WORK TO DEVELOP PARTNERSHIPS WITH OUR CUSTOMERS. THAT'S OUR GOAL, AND WE DO IT BY EXCEEDING OUR CUSTOMERS' EXPECTATIONS WITH QUALITY PRODUCTS DELIVERED ON TIME AND ON BUDGET," SAYS BOBBY BRADLEY, COMPUTER SYSTEMS TECHNOLOGY, INC.'S PRESIDENT AND CEO.

PROVIDING INFORMATION TECHNOLOGY AND SYSTEMS ENGINEERING SUPPORT, COMPUTER SYSTEMS TECHNOLOGY, INC. (CST) IS PLANNING ON THE FUTURE TO ACHIEVE SUCCESS AS YOUR BUSINESS PARTNER.

MEVATEC CORPORATION HAS ACHIEVED AN OUTSTANDING REPUTATION AS A HIGH-TECH SMALL BUSINESS FOCUSED ON DELIVERING QUALITY PRODUCTS AND SERVICES TO GOVERNMENT AND COMMERCIAL CUSTOMERS AT A COMPETITIVE PRICE. OVER THE PAST YEARS, MEVATEC HAS DIVERSIFIED BEYOND ITS TRADITIONAL AEROSPACE ENGINEERING TECHNICAL DISCIPLINES INTO MANAGEMENT SERVICES WHICH INCLUDES ACTIVITY-BASED COSTING/ACTIVITY-BASED MANAGEMENT (ABC/ABM) CONSULTING,

economic analysis, cost research, privatization studies, and other related areas. In addition, the company performs work in the area of enterprise solutions linked to the business process reengineering (BPR)-derived requirements.

MEVATEC's diverse capabilities in research and analysis; software engineering; systems design, development, and integration; management services; and technical support services have made it one of the nation's fastest-growing small businesses. Since 1989, it has grown from a four-person,

NANCY ARCHULETA, MEVATEC CEO

JENNIFER & COMPANY

family business into a $52 million company with 400 employees and six U.S. locations.

Although the Department of Defense remains MEVATEC's single largest customer, the company has taken steps to diversify into management services by developing expertise in BPR, economic analysis, enterprise software systems, and activity-based costing. These areas are designed to assist companies and government organizations in identifying opportunities to reduce the cost of operations.

"We use proprietary software tools and strong employee involvement to identify the true cost of activities within a company," says C. Thomas Houser, president of MEVATEC. "Our targets within any company or organization are those activities that are non-value-added. We quantify the cost of activities horizontally across an organization, determine those that are non-value-added, and recommend solutions. We can also assist in implementing those solutions when they involve information systems. Cost savings in the range of 10 to 20 percent are typical, but can be significantly greater."

Using MEVATEC's ABC/ABM approach, consultants helped a disbursing operation save $800,000 in costs, and a hospital increase profits from $15 million to $26 million over two years' time. MEVATEC's nine-step process of evaluation and appraisal reviews all segments of a company's day-to-day business activities, and is designed to find ways for a company to reduce costs.

"We are not always chartered to reduce a company's employee size or operational capabilities. What we are often asked to do

is help companies and their employees become more efficient to accommodate future growth without a parallel increase in support infrastructure," Houser says.

In both its government and its commercial work, MEVATEC strives to be a best value company that delivers the highest expected value to the customer considering risk. "We recognize that there are some business sectors that traditionally look for the lowest bidder, and this is usually appropriate. However, we tend to pursue opportunities that consider many factors other than just price," Houser says.

As a technical company, MEVATEC continues to achieve success in its research and analysis efforts, which include simulation and modeling of missile systems, lethality assessments, and requirements analysis. The company's software engineering efforts include database design; software reuse; and software design, development, testing, and documentation; while its efforts in systems design, development, and integration include network design and development, communications analysis, information management system design and support, and development of data libraries. The company also provides technical, programmatic, and testing support for military systems; and, through the acquisition of a small business in 1994, the firm offers services in the environmental area.

By maintaining its commitment to quality and customers on both government and commercial projects, MEVATEC is achieving success and offering its customers Today's Resource for Tomorrow's Technology.

AN EVOLUTION AT THE HUNTSVILLE OPERATIONS OF MAGNETEK, INC. HAS LED THIS MANUFACTURER OF ELECTRICAL AND ELECTRONIC EQUIPMENT TO TAKE A DIFFERENT PROFILE IN THE ELECTRONICS AND ELECTRICAL EQUIPMENT INDUSTRY. WITH A NEW FOCUS ON MANUFACTURING ADVANCED LIGHTING PRODUCTS, MAGNETEK IS EXPERIENCING EXCITING ADVANCES IN TECHNOLOGY, REVENUES, AND ASSOCIATE INVOLVEMENT. ✶ "WHEN WE FIRST CAME TO HUNTSVILLE IN 1993, WE WERE FOCUSED

on the high-volume production of electronic lighting ballasts," says Dan Hawkins, human resources director for MagneTek's Huntsville operations. "Since then, we've changed our charter to a technology and advanced manufacturing center with responsibility for new, global product development and manufacturing process development for electronic and magnetic ballasts."

A MagneTek Showcase

Today, Huntsville is the technology center for the global Lighting Products Group (LPG). The company employs approximately 250 people at its Huntsville operations, with more than a third of those employees being salaried professionals in the mechanical, electrical, and industrial engineering fields. The company occupies 125,000 square feet at its 40-acre site in Gateway Industrial Park near the Huntsville/Madison County Jetplex.

"With our corporate headquarters in Nashville less than two hours away, our Huntsville operations have become a customer showcase of MagneTek's most modern facilities," Hawkins says. "It is a convenient location for us, and one that puts us in a geographical market known for its technological advances in the electronics field."

Applications for MagneTek's lighting products include magnetic and electronic ballasts used in office buildings, factories, warehouses, automotive, neon signs, computers, office automation, residential lighting uses, and other areas involving power conversion for lighting systems. Of the $1.3 billion in revenues earned annually by MagneTek through its Power Electronics Group, Motors and Control Group, Lighting Products Group, and Drives and Systems

Group, close to $500 million comes from the LPG. Worldwide, MagneTek employs more than 14,000 associates in its four core business groups at 18 manufacturing plants in North America and eight overseas.

Contributing to Corporate Growth

The Huntsville facility is a key contributor to MagneTek's future growth, particularly the Lighting Products Group. As a technology and advanced manufacturing center, Huntsville operations are responsible for all new products, manufacturing process development, new program launches, and numerous best practices to be used at other MagneTek facilities. The facility is well equipped with surface-mount technology, radial insertion, test engineering, electronic and magnetic labs, demand

flow technology, six sigma quality programs, and other programs to help lead MagneTek into the next millennium.

"The renewed focus on Huntsville as LPG's technology and advanced manufacturing center is exciting for everyone," Hawkins says. "Our associates are involved in cutting-edge technologies and programs that will help lead MagneTek into the future.

"Companies will always need lighting systems in their buildings, factories, and products. They now realize that MagneTek's lighting products help provide a much more efficient way of supplying energy to these lighting fixtures and systems. Our products help our customers save energy and money by providing high-efficiency and high-performance lighting ballasts. MagneTek's products are Energy Engineered," says Hawkins.

MAGNETEK, INC. IN HUNTSVILLE EMPLOYS APPROXIMATELY 250 PEOPLE AT ITS 125,000-SQUARE-FOOT FACILITY ON A 40-ACRE SITE IN GATEWAY INDUSTRIAL PARK NEAR THE HUNTSVILLE/MADISON COUNTY JETPLEX. THE HUNTSVILLE FACILITY IS THE TECHNOLOGY AND ADVANCED MANUFACTURING FOR MAGNETEK'S LIGHTING PRODUCTS GROUP.

Triad Properties Corporation

HARD WORK, CAREFUL PLANNING, IN-DEPTH RESEARCH, INVESTMENT DISCIPLINE, CREATIVITY, AND LONG-TERM PERSPECTIVE. THESE QUALITIES FORM THE EQUATION AND CREATE THE COMPETITIVE ADVANTAGE THAT HAS MADE TRIAD PROPERTIES CORPORATION A SUCCESS IN MAJOR SOUTHERN MARKETS SUCH AS ATLANTA, DALLAS, HUNTSVILLE, MEMPHIS, NASHVILLE, AND SOUTH FLORIDA. AS A PERFORMANCE-ORIENTED, YIELD-DRIVEN, REAL ESTATE INVESTMENT AND OPERATING COMPANY, TRIAD

Properties specializes in acquiring, developing, managing, and leasing quality office and industrial properties in major metropolitan areas.

Since its inception in 1994, Triad has acquired and developed more than 4.4 million square feet of office and industrial space. During this time, the company has sold more than 2.1 million square feet, which has generated extraordinary financial returns for Triad's group of Huntsville- and Atlanta-based investors.

Exceptional Investments

Triad's principals, Tom Daniel, Lance Sallis, Gerry Shannon, Mark Smith, and William Stroud, have made the company a leading commercial real estate firm by using their skills to identify, acquire, reposition, recapitalize, and re-package undervalued investments with the goal of exercising an institutional exit. After targeting opportunities, the company's investment discipline is reflected by its ability to negotiate transactions in a patient, persistent, and tenacious manner. Triad's diligence, extensive market knowledge, negotiating abilities, and sound underwriting result in a focus on capital preservation, long-term value enhancement,

and extraordinary risk-adjusted returns.

For example, Triad completed the sale of a five-building, 740,000-square-foot office portfolio in Atlanta to a national real estate investment trust, Highwoods Properties Inc., for $103 million. The portfolio was developed over an 18-month period, and the sale generated a 39 percent internal rate of return for its investors. Although the newly developed buildings were constructed on a speculative basis, they were leased upon completion to a tenant roster including IBM,

Nortel, BellSouth, Prudential, the Travelers, and Hartford Insurance.

"We worked hard to achieve a unique disposition structure so our investment partners could elect to receive their return in the form of cash, or they could elect to defer taxes and monetize their investment by exchanging their profits for Highwoods stock," says Shannon.

"The capital market arena we operate in favors companies that are transitioning from traditional partnership ownership of real estate into a public and corporate format,"

TOP: LOCATED IN NASHVILLE, 3322 WEST END OFFERS 11 STORIES OF PRESTIGIOUS OFFICE SPACE.

BOTTOM LEFT: BROOKRIVER CENTER CONSISTS OF TWO CLASS A BUILDINGS TOTALING MORE THAN 313,000 SQUARE FEET IN DALLAS.

RIGHT: THE BELVEDERE IN DALLAS IS HOME TO TRIAD PROPERTIES' SOUTHWESTERN REGIONAL OFFICE.

Stroud says. "As this environment evolves, we are going to continue raising funds, investing, and aggregating portfolios of property with the goal of building a vertically integrated real estate company with a track record of delivering superior risk-adjusted performance to our partners. We offer integrity, performance, and experience."

Local financial institutions; regional banks; AMRESCO, a Dallas-based real estate mezzanine lender; and Bankers Trust, a Wall Street bank, provide the debt and mezzanine capital for Triad's projects. Triad co-invests with capital partners, many of which are Huntsville-based, to provide equity.

Expanding Regional Presence

Although founded and headquartered in Huntsville, Triad conducts much of its business in Atlanta and Dallas. The firm took its experience in Atlanta's commercial real estate market and exported the strategy to Dallas. To allow its partners to capitalize on the momentum Triad has established, the company expanded its operations in Texas. Led by Dallas-based principal Lance Sallis, Triad merged with a Texas real estate company and acquired another Texas operating company, resulting in a total employee base of 30 people.

Since then, Triad has acquired a 1,055,240-square-foot office portfolio valued at $112 million. Included in the portfolio is an 11-story, 222,711-square-foot office building in Nashville. In addition, Triad started the development of 767,698 square feet in Atlanta val-

ued at $41.5 million. Currently, Triad manages and leases more than 1.2 million square feet of space in Atlanta, Dallas, Nashville, Memphis, South Florida, and Huntsville. "If you are doing business in the Southeast, you have to go through Atlanta," Shannon says. "Likewise, if you are doing business in the Southwest, you have to go through Dallas."

"With corporate headquarters in Huntsville and regional offices in Atlanta and Dallas, Triad's employees are positioned to successfully analyze, trade, structure, and underwrite a variety of real estate transactions," according to Atlanta-based principal Tom Daniel. The firm has sold properties to pension fund advisers from Boston to San Francisco, contributed property in exchange for stock in real estate investment trusts, received institutional investment capital from university endowment funds and mezzanine lenders, and partnered with international real estate giant Trammell Crow Company on more than 20 projects.

Competitive Advantage

Triad's history of successful transactions reflects its principals' extensive, in-depth knowledge of real estate operations, capital markets, and securitized transaction structures. As members of the American Institute of Certified Public Accountants, Stroud and Shannon play an active role in directing the company. This financial background allows Triad to enjoy a competitive advantage in the local real estate investment community.

"By bringing financial engineering capabilities to the table, we are able to optimize the debt and equity structures to maximize return on the dollar invested," Stroud says.

A proven financial background, coupled with Triad's commercial real estate success, has helped the company build a supportive group of investors and clients. "Hard work, careful strategic planning, and investment discipline—paired with a long-term perspective—have allowed Triad and its capital partners to experience significant growth on an extraordinarily profitable basis," says Mark C. Smith, Triad co-owner and a member of the board of directors.

As real estate markets continue to improve and as the need for acquisition capital increases, Triad Properties Corporation will play a major role in creating highly innovative and soundly underwritten investments to meet the demands of prudent advisers, astute investors, and informed clients.

CLOCKWISE FROM TOP LEFT: ONE OF TRIAD PROPERTIES CORPORATION'S DISTRIBUTION CENTERS IN ATLANTA, WEST OAK COMMONS

LOCATED IN FORT MYERS, TRIAD PROPERTIES HAS PRIME OFFICE SPACE IN METRO PARK.

MCGINNIS PARK IN ATLANTA IS HOME TO TRIAD PROPERTIES' SOUTHEASTERN REGIONAL OFFICE.

WHEN EXECUTIVES AT WOLVERINE TUBE, INC. WERE SEARCHING FOR A NEW CORPORATE HEADQUARTERS, THEY DIDN'T HAVE TO LOOK FAR FROM THEIR DECATUR, ALABAMA, OFFICES. AFTER STRIKING NASHVILLE, BIRMINGHAM, AND ATLANTA FROM THE LIST OF POSSIBILITIES, THE COMPANY TURNED ITS FOCUS TOWARD NEIGHBORING HUNTSVILLE. THE NEW HEADQUARTERS, ESTABLISHED IN 1994 AT HUNTSVILLE'S PERIMETER PARK, FIT WOLVERINE'S OVERALL PLAN

to strategically locate its corporate offices in a city that offered the amenities of an international business community.

"We wanted to establish our corporate offices in a larger city that had hotel and restaurant accommodations for our customers," says James E. "Jed" Deason, executive vice president and chief financial officer. "But we didn't want to move too far away from our manufacturing facility in Decatur, where our corporate headquarters had been since the 1970s. Many of our executives had grown up in the Decatur plant, and we didn't want to lose them with a move several hundred miles away."

Leading the Competition

As the leading North American manufacturer and distributor of copper and copper alloy tubular products, as well as a variety of other fabricated tubular products, Wolverine enjoys annual sales

of more than $600 million. The company's products—such as industrial, technical, and copper alloy tubing—are manufactured to demanding customer specifications and international standards. While used in a myriad of applications, Wolverine's products are marketed primarily to the air-conditioning, appliance, refrigeration, plumbing, automotive, and energy industries.

"We have a number of competitors, but we are the market share leader in all of our major product

lines. As a result of Wolverine's strategically positioned manufacturing locations and technological excellence, the company stands out from the competition by offering an extensive line of high-quality, cost-efficient commercial products," Deason says.

Wolverine is also recognized worldwide as the technological leader in nonferrous products that serve the heat transfer, industrial, power and process, electrical, electronic, automotive, and consumer product markets. The

AT WOLVERINE'S NEW $5 MILLION RESEARCH AND DEVELOPMENT CENTER IN DECATUR, ALABAMA, THE COMPANY IS CONTINUALLY EXPLORING OPTIONS FOR IMPROVED HEAT TRANSFER EFFICIENCY IN ITS PRODUCT LINE (TOP).

WOLVERINE'S CAPITAL INVESTMENTS HAVE POSITIONED THE COMPANY TO PROVIDE BETTER SERVICE TO CUSTOMERS, IMPROVE QUALITY, LOWER COSTS, AND CAPITALIZE ON THE DEMAND FOR COPPER TUBE PRODUCTS (BOTTOM).

company's $5 million Technology Center and Research Laboratory in Decatur allows Wolverine to continue its dominance in heat transfer technology. By supporting the engineering and testing of specialized products, Wolverine is meeting the market demand for more environmentally friendly products that will reduce greenhouse gas emissions. "One of the drivers behind this technology center was the movement started in January 1996, when 40 countries stopped the production of chlorofluorocarbon [CFC] refrigerants. Before then, it was the refrigerant of choice," Deason says. "Our facility is developing and testing new tubes for use with non-CFC refrigerants. There is a constant demand for products going into non-CFC applications, and Wolverine is very involved in supporting the transition to environmentally friendly refrigerants."

Globally Focused, Technologically Advanced

Wolverine is today a publicly owned company with more than 3,600 employees worldwide. In addition to manufacturing facilities in Alabama, Tennessee, Mississippi, Oklahoma, North Carolina, Texas, Pennsylvania, Canada, and China, the company maintains sales and business development offices in France, England, and Hong Kong. Its North American and international marketing campaigns are coordinated from the Huntsville corporate headquarters. "Wolverine has 11 plants in North America and one plant in Shanghai. Huntsville has an international business community that complements the worldwide scope of our business," Deason says.

Locating a facility in Shanghai marked Wolverine's first step in a strategic plan to expand its manufacturing and distribution capabilities worldwide in support of customer growth overseas. The $7 million plant manufactures high-value technical tubing for both North American companies currently established in China and Asian manufacturers of commercial air-conditioning products. By

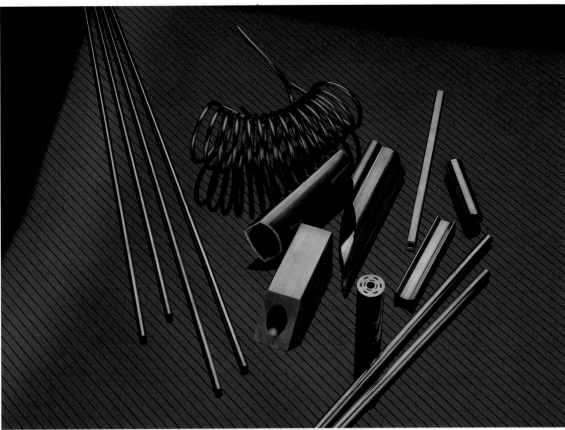

locating near the overseas facilities of its North American customers, Wolverine can deliver products on a timely and cost-efficient basis, thus further solidifying those relationships.

The acquisition of other companies is also an important component in Wolverine's mission to enhance and broaden its commercial product base while becoming a global supplier and a world-class organization. Many of these acquisitions have provided entry into complementary markets through the company's fabricated products group. For example, the recent purchase of a Korean manufacturer gives Wolverine—already known for its seamless tubing—the additional capability of producing welded tube for industrial use. Wolverine is also marketing its fabricated product capabilities to North American companies that are outsourcing subassembly and final assembly of products.

"We can provide outsourcing production more economically because we already have the raw materials needed in-house," Deason says. "Having those raw materials makes us more competitive. We want to leverage our raw materials and heat transfer tech-

nology into other applications, such as in computer and automotive products that can use our heat transfer technology to eliminate the use of fans."

While Wolverine is an established manufacturer and distributor of metal tubing products, its expertise goes beyond the manufacturing process to include the development of new applications for metal products. Through ongoing investments in technology and a commitment to addressing changing customer needs, Wolverine Tube has proved its reputation as a Technology Company in the Metals Marketplace.

WOLVERINE PRODUCES A WIDE RANGE OF COPPER ALLOY PRODUCTS USED IN A VARIETY OF INDUSTRIES, INCLUDING CONSUMER APPLIANCE, REFRIGERATION, AND AIR CONDITIONING (TOP).

WOLVERINE'S TECHNOLOGICALLY-ADVANCED TURBO-A, TURBO-B, AND TURBO-C PRODUCT LINES ARE INDUSTRY LEADERS (BOTTOM).

IN HUNTSVILLE, MORE THAN ANYWHERE ELSE IN THE SOUTH, CONSUMERS AND BUSINESSES HAVE EMBRACED THE NEW CELLULAR TECHNOLOGY OFFERED BY POWERTEL, INCORPORATED. SINCE LOCALS WERE INTRODUCED TO POWERTEL TECHNOLOGY IN EARLY 1997, NORTH ALABAMA HAS BECOME ONE OF POWERTEL'S MOST DYNAMIC AND FASTEST-GROWING MARKETS, WITH A MARKET SHARE OF THOUSANDS OF CUSTOMERS. ✳ "WE ARE THE FIRST DIGITAL PERSONAL COMMUNICATIONS SERVICES COMPANY IN THE HUNTSVILLE MARKET,"

says Elbert Balch, Powertel's marketing manager in North Alabama. "In Huntsville, there is certainly a market ready for new technology. People here understand and appreciate new technology. They embrace it and see the benefits."

Superior Digital Services

Digital, rather than analog, communications offer customers inherent security, high voice quality, and long battery life. In addition, Powertel's digital signals are transmitted at a higher frequency and are decoded differently in the transmission process to offer total security through the Global System for Mobile Communications (GSM), clearer reception, secure data transmission, and less expensive operation costs.

"Not only do we give you better voice transmission and security over cellular or analog phones, but we have also been able to

package many landline features into the small, handheld phones," Balch says. "We give you caller ID, call waiting, call forwarding, voice mail, and paging features at a very inexpensive rate. Users can use their phone to create a personal electronic phone book, and enhanced features are available for receiving E-mail and fax transmissions. And, because of the way we've designed the personal communications services network and the way we've placed the transmission towers in close proximity to each other, customers can use very small, handheld units with long battery life. Most phones will go two or three days without recharging, and recharging takes minutes rather than hours. These are definite advantages over cellular phones."

At 246,000 contiguous square miles, Powertel's licensed footprint is the largest of any personal

communications services carrier in the Southeast. Powertel's licenses encompass 12 states, including all or most of Georgia, Alabama, Mississippi, Tennessee, and Kentucky, and parts of Louisiana, Arkansas, Illinois, South Carolina, Indiana, Missouri, and North Carolina. And thanks to GSM, Powertel customers can also use their phones in more than 3,400 North American cities.

Building a High-Quality Network

In growing its service area, Powertel first worked to establish a presence in key markets and along major highways throughout the Southeast. Then, the firm became the first to build a network that delivers quality, dependable, easy-to-use, and affordable wireless service to these markets.

"It has always been our company's overall strategy to build out our network into the larger cities and major interconnecting highways in the Southeast," Balch says. "We've concentrated on building the major cities, and, when we connect on major highway and interstate routes, we get the smaller cities, so that our coverage becomes quite extensive."

But before Powertel could establish its reach, it had to build a foundation of expertise in digital technology. That foundation began in 1990 when InterCel was established in West Point, Georgia. As InterCel developed its services for customers in west-central Alabama and southwest Georgia, it increasingly began to use digital technology for its wireless communications.

From 1995 to 1997, InterCel purchased 18 personal communications services licenses, giving the company the right to establish digital wireless communications in licensed areas and making it the largest service provider of its kind in the Southeast. In 1997, the

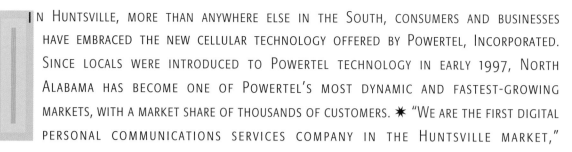

Powertel's Extensive Service Area

Powertel Licensed Footprint
Powertel PCS Service Area
Powertel Planned PCS Service Area

SINCE LOCALS WERE INTRODUCED TO POWERTEL TECHNOLOGY IN EARLY 1997, NORTH ALABAMA HAS BECOME ONE OF POWERTEL'S MOST DYNAMIC AND FASTEST-GROWING MARKETS.

HUNTSVILLE HAS EMBRACED THE NEW DIGITAL PERSONAL COMMUNICATIONS SYSTEMS OFFERED BY POWERTEL.

company's digital business was renamed Powertel, and began trading on the Nasdaq stock exchange as PTEL.

Making Wireless Affordable

Powertel offers its customers affordable rate plans, with fees based on the number of minutes used. In addition, Powertel phones offer features that make using them much less expensive. For instance, users who purchase local Powertel service in their home cities can travel to any other Powertel service area and make calls there at their home-based local rate.

In addition, the first minute of inbound calls on Powertel phones is free time, which is causing

a change in the paradigm of wireless service. "In the past, users have been reluctant to give out their phone number because they don't want to run up their bill," Balch says. "Now, you can give your number out freely and use caller ID to screen your calls before answering. You can choose to let the voice mail answer a call or you can choose to answer the call and disconnect within a minute without being charged."

Wireless communication has also begun to replace traditional communications devices wired into the home or business. "A temporary employee who is only here for a few months to a year could choose to use one of our

phones rather than go through the installation and then later the disconnection of a landline phone," Balch says. "Powertel is less expensive, much more convenient, and it's a service that can continue if the employee moves to another area within our 12-state service area."

As consumers continue to discover the benefits of its services, future growth for Powertel seems limitless. "The sky's the limit with personal communications services," Balch says. "Everyone has a need to communicate, and future predictions indicate that personal communications services will become a part of everyday living for people from all walks of life."

HERITAGE BANK OF HUNTSVILLE IS CONFIDENTLY RELYING ON THE COMBINATION OF A CORE GROUP OF VERY COMPETENT BANKING PROFESSIONALS AND THE ECONOMIC STRENGTH AND MOMENTUM OF HUNTSVILLE AND MADISON COUNTY TO QUICKLY PROPEL IT TO THE POINT WHERE IT SIGNIFICANTLY IMPACTS THE AREA'S FINANCIAL SERVICES MARKET. ALTHOUGH IT IS ONE OF THE AREA'S NEWEST FINANCIAL INSTITUTIONS, HERITAGE HAS ALREADY BEGUN TO FIRMLY ESTABLISH ITSELF BY

ESTABLISHED IN EARLY 1998, HERITAGE BANK OF HUNTSVILLE HAS ENJOYED AN OVERWHELMINGLY POSITIVE RESPONSE FROM THE COMMUNITY. TREMENDOUS GROWTH HAS CONTINUED, FOLLOWING THE BANK'S MOVE TO A PERMANENT MAIN OFFICE ON THE FIRST FLOOR OF A NEW, $4 MILLION OFFICE BUILDING ON BALMORAL DRIVE.

"HERITAGE BANK OF HUNTSVILLE IS A TOP-NOTCH COMMUNITY BANK THAT HAS, AS ITS MAIN FOCUS, A HIGH LEVEL OF UNDERSTANDING OF THE HUNTSVILLE MARKET," SAYS VERNON BICE, PRESIDENT.

JENNIFER & COMPANY

offering residents and businesses the opportunity to work with a full-service bank that is focused on the local market. The bank's growth has resulted from the competence of its banking professionals and the consistent high quality of its banking services, including a wide variety of checking and money market investment accounts, certificates of deposit, individual retirement accounts, home mortgages, consumer loans, and business loans. Heritage is very familiar with all forms of real estate financing in the market.

"Heritage Bank of Huntsville is a top-notch community bank that has, as its main focus, a high level of understanding of the Huntsville market," says Vernon Bice, president. "Members of our board of directors and our stockholders are from the Huntsville area. So, too, are our bankers, who have established reputations in the local banking community and who are committed to providing professional financial services to local customers who have reached a certain level of complexity in their financial affairs. We are working to build a bank that is responsive to the Huntsville community."

Growing with Huntsville

Established in early 1998, Heritage Bank of Huntsville has

enjoyed an overwhelmingly positive response from the community. Tremendous growth has continued, following the bank's move to the first floor of our new, $4 million office building on Balmoral Drive, located in the densely populated Whitesburg Drive/Airport Road area of southeast Huntsville.

"Our facility is positioned between a high-traffic retail area and an emerging professional area," Bice says. "Customers prefer to bank where they live and shop, and we are providing them that convenience through the strategic placement of our main office and the future locations of our branch offices."

Regional Community Banking

Heritage Bank of Huntsville is affiliated with Heritage Bank in nearby Decatur. As a result, the business relationship has provided the Huntsville institution with a charter, a data processing system that was already on-line, and numerous competitive advantages. This affiliation allowed the Huntsville bank to bypass delays often associated with establishing a new financial institution.

In Huntsville, Heritage is very much its own operation, with a board of directors that includes

Bice and several other local leaders: Larry Landman, president of L&L Lumber Company; Greg Parker, president of Fountain, Parker, Harbarger & Associates; E.C. "Pony" Lee, president and chief executive officer of Summa Technology; Ben Walker, president of United Property Management; Rod Steakley, partner with Sirote & Permutt, P.C.; Johnny Moss, president of Moss Lumber Industries; Mark Yokley, president of G.W. Jones & Sons; Bill Salter, president of Intergraph Federal Systems; and Shirley Hale, civic leader and former director of the Huntsville Hospital Foundation. It is this group of directors, along with the bank's stockholders and employees, who give Heritage Bank its local strength.

"Huntsville is a very demanding banking market," Bice says. "We can make better decisions quicker for our customers because we know the local market and, hopefully, we can provide them with more flexibility to address their individualized needs." By offering professional financial services in conjunction with a high level of local market awareness, Heritage Bank will continue gaining the patronage of those who wish to do business with a bank that calls Huntsville home.

Southern Bank of Commerce

SOUTHERN BANK OF COMMERCE KNOWS THE IMPORTANCE OF PERSONAL BANKING RELATIONSHIPS. THE BANK'S GROWTH IS DEPENDENT ON THE PERSONAL SERVICE ITS EMPLOYEES EXTEND TO LOCAL CUSTOMERS, AND THESE RELATIONSHIPS ARE PAVING THE WAY FOR SOUTHERN BANK OF COMMERCE'S SUCCESSFUL DEVELOPMENT IN HUNTSVILLE AND NORTH ALABAMA. ✳ "WE DELIVER A QUALITY PRODUCT TO OUR CUSTOMERS. BUT INSTEAD OF BEING TRANSACTION ORIENTED, WE ARE RELATIONSHIP ORIENTED,"

says W. Evans Quinlivan, Southern Bank of Commerce's Huntsville/ Madison County president. "We want to give our customers predictability, consistency, and availability in their banking relationship."

Banking Decisions Made Locally

Since opening for business in Eufaula, Alabama, in 1926, Southern Bank of Commerce has been expanding its operations in both North and South Alabama. As the company enters a new market, banking executives familiar with the business climate are put in place to ensure that financial decisions reflect local expectations. As a result, Southern Bank of Commerce employees in Huntsville and Madison County can offer progressive products, combined with traditional, personalized services and the management insight of local banking executives.

"What's happening in the industry is that big banks continue to get bigger," says Quinlivan, who has 15 years of banking experience in the Huntsville market. "A byproduct of that growth is they have to become much more systematic, much more black and white in their policies, and much more procedure oriented. With that, the overall pro-

cess in banking decisions becomes less personal, friendly, and flexible. At Southern Bank of Commerce, we are putting the personal relationship back into banking."

In response to ongoing economic development and market growth in Huntsville/Madison County, Southern Bank of Commerce opened its local operations in mid-1998. Currently housed in a new facility at the intersection of Meridian, Monroe, and Washington streets, Southern Bank of Commerce maintains a branch in Madison, with plans to open other branch locations in the near future.

Serving Small Businesses

Our target market is primarily small businesses that need a consistent relationship with banking executives who understand their potential for growth and who can provide them the flexibility needed when making substantial capital investments," Quinlivan says. "We are also providing real estate loans for residential development and full-service commercial banking, all offered with local decision making and personal banking relationships."

Because of its focus on personal, localized banking, Southern Bank

of Commerce sought out a board of directors whose members reflect the entrepreneurial spirit of Huntsville/Madison County. The board members include Frank McWright and John Wynn of Lanier, Ford, Shaver & Payne; Gerry Shannon of Triad Properties; Mike Patterson of G.W. Jones & Sons; Russ Burns of Universal Construction; Steve Siniard of Bestline Builders; Bobby Bradley of Computer Systems Technology; and William P. "Bud" Albritton of Amtec Corporation.

While Southern Bank of Commerce offers consumers a full range of services, its progressive policies and procedures greatly benefit the small-business owner.

"Huntsville obviously has a tremendous entrepreneurial spirit," says Quinlivan. "We want to support that spirit through our knowledge of the potential in this market, our understanding of the business challenges and opportunities that small-business owners face, and our commitment to provide them with a bank that makes loan decisions based on the local market, not on the policies and processes of a bank that makes decisions only at its corporate headquarters."

Southern Bank of Commerce is offering Huntsville a new bank managed by old friends.

SOUTHERN BANK OF COMMERCE OPENED OPERATIONS IN MID-1998 IN HUNTSVILLE/ MADISON COUNTY IN A NEW FACILITY— PICTURED HERE IN AN ARTIST'S RENDERING— AT THE INTERSECTION OF MERIDIAN, MONROE, AND WASHINGTON STREETS. THE BANK OFFERS PROGRESSIVE PRODUCTS, COMBINED WITH TRADITIONAL, PERSONALIZED SERVICES AND THE MANAGEMENT INSIGHT OF LOCAL BANKING EXECUTIVES.

BEGINNING AS A SMALL PUBLISHER OF LOCAL NEWSPAPERS IN THE 1930S, TOWERY PUBLISHING, INC. TODAY PRODUCES A WIDE RANGE OF COMMUNITY-ORIENTED MATERIALS, INCLUDING BOOKS (URBAN TAPESTRY SERIES), BUSINESS DIRECTORIES, MAGAZINES, AND INTERNET SITES. BUILDING ON ITS LONG HERITAGE OF EXCELLENCE, THE COMPANY HAS BECOME GLOBAL IN SCOPE, WITH CITIES FROM SAN DIEGO TO SYDNEY REPRESENTED BY TOWERY PRODUCTS. IN ALL ITS ENDEAVORS, THIS

Memphis-based company strives to be synonymous with service, utility, and quality.

A Diversity of Community-Based Products

Over the years, Towery has become the largest producer of published materials for North American chambers of commerce. From membership directories that enhance business-to-business communication to visitor and relocation guides tailored to reflect the unique qualities of the communities they cover, the company's chamber-oriented materials offer comprehensive information on dozens of topics, including housing, education, leisure activities, health care, and local government.

In 1998, the company acquired Cincinnati-based Target Marketing, an established provider of detailed

city street maps to more than 300 chambers of commerce throughout the United States and Canada. Now a division of Towery, Target offers full-color maps that include local landmarks and points of interest, such as parks, shopping centers, golf courses, schools, industrial parks, city and county limits, subdivision names, public buildings, and even block numbers on most streets.

In 1990, Towery launched the Urban Tapestry Series, an award-winning collection of oversized, hardbound photojournals detailing the people, history, culture, environment, and commerce of various metropolitan areas. These coffee-table books highlight a community through three basic elements: an introductory essay by a noted local individual, an exquisite collection of four-color photographs, and profiles of the companies and organizations that animate the area's business life.

To date, more than 80 Urban Tapestry Series editions have been published in cities around the world, from New York to Vancouver to Sydney. Authors of the books' introductory essays include former President Gerald Ford (Grand Rapids), former Alberta Premier Peter Lougheed (Calgary), CBS anchor Dan Rather (Austin), ABC anchor Hugh Downs (Phoenix), best-selling mystery author Robert B. Parker (Boston), American Movie Classics host Nick Clooney (Cincinnati), Senator Richard Lugar (Indianapolis), and Challenger Center founder June Scobee Rodgers (Chattanooga).

To maintain hands-on quality in all of its periodicals and books, Towery has long used the latest production methods available. The company was the first in the country to combine a desktop workstation environment with advanced graphic systems to provide color

separations, image scanning, and finished film delivery under one roof. Today, Towery relies on state-of-the-art digital prepress services to produce more than 8,000 pages each year, containing well over 30,000 high-quality color images.

An Internet Pioneer

By combining its long-standing expertise in community-oriented published materials with advanced production capabilities, a global sales force, and extensive data management expertise, Towery has emerged as a significant Internet provider. In keeping with its overall focus on community-based resources, the company's Internet sites represent a natural step in the evolution of the business. There are two main product lines within the Internet division: introCity™ and the American Community Network (ACN).

Towery's introCity sites introduce newcomers, visitors, and longtime residents to every facet of a particular community, while also placing the local chamber of commerce at the forefront of the city's Internet activity. The sites include newcomer information, calendars, photos, citywide business listings with everything from nightlife to shopping to family fun, and on-line maps pinpointing the exact location of businesses, schools, attractions, and much more.

ACN, Towery's other Internet product, is the only searchable on-line database of statistical information for all of the country's 3,141 counties and 315 metropolitan statistical areas. Each community's statistical profile includes vital information on such topics as population, workforce, transportation, education, taxes, and incentives. ACN serves as a national gateway to chambers of commerce, private

TOWERY PUBLISHING PRESIDENT AND CEO J. ROBERT TOWERY HAS EXPANDED THE BUSINESS HIS PARENTS STARTED IN THE 1930S TO INCLUDE A GROWING ARRAY OF TRADITIONAL AND ELECTRONIC PUBLISHED MATERIALS, AS WELL AS INTERNET AND MULTIMEDIA SERVICES, THAT ARE MARKETED LOCALLY, NATIONALLY, AND INTERNATIONALLY.

STEVE DAVIS

companies, and other organizations and communities on the Web, making it an ideal resource for finding and comparing data on communities suitable for a plant or office location.

Decades of Publishing Expertise

In 1972, current President and CEO J. Robert Towery succeeded his parents in managing the printing and publishing business they had founded nearly four decades earlier. Soon thereafter, he expanded the scope of the company's published materials to include *Memphis* magazine and other successful regional and national publications. In 1985, after selling its locally focused assets, Towery began the trajectory on which it continues today, creating community-oriented materials that are often produced in conjunction with chambers of commerce and other business organizations.

Despite the decades of change, Towery himself follows a long-standing family philosophy of unmatched service and unflinching quality. That approach extends throughout the entire organization to include more than 130 employees at the Memphis headquarters,

another 60 located in Northern Kentucky outside Cincinnati, and more than 50 sales, marketing, and editorial staff traveling to and working in a growing list of client cities. All of its products, and more information about the company, are featured on the Internet at www.towery.com.

In summing up his company's steady growth, Towery restates the essential formula that has driven the business since its first pages were published: "The creative energies of our staff drive us toward innovation and invention. Our people make the highest possible demands on themselves, so I know that our future is secure if the ingredients for success remain a focus on service and quality."

TOWERY PUBLISHING WAS THE FIRST IN THE COUNTRY TO COMBINE A DIGITAL DESKTOP ENVIRONMENT WITH ADVANCED GRAPHIC SYSTEMS TO PROVIDE COLOR SEPARATIONS, IMAGE SCANNING, AND FINISHED FILM DELIVERY UNDER ONE ROOF. TODAY, THE COMPANY'S STATE-OF-THE-ART NETWORK OF MACINTOSH AND WINDOWS WORKSTATIONS ALLOWS IT TO PRODUCE MORE THAN 8,000 PAGES EACH YEAR, CONTAINING WELL OVER 30,000 HIGH-QUALITY COLOR IMAGES (TOP).

THE TOWERY FAMILY'S PUBLISHING ROOTS CAN BE TRACED TO 1935, WHEN R.W. TOWERY (FAR LEFT) BEGAN PRODUCING A SERIES OF COMMUNITY HISTORIES IN TENNESSEE, MISSISSIPPI, AND TEXAS. THROUGHOUT THE COMPANY'S HISTORY, THE FOUNDING FAMILY HAS CONSISTENTLY EXHIBITED A COMMITMENT TO CLARITY, PRECISION, INNOVATION, AND VISION (BOTTOM).

Roger Bickel is a Bingham Farms, Michigan, photographer who specializes in travel and nature images. During visits to Huntsville, he has found that the area offers a variety of opportunities for unique and interesting photography. Bickel's work has appeared in Towery Publishing's *Cincinnati: Crowning Glory; Dayton: The Cradle of Creativity; Discover Columbus; Greater Grand Rapids: The City That Works*; and *Greater Detroit: Renewing the Dream*.

Bernd Billmayer was born in Germany, but has lived in Huntsville since 1958. A professional photographer, he has been manager of Intergraph's photography department for the past 19 years. Billmayer's personal photography has appeared in more than 50 shows and exhibits, including three one-man shows. His commercial, industrial, and advertising work is published worldwide.

David A. Dobbs has amassed a clientele that includes Ingram Micro, Blount International, Vulcan Materials, the Center for Disease Control and Prevention, and BellSouth Telecommunications. He photographed a 1993 piece for *National Geographic Traveler*

on the Carter Center in Atlanta. Dobbs currently runs David Dobbs Photography in Decatur, Georgia.

Bob Gathany, originally from upstate New York, owns and operates Huntsville Photo Lab with his wife, Lou. The photography gene runs in his family: His grandmother also operated a studio in Pennsylvania in the early 1900s. Gathany specializes in the copying and restoration of old photographs and images of business and industry. He is an assistant scoutmaster with the Boy Scouts of America and he photographs Scout activities for the Greater Alabama Council.

Jim Hargan practices freelance photography and writing full-time from his home in the mountains of North Carolina. His work has appeared in numerous magazines, calendars, postcards, and books, including *Compass American Guides: North Carolina*; the *New York Times*; the *Atlanta Constitution*; and *Farm & Ranch Living*, as well as Towery Publishing's *Charlotte: Nothing Could Be Finer* and *Celebrating a Triangle Millennium*. Hargan and his wife live in the Smoky Mountains community of Possum Trot.

Hillstrom Stock Photo, established in 1967, is a full-service stock photography agency based in Chicago. Its largest files include images of architecture, agriculture backgrounds, classic autos, gardens, and high-risk adventure/sports.

Monica M. Martin teaches black-and-white darkroom techniques through the Continuing Education program of the University of Alabama in Huntsville. A graduate of the University of California in Santa Barbara, she moved to the Huntsville area in 1988. Martin's photography has been used by the Huntsville Arts Council for annual reports and PANOPLY guides.

Muril Robertson, a freelance art, commercial, and nature photographer, works for Quality Research as an applied mathematician. He has been named the top photographer of the year by the Huntsville Photographic Society for a record four times and also received second prize in the 1994 Robert Huntzinger photography contest sponsored by Kodalux. Robertson's images have appeared in *American Photo, Ladies' Home Journal*,

the *Washington Post, Tennessee Valley's Hometown Press*, and *Alabama Magazine*.

Charles Seifried, a graduate of the University of Missouri, moved to the Huntsville area 21 years ago. The recipient of numerous ADDYs over the years, he specializes in industrial, commercial, and nature photography. Seifried owns and operates Charles Seifried Photography in Decatur, Alabama.

Sam Tumminello, a native Huntsvillian, attended Huntsville High School as well as the University of Alabama in Huntsville. He is employed by PPG Industries in the Aircraft Products Unit as a senior customer service representative. A freelance photographer, Tumminello recently documented the construction of the Capt. William J. Hudson (Steamboat Bill) Bridge in Decatur, Alabama.

Other photographers and organizations that contributed to *Huntsville/Madison County: To the Edge of the Universe* include Roy Simmons and the National Aeronautics and Space Administration.

INDEX OF PROFILES

◆ © MURIL ROBERTSON

Davis, Jan, 1953-
    Huntsville/Madison County : to the edge of the universe /
introduction by Jan Davis.
        p.   cm. — (Urban tapestry series)
    "Sponsored by the Chamber of Commerce of Huntsville/Madison
County."
    Includes index.
    ISBN 1-881096-70-X (alk. paper)
    1. Huntsville (Ala.)—Civilization.   2. Huntsville (Ala.)
Pictorial works.   3. Business enterprises—Alabama—Huntsville.
4. Huntsville (Ala.)—Economic conditions.   5. Madison County
(Ala.)—Civilization.   6. Madison County (Ala.) Pictorial works.
7. Business enterprises—Alabama—Madison County.   8. Madison County
(Ala.)—Economic conditions.   I. Title   II. Series.
F334.H9D38   1999
976.1'97—dc21X   99—26352

TOWERY PUBLISHING, INC.
The Towery Building,
1835 Union Avenue,
Memphis, TN 38104

PUBLISHER: J. Robert Towery ✳ EXECUTIVE PUBLISHER: Jenny McDowell ✳ NATIONAL SALES MANAGER: Stephen
Hung ✳ MARKETING DIRECTOR: Carol Culpepper ✳ PROJECT DIRECTOR: Pat Patterson ✳ EXECUTIVE EDITOR:
David Dawson ✳ MANAGING EDITOR: Lynn Conlee ✳ SENIOR EDITOR: Carlisle Hacker ✳ EDITOR/PROFILE
MANAGER: Heather Ramsey ✳ EDITORS: Mary Jane Adams, Jana Files, John Floyd, Brian Johnston ✳ ASSISTANT
EDITOR: Rebecca Green ✳ EDITORIAL ASSISTANT: Sunni Thompson ✳ PROFILE WRITER: Kari J.
Hawkins ✳ CAPTION WRITER: Sunni Thompson ✳ CREATIVE DIRECTOR: Brian Groppe ✳ PHOTOGRAPHY
EDITOR: Jonathan Postal ✳ PHOTOGRAPHIC CONSULTANT: Dennis Keim ✳ PHOTOGRAPHY COORDINATOR: Robin
Lankford ✳ PROFILE DESIGNERS: Laurie Beck, Kelley Pratt, Ann Ward ✳ PRODUCTION ASSISTANTS: Loretta
Drew, Melissa Ellis ✳ PRODUCTION RESOURCES MANAGER: Dave Dunlap Jr. ✳ PRODUCTION COORDINATOR:
Brenda Pattat ✳ DIGITAL COLOR SUPERVISOR: Darin Ipema ✳ DIGITAL COLOR TECHNICIANS: Amanda Bozeman,
Eric Friedl, Deidre Kesler, Brent Salazar ✳ PRINT COORDINATOR: Tonda Thomas